OXFORD STUDIES IN AFRICAN AFFAIRS

General Editors
John D. Hargreaves, Michael Twaddle,
Terence Ranger

FAMINE THAT KILLS

D0071763

Famine that Kills
Darfur, Sudan

Revised Edition

Alex de Waal

OXFORD
UNIVERSITY PRESS

OXFORD
UNIVERSITY PRESS

Oxford   New York
Auckland   Bangkok   Buenos Aires   Cape Town   Chennai
Dar es Salaam   Delhi   Hong Kong   Istanbul   Karachi   Kolkata
Kuala Lumpur   Madrid   Melbourne   Mexico City   Mumbai   Nairobi
São Paulo   Shanghai   Taipei   Tokyo   Toronto

Copyright © 1989, 2005 by Alex de Waal

First published in 1989 by Oxford University Press, Inc.
198 Madison Avenue, New York, New York 10016

www.oup.com

Oxford is a registered trademark of Oxford University Press

All rights reserved. No part of this publication may be reproduced,
stored in a retrieval system, or transmitted, in any form or by any means,
electronic, mechanical, photocopying, recording, or otherwise,
without the prior permission of Oxford University Press.

Library of Congress Cataloging-in-Publication Data
De Waal, Alexander.
Famine that kills : Darfur, Sudan, revised edition / Alexander de Waal
p. cm.—
Bibliography: p.
ISBN-13 978-0-19-518163-0

1. Famines—Sudan—Darfur. 2. Darfur (Sudan)—Economic Conditions.
3. Darfur (Sudan)—Rural conditions. 4. Food relief—Sudan—Darfur. I. Title.
II. Series.
HC835.Z9F335 1989 363.8'09627—dc20   89-9254

7 9 8

Printed in the United States of America
on acid-free paper

ACKNOWLEDGEMENTS

This study originally formed a doctoral thesis at Oxford University. While doing the research I was supported by a grant from the Economics and Social Research Council, and for one year in Sudan by the Save the Children Fund. All interpretations of evidence and opinions in this book are of course entirely my own.

Thanks are due to many people. Wendy James, Peter Collett, Clyde Mitchell, and Megan Vaughan have provided academic supervision., Hussein Abdel Gadir and WSDC helped me to travel to Darfur, and Ibrahim Khatta put me up when I arrived. Fatih Sadig Jamil, Brian Kerr, Mohammed el Hassan Mukhtar, Abu Hamed Hasabollah, Mark Pearson, David Hughes, Jim Harvey, Marianne Nolte, Sabil Adam Yagoub, and Ibrahim Yahya Adam taught me most of what I known about Darfur. Mohammed A. Osman first persuaded me to work with Save the Children Fund. Thereafter, support from the office, transport, and field staff of SCF was critical to the success of this project. Particular mention should be given to Ruth Buckley, Rae McGrath, Wendy Fenton, Mick Dick, Chris Eldridge, Iain Russell, John King and family, Jane MacAskill, Peter Johnson, Bob Strickland, Iain Russell, Anne Lefond, Simon Mollison, Khalid Roy, Haj el Nur Ahmad, Julian Pitcher, Jon Dixon, Mike Pring, Ahmad Osman, Mohammed Ajeli, and many others: the work I did would not have been possible without them. While in the field I worked with many people: Mohammed Imam, Mohammed Abdel Gadir, Jaafar Ali, Mahadin Ahmad, Abdel Aziz Ahmad, Hafiz Abbaker and Mohammed el Nil during 1985; Abdalla Mohammed, Abdel Moniem Mohammed, Musa Ahmad, Gibriel Baraka, Omar Abdu, Ibrahim Hamed, Ahmad Ishag, Mojtaba el Zaki, Hamed Esh, Rob Stirling, and Stuart Lloyd during 1986. John Seaman in London provided intellectual stimulation and practical support. Atul Vadher has given much moral support. While analysing and writing I have received many useful comments in the seminars I have given in Khartoum, Oxford, Sussex, and Liverpool. A number of people have also provided information and advice, or commented in more detail on versions of the text, especially Ruth Buckley, David Hughes, Simon Mollison, Nigel Taylor, Stephen Devereux, David Keen, Ahmad Karadawi, David Turton, Matthew

Lockwood, Louisa Gosling, Jay Kynch, Douglas Johnson, and Robert Chambers. Many thanks are due to my wife, Astier Mesghenna Almedom, for her tolerance and support. Above all, thanks is due to Malek Mohammed el Amin, my constant and invaluable companion in the field; a single credit cannot do justice to the contribution of his work.

★

Author and publisher would like to thank the Save the Children Fund for their generous subsidy of the production costs of this book.

PREFACE TO 2005 EDITION

The fifteen years since the publication of *Famine that Kills* have not been a good time for the people for whom Darfur is home. Twenty years since the drought that precipitated the famine of which this book is a study, the crisis in Darfur has been variously labelled the 'world's worst humanitarian disaster' and 'genocide.' I left Darfur in 1987, optimistic that Darfurians' resilience, tenacity, and readiness to innovate would ensure that they could prevail in the face of most adversities. But the famine of 1984–85 is matched and probably surpassed by the disaster now unfolding.

What has changed in the meantime? Has the humanitarian international learned to respond effectively to famines and crises of massacre and mass displacement? What augurs of the current violence can be detected in the ethnography of 1984–85? In this preface, I reflect upon famine theory and humanitarian practice and how they have changed over a decade and a half, and also on the developments that have brought a different kind of catastrophe down on the long-suffering people of Darfur.

Famine Theory and Humanitarian Practice

John Maynard Keynes is reputed to have responded to a criticism of inconsistency, 'when the facts change, I change my opinion. What do you do, sir?' Much has changed, both in the nature of famines and in the capacity of humanitarian responses. *Famine that Kills* could not be published today without howls of protest over its methodological and analytical deficiencies. That, I hope, says as much about the considerable progress in the field of humanitarian studies in the intervening period as it does about the shortcomings of the book itself. But it is also distressing to see how much of the book is still relevant.

One benefit of the infancy of the field of famine studies in the 1980s was that it was still possible to write a book with a grand sweep. Today, each of the subjects addressed, namely the history of famine, livelihood strategies under stress, and the epidemiology of famine mortality, would be more than sufficient for a monograph in itself. By the same token, a full review of developments in the field over the last fifteen years would be long indeed. And such a review would need a special focus on the role of violence—not just structural or 'silent violence,' but also manifest or 'loud' violence—in creating particularly virulent forms of famine.

The discipline of humanitarian studies has grown in size and sophistication since the 1980s, when an aspiring student of humanitarian affairs would have been hard pressed to find more than one or two academic institutions offering courses on the subject. Today, there are plentiful courses, diplomas and degrees, and their graduates are staffing the ranks of humanitarian agencies and donor institutions. The result is a huge increase in the knowledge base about famines and how to respond to them. (And I hope that my writings may have modestly contributed to this change.) There is a far greater readiness to canvass criticism and acknowledge difficulty. Nobility of purpose no longer confers immunity from sociological critique. Professional standards and codes of conduct have been debated, adopted, and revised.

But has increased expertise translated into more effective relief operations? Sadly, much is still wanting. In August 2003, more than 60,000 Darfurians fled to Chad. Almost a year later, the relief operation still lacks many essentials, including sound logistics and decent primary health care. With the last two decades' investment in professionalizing relief responses, such shortcomings are inexcusable.

There is still a vast gap between understanding rural poverty and vulnerability, and social and economic policymaking. The people who suffer famines are rarely, if ever, given the opportunity to define the event as they see fit and respond using their expertise. One of the most remarkable lacunae in current poverty reduction strategies is the neglect of the need to support the risk-minimization strategies of rural people. A case in point is Ethiopia, a country faced with recurrent drought and wild price fluctuations for its basic export, coffee. Between 1991–2000, Ethiopia managed an average GDP growth of 2.9% per annum, a figure that masks considerable volatility—in the best years the economy grew by 9.4% and in the worst it shrank by 3.64% (Fedelino and Kudina 2003, pp. 12–13). For most rural Ethiopians today, as for Darfurians in the 1980s, the priority is preserving livelihoods in the face of such predictable adversities—theirs is a human security approach (cf. Alkire 2003). Macro-economic figures show that more people are plunged into poverty by an economic contraction than are lifted out of it by a comparable expansion (Easterly 2002, p. 13). While rural people may be resilient to a single shock, repeated adversities force people to adapt livelihoods and reduce many to long-term destitution (Davies 1995).

The International Monetary Fund (IMF) Staff Assessment of Ethiopia, preparatory to granting debt relief under the Highly-Indebted Poor Countries (HIPC) initiative in April 2004, suggests that the country should be able to double its growth rate to an average of 6% per annum, thereby enabling it to halve its number of poor people by 2015 (IMF 2004). But the IMF smuggles a caveat into this rosy outlook: 'While this is an ambitious objective, in the view of the staffs it is achievable if the government pursues an ambitious reform agenda and sound macroeconomic policies that would promote higher private savings and investment, and *provided there is adequate rainfall and a favorable external environment*' (p. 4, emphasis added). What a dumbfounding assumption is contained in that final clause! An *average* of 6% growth in a volatile economy may lead to little or no decrease in the poverty headcount whatsoever.

Meanwhile, because of this obliviousness to shocks, the Ethiopian government has virtually no year-on-year flexibility in responding to variable conditions. When faced with a drought that left fifteen million Ethiopians facing hunger in 2002, the fiscal conditionalities for staying on-track for HIPC meant that the government had to reduce its spending. The proven policies for responding to such a crisis, through employment guarantee schemes or purchasing food in surplus-producing areas, for example, were prohibited. Thus Ethiopia had to rely on international agencies to bring in huge quantities of food aid, which was done with remarkable efficiency. This, of course, flooded the market and meant that many farmers who had bought fertilizer on credit could not repay their debts without selling assets.

This is an example of shockingly bad policy that fails to pass the simple test of being consonant with the realities facing rural people. Should we condemn the macro-economists for ignoring the micro-level research on livelihoods and coping strategies? Or should we also criticise those who study rural economies and have failed to make an impression on macro-economic thinking? Either way, the lack of progress is lamentable.

Another challenge is the abiding neglect of famine demography. When writing *Famine that Kills,* I assumed demographic surveys of the general population of famine-stricken areas would become routine. Today, it is remarkable how few such investigations there have been. Students of famine demography are still advised to consult nineteenth-century Indian statistics in preference to contemporary African ones. We know almost nothing about mortality levels in the major humanitarian crises of the 1990s across Africa, and it is quite possible that the death rates in the Darfur crisis of 2004 will be less well-documented than 1984–85.

The central challenge thrown down by *Famine that Kills* is to problematize the concept of 'famine.' I sought to challenge the assumption that 'we' (outsiders, English speakers) intuitively know what famine is, and instead attempted to privilege the insights of local people who are the proven experts in the subject. A conceptual and definitional exercise lies at the heart of this. This is not resolved. There are inconsistencies in defining 'famine,' which reflect both the slipperiness of the concept and my own deliberate refusal to define it too precisely. The three-way distinction between Malthus's Famine (gigantic and inevitable, and also imaginary), 'famine' in the common English sense of mass starvation unto death, and famine as a lived social experience, needs repeating and refining. In this respect, *Famine that Kills* should be read alongside my critique of entitlement theory (de Waal 1990), wherein I borrowed and adapted the concept of the famine 'thermometer' from John Rivers and his colleagues (Rivers et al. 1976), and used it to identify various points at which different diagnoses and definitions of famine can become applicable.

For some years, this definitional debate seemed to be no more than an academic sideshow, principally because the major humanitarian crises of the 1990s were caused by war, and the political and theoretical questions of defining the level of suffering induced were justifiably seen as beside the point. The currency of the anodyne term 'food security' and its correlates also helped defuse the issue. Driven by the laudable aim of improving food policy, the food security paradigm has contributed to unfortunate conceptual regressions, including a focus on food to the exclusion of livelihoods, health and social cohesion, and a focus on food production, which obscures the multiple causes of malnutrition.

However, the droughts and food crises of 2002 in southern Africa and Ethiopia, occurring during a Republican administration in the Untied States whose leaders have vowed 'no famine on our watch,' have revived the salience of defining 'famine.' In southern Africa, the co-occurrence of a generalized HIV/AIDS epidemic and drought caused a crisis that I dubbed 'new variant famine' (de Waal and Whiteside 2003), to the dismay of those who argued that the lack of widespread starvation unto death ruled out the experience from being classed as 'famine.' The word 'famine' was challenged as being extreme and alarmist. To the contrary, I would contend that the slow but inexorable downward slide of well-being associated with the impact of HIV/AIDS on poor communities, which leaves affected households 'not coping but struggling,' in the apt words of Gabriel Rugalema (2000), means that the word 'famine' is arguably too mild to describe the as-yet-unnamed crisis of social reproduction that the epidemic will bring in its wake. The single greatest change in the nature of famine in the last decade is the impact of HIV/AIDS on vulnerability to hunger and destitution, and we are only at the beginning of understanding what it means.

In Ethiopia, a major relief operation distributed immense quantities of free food to about fifteen million people, and the government and most of its donors concurred that no famine occurred. The affected people were not consulted over this, and the data that might reveal excess mortality are only now being collected and analysed (July 2004). Meanwhile, in a more theoretical manner, Stephen Devereux and Paul Howe are seeking to develop 'famine scales' that measure the scale and intensity of famine.

Famine that Kills became perhaps best known for its strong claims about the epidemiology of excess mortality in famine. The finding that infectious diseases were the principal cause of famine mortality was nothing new, and in retrospect it is astonishing that such an elementary fact of disaster epidemiology should have caused such a stir. There is no doubt that the position that I argued is too strong. The striking and unexpected finding that socio-economic indicators had almost no correlation with mortality levels led me to search for an alternative explanation, which I duly found in the health crisis model. This residual hypothesis was then forwarded, perhaps not cautiously enough. There are so many intermediate variables between income and food access and the nutritional status of children that the inference that nutritional factors played almost no role cannot be sustained by the data. As Helen Young and Susanne Jaspars subsequently pointed out, *nutrition matters* (1995). For good measure, they derived their data from Darfur. I stand corrected. But my chief point, that food consumption failures cannot account for famine mortality in the absence of analysis of disease, is correct. And the practical recommendation that measles immunization, malaria control and clean water supplies are at least as important as emergency food relief, still stands.

There is a striking contrast between the level and pattern of famine deaths in Darfur in 1984–85 and that in the camps for displaced Dinka in places such as el Meiram and Abyei in southern Kordofan in 1988. In those camps, death rates were about sixty times greater than in the general population of Darfur in 1985 and four times higher than in the camp at Korem, Ethiopia, in the worst days of 1984 (de Waal 1994a, p. 158). The reason was that the inhabitants of these camps were being deliberately starved: they had been robbed of all their possessions, were denied relief assistance (which in the case of Babanusa camp, was standing in railway trucks just a few hundred metres away), and were prevented from moving freely, so that they could not pursue any coping strategies. Rates of malnutrition reached astonishing levels: 74% of children were severely malnourished according to one survey. A threshold had been crossed in which frank starvation became commonplace; the logarithmic relation between undernutrition and mortality meant that, to apply Rivers' (1976) metaphor, cold water had turned to ice. This was famine as policy (Keen 1994). As prophetically emphasized by one of my Dinka informants in 1986, 'to starve' is transitive: it is something people do to each other.

Famine and untreated epidemics can be genocidal, and in this and several subsequent cases, Sudanese military officers used them in precisely this way. As David Maybury-Lewis notes, regarding the annihilation of indigenous peoples, 'discussion of genocide . . . should not focus solely or even principally on deliberate attempts to massacre entire societies. Often the widespread dying resulted not so much from deliberate killing but from the fatal circumstances imposed by the imperialists on the conquered' (2002, p. 45). Regrettably, Sudan has a rich archive on this issue. To give just one instance, Médecins Sans Frontières estimates that 'at least one third of the original population of western Upper Nile have lost their lives to kala azar and other treatable diseases' (MSF 2002, p. 33). The project of codifying 'famine crimes' into law (Marcus 2003) converges with the project of refining and implementing the Genocide Convention. Ethnographers of famine and genocide have much to learn from one another. In Darfur today, where much violence is directed at destroying livelihoods, including cutting down fruit trees and breaking irrigation ditches, which signify claims to land, the convergence is evident.

In contrast to my subsequent writings, *Famine that Kills* is light on the politics of famine creation. But the basic analysis in this book is what underpins the political arguments I later developed, most notably in *Famine Crimes* (1997). The analysis of famine as a social experience rather than a technical malfunction is the foundation of the case for politicizing famine. When famine moves an electorate to anger, it will be prevented. Also, in order to appreciate my later critique of the ineffectiveness of international agencies' interventions, it is essential to understand the modest impact of external relief programmes, relative to the far greater contribution to survival and the maintenance of livelihoods by people's own efforts. Humanitarian outsiders can only make a positive difference if they realise that they can only make a small difference. As I write, most international writing on the current famine in Darfur mistakenly assumes that relief food will make the biggest difference to the survival of Darfurians. The biggest lesson from this book is that it is people's own efforts, made possible by security in rural areas and health services, that will do that.

A few mis-representations need to be corrected. Martin Adams' account of the 1973 drought is unfairly caricatured on page 71: his concern was with the successful spontaneous resettlement of farmers and herders in southern Darfur. The critique of nutritional surveillance is overly polemical—but something still needs to be done to reinvigorate mortality surveillance. Alternative analyses of the mortality data are possible. For example, the estimates for child and infant mortality may be too low: the apparent drop in fertility in 1982–83 might in fact point to under-reporting of child deaths during the famine. The enigmatic remark about lost trains on page 124 could have benefited from elaboration: the trains may have disappeared but the wagons did not, and the pilot whom USAID requested to fly above the railway track in a fruitless attempt to locate a missing train was the victim of a category mistake. I make no apology, however, for the combative tone of some of my writing: famine should make us angry and should make us think hard about our failings, including our intellectual failings. Complacency or unwillingness to injure feelings is a banal reason for allowing people to die, but reprehensible nonetheless.

Origins of the Darfur Crisis of 2003–2004

When I lived in Darfur, the region was at peace. Barely a month after I left, more than one thousand displaced Dinka were murdered in ed Da'ien, marking the beginning of Darfur's current era of bloodshed. In retrospect, the ability I had to travel the entire length and breadth of the region, with minimal security worries and no travel permit required, was a luxury that no subsequent researcher or aid worker has had. By 1987, political processes were in motion that led ultimately to the outbreak of war in 2003 and its escalation into genocidal massacre and displacement. It is deeply sad that Darfur should not only be a textbook study of famine, but of genocide as well.

Throughout *Famine that Kills* there are hints of coming violence. The discussion of the strained relations between the Fur farmers of Nankose and the nearby pastoralists (p. 52), and the disputes associated with moving herds through the settled areas of Goz Dango (pp. 155–56) are examples. But perhaps the most significant clue lies in Sheikh Hilal Musa's comments on the disturbed moral geography of Darfur consequent on drought (p. 87). It was in long discussions with the ageing *nazir* of the Jalul Rizeigat at Aamo near Fata Borno in November 1985, that I became aware of how the changing ecology of Darfur also profoundly disturbed the moral order of society. Sheikh Hilal upbraided me for not speaking Arabic like an Englishman (colonial officers were trained in classical Arab), served sweet tea on a silver platter, presented me with a giraffe-tail fly whisk, and told me the world was coming to an end.

The entire text of *Famine that Kills* contains not a single reference to 'Africans,' whether 'black' or 'indigenous.' The terminology and the concepts that underlie it were simply not in use. Identities were complex and overlapping. Individuals and groups could shift from one category to another. For example, the Gimir people appear to have become 'Arabs' in the last two decades. In short, Darfur showed a characteristic 'Sudanic' pattern of permeable ethnic boundaries. Racism existed, evident in the reciprocal insults of Arab and Fur at Nankose when arguing over pastures. But Darfur's Arab-African dichotomy is an ideological construct that has emerged very recently, largely as a result of events outside the region. Arab supremacism in Darfur was born in 1987 along with the region's 'Arab Alliance,' which owes more to Khartoum and Libya than to any realities in Darfur. This in turn led Fur and Masalit militants to adopt the label 'African,' emphasizing a common political identity with Southerners and the Nuba. This simplistic dichotomization was encouraged by foreign commentators' casual use of the same terminology to interpret Sudan's civil war.

But neither must we create an idealized harmonious past for Darfur. Just as the point of historical reference for 1984–85 was the *julu* famine of seventy years earlier, there are obvious historical parallels for today in the 'turmoil and bloodshed' that marked the decades after 1874. Amid the struggles for resource and state power of those years we can identify millenarian and racist ideology. By the same token, what we know about the nature and scale of the atrocities committed today may give us insight into the unrecorded human experience of war, massacre, pillage, and rape a century ago.

How did the conflict and massacres of 2003–04 originate? There is little writing in English on this issue worthy of note (for an exception, see International Crisis Group 2004). Let me briefly examine the roles of land, settlement of disputes, national politics, and ideology.

Land rights are key to understanding Darfur and the conflicts therein. One important set of issues surrounds communal land jurisdiction, notably the question of the still-uncertain legal status of the concept of a tribal *dar*, *hakura*, or homeland. In his overview of Sudan's land laws, Saeed el Mahdi noted cautiously that tribes have become '*almost* the owners of their homelands' (1979, p. 2, emphasis added; see also Rünger 1987). Let us note the anomalous situation of several pastoral groups that were not awarded *dars* by the colonial authorities. While the large Baggara groups of southern Darfur were all awarded de facto jurisdiction over substantial tracts of territory, smaller and more itinerant groups were either given more limited *dars* (Beni Hussein, Zayadiya) or none at all (Salamat and the three branches of the northern Rizeigat, namely Jalul, Mahariya and Ereigat). These latter groups were inevitably more dependent on the stability of the 'moral geography' of Darfur. When land was plentiful, this was rarely problematic, but the rapid using-up of free cultivable land and the degradation of the range meant that land disputes became more common and more bloody in the 1980s. Recall Sheikh Hilal's interpretation of the ecological changes in moral and cosmic terms. Perhaps it is no coincidence that his son Musa is the leader of the *Janjawiid* militia, and that the northern Rizeigat are the backbone of this force.

The maintenance of law and order and the resolution of disputes are two of the most basic functions of government. Neither has been consistently performed in Darfur since the 1980s. President Nimeiri's creation of a Darfur regional government in 1980, and his failure to provide it with resources, meant that local administration went into a steep decline from which it has not recovered. In the mid-1980s, the two big development projects in the region (Western Savanna Development Corporation and Jebel Marra Rural Development Project) and Save the Children Fund, which was handling food aid distributions on behalf of USAID, had larger budgets, more vehicles, and greater capacity to operate in rural areas than the government. If the police wanted to conduct an operation against brigands, they needed to commandeer agency vehicles and fuel. The governor was no longer able to cover the costs of lengthy or well-attended inter-tribal conferences.

As a result, law enforcement collapsed almost entirely, and the authorities compensated for the rarity of apprehending bandits with the savagery of the punishments they meted out. Communities acquired guns to deter armed robbers. Herders, having more valuable and more mobile capital stock, armed themselves more. Without mediation, disputes escalated. When inter-communal conferences were convened, the government did not have the capacity to implement the decisions reached. The division of Darfur into three states and the revival of the Council of Native Administration, both in 1994–95, did nothing to address the basic problem of empty local coffers. On the contrary, assigning *amarat* ('principalities'—the new form of *dars*) on an ethnic basis became simply a charter for militarized ethnicity and its corollary, ethnic cleansing.

Darfur has managed well in the past with a light hand of administration. Manipulation by successive governments in Khartoum led to war. The first conflict was sparked in 1987 when the Libya-Chad war overflowed into Sudan. For some years, Libya had hosted exiles from Sahelian Arab groups that ranged from the Sudanese Ansar (followers of the Mahdi, in exile opposed to the Nimeiri government) to Tuareg rebels from Mali. Colonel Muammar Gaddafi armed and trained them and recruited many into an 'Islamic Legion,' which served as a spearhead for his war in Chad. He nursed the dream of an 'Arab belt' across the entire Sahel. After 1986, through Gaddafi's partnership with Prime Minister Sadiq el Mahdi, Libyan-backed militia used Darfur as a rear base, and flooded Darfur with automatic weapons, advertised the impotence of local government, and brought an ideology of Arab supremacism. In response, the Fur organized village defence groups. It became a Darfurian civil war. Belatedly, in May 1989, popular pressure compelled al Mahdi to convene a peace conference in el Fasher.

Brigadier Omer al Bashir launched his coup d'etat while this conference was in session. At first, many Darfurians welcomed the coup, hoping that a military government would show the resolve to ensure security in the region. But political polarization was well in train, exemplified by the defection of a leading Fur Islamist, Daud Bolad, to the Sudan People's Liberation Army (SPLA), whose leader, Dr. John Garang, was seeking an alliance of all of Sudan's marginalized 'African' peoples. In 1991, Bolad led an ill-fated military expedition into the region, aiming to ignite an insurrection among the Fur. Bolad was captured by the military governor of Darfur, Tayeb Ibrahim 'Sikha'—his nickname meaning 'iron bar,' for his skill at wielding that instrument at student demonstrations when he was bodyguard to none other than Bolad. Helped by his capture of Bolad's notebooks, Ibrahim quietly and ruthlessly rounded up the rebellion's supporters. The Beni Halba militia, known as *fursan* (cavalry), which had fought the SPLA unit, were rewarded with the provocative renaming of their district capital Idd al Fursan (it was formerly Idd al Ghanam). But Ibrahim also reached out to Darfur's non-Arabs, seeking to neutralize the Darfurian critique of their continuing marginalization in Khartoum politics. He praised their piety and stressed that citizenship was founded on Islamic faith, not race. It was an expedient stratagem, which reflected the wider ambition of Sudan's Islamist leader, Hassan al Turabi, to broaden the base of the Islamic movement from the riverain Arab elites to non-Arab Moslems.

The project of militant Islam in Sudan reached its peak in the mid-1990s. Thereafter, weakened by internal contradictions and regional antagonism, it began to implode (de Waal and Abdel Salam 2004). The movement split in 1999, when President Bashir dismissed Turabi from his position as Speaker of the National Assembly and later arrested him. Many of the leaders and most younger cadres followed Turabi into opposition. This split had several ramifications. One was that henceforth, the government's Islamism was rhetorical and defensive: it had abandoned its ambitions at social transformation. Another was that the division took on a regional or ethnic dimension. Most of the 'westerners' (from Darfur and Kordofan) went into opposition, while most of the riverain Arabs (and security officers) stayed in government. Shortly afterwards, Islamist 'westerners' produced the 'Black Book,' which detailed how successive governments had marginalized Darfur and Kordofan. Some Islamists formed the Justice and Equality Movement (JEM) to fight in Darfur, and others supported it more or less openly. One dimension to the Darfur war is a civil war among the Islamists. The intimacy of this conflict among former comrades militates against its easy resolution.

Meanwhile, conditions were ripe for Darfur's radical secularists to revive the resistance movement that had been aborted in 1991. The backbone of this is lawyers, schoolteachers, and community leaders from the Fur, Masalit, and Zaghawa, who formed the Darfur Liberation Front. After beginning military operations in early 2003, they renamed themselves the Sudan Liberation Movement/Army, in a deliberate echo of the SPLA. The Islamist and radical secularists found themselves in an improbable coalition. The SLA quickly showed military panache and capacity, attacking (among other targets) el Fasher airport and destroying military aircraft.

The Sudanese state is weak, but for short periods of time it can unleash formidable destructive forces. For a decade, the Islamist alliance shielded Darfurians from the historic processes of violent depredation of the Sudanese peripheries by the Sudanese state. When that shield was lifted, war and massacre duly followed. Was this assault driven by a powerful and explicit ideology (cf. Kuper 1981)? For its 1992 Kordofan *jihad*, the government had sought an elaborate *fatwa* to justify their onslaught. Other genocidal episodes in the Sudanese civil war, including the militia raids into Bahr el Ghazal in the late 1980s and the clearing of the oilfields of western Upper Nile during 1998–2002, had only the thinnest ideological veneer. No Islamist legitimation has been attempted for the Darfur campaign—not least because the JEM has better Moslem credentials than the government forces, which have further spoiled their record by desecrating mosques. The latent 'ideology' of 'Sudanization,' namely the spread of specific social and cultural values, economic and political relations, associated with the riverain core of the Sudanese state, is at work in tandem with the Arab supremacism of the *Janjawiid* leadership. However, the conjunction of these specific forms of Arabization is surely too weak an explanation for the viciousness of today's assault.

The Sudan government's military strategy is the principal reason for the massacre and displacement. Following a twenty-year-old practice, it has fought a low-budget counter-insurgency, using self-financing militias and the cheap weapons of scorched earth and famine. Local components contributing to the growth of militias include economic deprivation and failure to resolve disputes (de Waal 1994b), but the most important factor is the strategy adopted by security agencies, notably military intelligence. Recurrent untrammelled violence by paramilitaries has been a particularly horrible feature of the war. More Sudanese citizens have died from hunger and disease than by massacre and assassination. In pursuing the militia strategy, the security cabal has often acted beyond the purview of the legislature and executive, and even in opposition to senior officers of the regular army. The security-militia nexus has thrived amid the division and irresolution of different ruling cliques and institutions. It has regularly sought to delay or derail peace negotiations with the SPLA. Arguably, it is the very core of the Sudanese state.

In this context, it is not surprising that when the SLA and JEM insurrection intensified in 2003, the security cabal would seek out a local militia to arm and support. Candidates were available including the Beni Halba *fursan* and other local militias, armed as part of the Popular Defence Forces. The result was the *Janjawiid*. The motives are power, pride, greed, and the sheer habit of taking counter-insurgency to its annihilatory extreme.

Is it genocide? Here we encounter problems of definitional bluntness, similar to those encountered when asking what counts as famine. In contrast to the rich conceptual history of 'famine,' the term 'genocide' is a neologism barely sixty years old, whose coinage was coincident with its legal definition in the 1948 Genocide Convention. Because it is a crime, the diagnosis of 'genocide' hinges on the perpetrators' intent. Its lay usage is identified with the extreme and paradigmatic case, the Nazi Holocaust of European Jewry. What is happening in Darfur is not Genocide (capitalized) in this sense of the absolute extermination of a population. It does, however, fit the definition contained in the Genocide Convention, which is much broader and encompasses systematic campaigns against ethnic groups with the intention of eliminating them in part or whole. This (uncapitalized) 'genocide' is a legal term of art, and there is no a priori reason why it should straightforwardly correspond to lived experience or ethnographic complexity. Despite the caveats outlined above, Darfur's ethnic groups are readily identifiable (e.g., by native language). Moreover, genocidaires invariably seek to obliterate any ethnic complexities and indeterminacies with a simplistic labelling of their target group, exactly as is occurring now. The violence is far in excess of what would be considered proportionate for counter-insurgency purposes, including the deliberate killing, raping, and starving of civilians, and the destruction of their livelihoods. Genocidal intent can be shown.

When genocide is diagnosed we must respond. Leaving aside the question of military intervention, we should note that an effective response to Darfur's crisis will be complicated, comprehensive, and long. Moreover, in the spirit of *Famine that Kills*, we should attend to the understandings of genocide and its cognates by the people of Darfur (victims, perpetrators, and bystanders), and take these concepts and viewpoints into account rather than privileging an external viewpoint, however legally expert that may be. Let me conclude with just one preliminary observation on the challenge of an ethnographically-literate response to genocide in Sudan. Outsiders should be humble in the face of the lived experience of surviving genocide. The people of the Nuba Mountains, forgotten by the world, withstood the genocidal assaults of 1988–92 entirely through their own efforts (African Rights 1995). It would have been preferable for them not to have been tested to such limits. But, given that these remarkable people have faced oblivion and survived, scholars, activists, and practitioners need to learn from their demonstrated expertise. The people of Darfur have shown comparable resilience in surviving famine: let us hope they have the same skills when faced with genocidal massacre.

Conclusion

The text of *Famine that Kills* is unchanged from the 1989 edition. The analysis is a product of its time. Today I would write a very different book, but not necessarily a better one. The angry optimism would be modulated by more modest expectations of what we can expect from international relief agencies, and by the bewildering, demoralizing and all-encompassing impacts of the HIV/AIDS epidemic, which has yet to devastate Darfur, but which hangs like a shadow over the whole continent. But there is plenty to rage against: the inhuman cruelty of so many of Sudan's leaders, the poor policy based on poor analysis of so many international civil servants, and the needless deaths of so many thousand people, most of them children, who deserve better. And there is still plenty of reason for optimism. If the people of Darfur, objects of my immense admiration, are provided with security, human rights, political representation, and the opportunity to pursue their livelihoods and develop their region, they will use their energy and determination to good effect.

Alex de Waal
Addis Ababa, July 2004

Bibliography

African Rights (1995, July). *Facing Genocide: The Nuba of Sudan* (London, African Rights).

Alkire, S. (2003). 'Concepts of Human Security,' in L. Chen, S. Fukuda-Parr and E. Seidensticker (eds.), *Human Insecurity in a Global World* (Cambridge MA, Global Equity Initiative).

Davies, S. (1995). *Adaptable Livelihoods: Coping with Food Insecurity in the Malian Sahel* (London, Macmillan Palgrave).

de Waal, A. (1990). 'A Reassessment of Entitlement Theory in the Light of Recent Famines in Africa', *Development and Change*, 21, 469–90.

de Waal, A. (1994a). 'Starving out the South,' in M. Daly and A. Alsikainga (eds.), *Civil War in Sudan* (London, IB Taurus).

de Waal, A. (1994b). 'Some Comments on Militias in Contemporary Sudan,' in M. Daly and Alsikainga, A. (eds.), *Civil War in Sudan* (London, IB Taurus).

de Waal, A. (1997). *Famine Crimes: Politics and the Disaster Relief Industry in Africa* (London, International African Institute and James Currey).

de Waal, A., and Abdel Salam, A. H. (2004). 'Islamism, *Jihad* and State Power in Sudan,' in A. de Waal (ed.), *Islamism and its Enemies in the Horn* (London, C. Hurst and Co).

de Waal, A., and Whiteside, A. (2003). '"New Variant Famine": AIDS and Food Crisis in Southern Africa', *The Lancet*, 362: 1234–37.

Easterly, W. (2002). *The Elusive Quest For Growth: Economists' Misadventures in the Tropics* (Cambridge, MA, MIT Press).

Fedelino, A., and Kudina, A. (2003, September). 'Fiscal Sustainability in African HIPC Countries: A Policy Dilemma?' (IMF Working Paper WP/03/187).

IMF (2004, March). 'The Federal Democratic Republic of Ethiopia: Joint Staff Assessment of the Poverty Reduction Strategy Paper Annual Progress Report,' IMF Country Report No. 04/59.

International Crisis Group (2004, 25 March). 'Darfur Rising: Sudan's New Crisis' (Washington and Brussels, ICG).

Keen, D. (1994). *The Benefits of Famine: A Political Economy of Famine and Relief in Southwestern Sudan, 1983–1989* (Princeton, Princeton University Press).

Kuper, L. (1981). *Genocide: Its Political Use in the Twentieth Century* (Harmondsworth, Penguin).

Marcus, D. (2003). 'Famine Crimes in International Law', *American Journal of International Law*, 97, 245–81.

Maybury-Lewis, D. (2002). 'Genocide Against Indigenous Peoples', in A. L. Hinton (ed.), *Annihilating Difference: The Anthropology of Genocide* (Berkeley, University of California Press).

Médecins Sans Frontières (2002, April). 'Violence, Health and Access to Aid in Unity State/Western Upper Nile, Sudan' (Brussels, MSF).

Rivers, J., Holt, J., Seaman, J., and Bowden, M. (1976), 'Lessons for Epidemiology from the Ethiopian Famines', *Annales Société Belge de Médecin Tropicale*, 56, 345–57.

Rünger, M. (1987). *Land Law and Land Use Control in Western Sudan: The Case of Southern Darfur* (London, Ithaca).

Rugalema, G. (2000). 'Coping or Struggling? A Journey into the Impact of HIV/ AIDS in Southern Africa', *Review of African Political Economy*, 26, 537–45.

Saeed Mohamed El-Mahdi (1979). *Introduction to Land Law of the Sudan* (Khartoum, Khartoum University Press).

Young, H., and Jaspars, S. (1995). *Nutrition Matters: People, Food and Famine* (London, IT Publications).

CONTENTS

LIST OF FIGURES

LIST OF TABLES

LIST OF ABBREVIATIONS

ELSU	Economic Livestock Unit
FAO	Food and Agriculture Organization
HTS	Hunting Technical Services
IMR	Infant Mortality Rate
JMRDP	Jebel Marra Rural Development Project
kg	Kilogramme
LMMC	Livestock and Meat Marketing Corporation
SCC	Sudan Council of Churches
SCF	The Save the Children Fund
UNHCR	United Nations High Commission for Refugees
UNICEF	United Nations Childrens Fund
USAID	Unites States Agency for International Development
WSDC	Western Savanna Development Corporation
WFP	World Food Programme
£s	Sudanese Pound (One Sudanese pound equals 100 piastres)

FURTHER READING

I have treated aspects of the evidence and arguments contained in this book in greater detail in the following publications:

'Famine Mortality, a Case Study of Darfur, Sudan 1984–85', *Population Studies*, 43 (1989), pp. 5–24 (see Chapter 7 below).

'Is Famine Relief Irrelevant to Rural People?' *I.D.S Bulletin*, 20/2 (1989), pp. 63–67 (see Chapter 8 below).

'The Sudan Famine Code of 1920: Successes and Failures of the Indian Model of Famine Relief in Colonial Sudan', Report to ActionAid, London (1988) (see Chapter 8 below).

'Refugees and the Creation of Famine: The Case of Dar Masalit, Sudan', *Journal of Refugee Studies*, 1 (1988), pp. 127–140 (see Chapter 9 below).

'A Re-assessment of Entitlement Theory in the Light of Recent Famines in Africa', Luca d'Agliano (Turin) and Queen Elizabeth House (Oxford) Development Studies Working Papers No. 4 (1988) (see Chapter 1 below).

'Famine Early-Warning Systems and the Use of Socio-Economic Data', *Disasters*, 12 (1988), pp. 82–92 (see Chapter 8 below).

'The Perception of Poverty and Famines', *International Journal of Moral and Social Studies*, 2 (1987), pp. 251–262 (see Chapter 1 below).

'Famine that Kills, Darfur 1984–85', Report to the Save the Children Fund, London (1987) (see Chapters 2–9 below).

I have seen people
Who were remarkable—
Highly deserving of your admiration
For the fact that they
Were alive at all

Bertholt Brecht

In the dark times
Will there also be singing?
Yes, there will also be singing
About the dark times

Bertholt Brecht

INTRODUCTION

This book is a study of the famine which struck Darfur, Sudan, during 1984/5. Most books about famines are written from the viewpoint of outsiders, such as relief agencies and other organizations which have taken it upon themselves to prevent or alleviate famines. This book is different. It analyses a famine from the perspective of the rural people who suffered it. The story of the huge international famine-relief operation forms only a marginal part in the analysis, reflecting the minor role that it played in the lives of the famine sufferers.

In writing this book, I am trying to change the way that we, that is, the affluent world, understand famines in poor countries, particularly in Africa. A change in this understanding should lead to profound changes in the way in which governments and relief agencies respond to the threats and occurrences of famines. I hope to do this by starting a dialogue. Currently there is no dialogue, no exchange of views, between relief organizations and the people they avowedly serve, the rural poor. Instead, the relief agenda is set entirely by the self-named 'donors' and their colleagues in the rich world. An agenda which is set by one party to a debate, without consulting the other parties, is likely to be largely sterile. This is the case with the current famine-relief agenda. If, however, we listen to the rural poor of Africa—not only to their voiced concerns but to an articulated understanding of the principles that underly their actions—a lively debate will follow, and a new agenda will be set. I am certain that this new agenda will be more fruitful.

In Chapter 8 I begin, in a hesitant manner, to suggest how famine relief might have been better implemented in Darfur during 1984/5. These specific recommendations suggest a new agenda for famine relief, but they are not the main purpose of this book. This is for three reasons. One reason is that at this stage, specific proposals are premature. We still understand relatively little about indigenous conceptions of and responses to famine. There is a need to go deeper, to listen to more articulations of the problems (such as the conflicting articulations of different groups in society), before returning to the question of how to formulate policies. There is a danger that policies developed from the present partial understanding will be too shackled by current orthodoxies to represent the change that is needed. The second reason is that all famines are different, and so the methods of relieving them ought to be appropriately different. The recommendations of Chapter 8 do not fully apply to certain parts of Darfur—as explained in Chapter 9— let alone to other countries at other times. The third and most important reason is that to conclude with a specific programme for action would be a betrayal of the purpose of this book. I do not want to be part of the creation of a new orthodoxy, which will be imposed on poor societies which are vulnerable to famine. Instead, I am arguing for no orthodoxies, but instead a willingness to listen to, debate with, and understand people who suffer famine in each place. These people are, after all, the proven experts in surviving famines. One precondition for this dialogue is critical self-scrutiny by those involved with famine relief, another is a willingness to be patient, and to listen hard. In a world where thousands are dying preventably and millions are destitute, the time and effort needed to begin and sustain a dialogue of this kind may appear to be a luxury. Many will dismiss it as such: 'People are starving and that is all we need to know.' I hope to show that it is not a luxury, but that it is essential. Lives and livelihoods depend on it. This subject is too important for the tried, tested, and failed formula of platitudes and panic. Nevertheless, we cannot be inactive in the meantime; this is why I have included some suggestions for policies that should be adopted or abandoned.

Ethical Issues

Is it morally justifiable to do research on a famine, while it is occurring? It might be objected that it is unethical to stand by, notebook in hand, while people are suffering and dying.

I do not believe that this is true. Famines are not situations where dying people are constantly and everywhere to be seen. They are situations where acute poverty and destitution are most prominent. It is distasteful in some ways to build a career on the suffering of other people, but this is true of almost all the professions in which non-poor people work with poor people. In any case, this is not what gives rise to the qualm. Misgivings come with the feeling that unless one is a doctor or a nurse who is actually putting spoonfuls of food into the mouth of a starving child, one should not be there. This qualm underestimates the central role of logistics and planning in a relief operation, and of the role of information in these. In an emergency, doctors are scarce, but data are scarcer. Panic could be defined as acting in an emergency without information, or without interpreted information. Under this definition, aid agencies regularly panic. No general would think of fighting a war without intelligence; but the lack of information with which many relief programmes are planned and implemented remains remarkable. A few pieces of reliable information may be worth many thousands of tons of food or many crates of medicine.

To some, these answers may still appear inadequate or at least distasteful. Underlying this persistent unease is a vision of famine as something simple, huge, and apocalyptic. In the face of such an absolute, doing anything but directly saving lives is seen as an irrelevance. I attempt to analyse this important but misleading concept of famine in Chapter 1: it is responsible for many blunders in the field of famine relief.

It is difficult to be neutral about famine. All writers are 'against' famine. It is easy for moral judgements to cloud critical thought. Moral outrage cannot be indiscriminate. The 1984/5 famine was bad, unacceptably bad. But it was not as bad as it might have been (for instance, without rain in 1985, or without relief), or as bad as it was often said to be. It was of an order of magnitude worse than the famines of the colonial period and the first twenty-five years of the independent Sudan, but the famines of 1888–92 and 1913/14 were of an order of magnitude worse still.

Sources

Most of the information on which this book is based comes from eighteen months' field research in Sudan, almost all in Darfur, between mid-1985 and early 1987. The fieldwork was not based on the revered social-anthropological method of participant observation. It is one thing to convince oneself that it is morally justifiable to do anthropological field research during a famine, but it is another thing actually to do it. Observing a famine is possible, participating in it is more difficult. Consider a comparison: how would a social anthropologist participate in a war? By shooting people, by being shot? Few social scientists have been truly close to famine. Pitrim

Sorokin (ed. 1975) suffered the Russian famine of 1919–22, along with his compatriots, and his account is revealing of the problems a sociologist faces studying such a disaster. Colin Turnbull (1972) lived among the Ik during a famine, but the stresses of doing so appear to have reduced him to the state of a paranoid recluse, cooking meals in secret on the floor of his Land-Rover. Having spent some time living in villages in comparable circumstances, I can sympathize with Turnbull. Hospitality soon wore thin, and co-operation with the research soon gave way to demands for action from me and my 'brothers' in the relief agencies. The stresses of such a situation not only made life depressing but made research practically impossible. It would be interesting and valuable to discover how Raymond Firth (1959) was able to live through a famine in Tikopia, and then write about it with such insight. For my part, I distanced myself from any single community and instead made case-studies of eight villages, one peri-urban quarter, and one camp for famine migrants. With a team of research assistants, I spent a limited time in each one. This has resulted in significant gaps in the information collected, for instance I have very little material on how the stresses of the famine affected family life. But it made the gathering of at least some information possible. Through co-operation with the Save the Children Fund, I had access to resources, including transport, research assistants, and computers, that made this more extensive type of research possible. The collaboration of Malek el Amin, previously head of the Regional Department of Statistics, was critical to the success of the field research. The core of the field research consists of nearly 1,200 structured questionnaire interviews, several hundred unstructured interviews, and sundry other surveys and investigations mentioned in the text.

I have also used documentary evidence. I have used it sparingly because it has many shortcomings. It is possible for a researcher studying Darfur to collect every statistic, published and unpublished, in a single slender file, and have confidence that every number is almost certainly wrong. A few examples will suffice. Historical estimates for the population of Sudan are considered unreliable; modern estimates are also dubious. The Census of 1983 concluded that the rural areas of Um Kedada district contained 111,000 people. In 1985 the Area Council estimated the rural population at 168,000. In 1986 the SCF field officer for Um Kedada,

Maurice Herson, compiled the first (allegedly) complete list of villages in the district; different interpretations resulted in five different population estimates. Nobody who has witnessed a visiting official sitting down with a local sheikh and negotiating a figure for the number of local inhabitants will continue to have much faith in official population figures. I have quoted this example because matters are worse with respect to animal numbers and cultivated area. Pre-famine estimates of animal numbers in Darfur varied by factors of two-and-a-half, estimates of cropped area in 1985 varied by nearly as much. Market statistics can be misleading, as the principal markets (those for which figures are available) represent a varying proportion of animals and crops sold, and prices in these markets are varyingly representative of prices in rural markets. Even rainfall figures can mislead. During the 1980s, as the drought worsened, many rainfall monitors in north Darfur ceased recording, as they were no longer receiving payment for this task. Consequently, aggregate rainfall figures selectively underrepresent the recent dry years. Statistical data have the quality of becoming 'harder' the further one is from the process of their collection and analysis. It is best to limit their use, and be sceptical.

Most of the historical information used comes from oral sources. These sources include several accomplished amateur historians of Darfur, who are cited in the text. Other information comes from archival sources. Sudan's modern history is rich in archival material, and I have failed to do justice to the wealth of material available. This is partly for reasons of time; partly because the recorded impressions of administrators are likely to be misleading where poverty and famines are concerned (some famines, such as those of 1913/14 and 1930/1, appear to have caught the British administrators almost completely by surprise); and lastly because written sources often have the insidious effect of appearing more reliable than oral sources, and so displace the latter from their rightful place.

Outline of the Argument

This book is structured around our need to recognize the limitations of our conceptual viewpoint concerning famines. The argument has four stages. Stage one is to question and discredit what is commonly meant by the word 'famine' in English. Stage two is to introduce

Darfur, its social economy and prominent ideologies, and from these develop an appropriate local concept of famine. Stage three is to analyse the famine of 1984/5 in the light of this notion of famine, looking in turn at the constituent concepts of hunger, destitution, and death, and then at relief. Stage four consists in an exploration of the limits of the explanatory scheme.

Chapter 1 contains the first stage of the argument. Different concepts of 'famine' are compared. The English notion of 'famine' focuses on extremity, notably on mass starvation unto death. This contrasts with the more subtle terms used by people who suffer famines in other parts of the world. The English concept is an outcome more of social philosophy than of social experience. In particular it is the result of the nineteenth-century Malthusian debate. Malthus tied the concept of 'famine' to food shortage and mass death through starvation. Amartya Sen, in *Poverty and Famines*, has discredited the first component, but the second still persists. This erroneous concept is reinforced by the biasing manner in which outsiders, such as journalists and relief workers, are exposed to famines, as 'disaster tourists'. The gulf between Western and indigenous understandings of famine is illustrated with case-studies of the famines of the early 1970s in the west African Sahel and in Ethiopia. Who defines an event as a 'famine' is a question of power relations within and between societies. Certain famine-relief technologies, such as early-warning systems and nutritional surveillance, serve to give foreign relief organizations more power to define famines, at the expense of rural people.

Chapters 2, 3, and 4 develop stage two of the argument. Chapter 2 introduces Darfur, its geography, its peoples, its society and economy, and some of the central ideologies of rural life. An ideology of particular importance is that of the autonomous producer, who 'belongs' in a community as an equal. The opposite of this state is dependence, exclusion from the community, and material poverty. During famine people strive to avoid this latter state, and to preserve the basis of an acceptable future livelihood. Chapter 3 chronicles the history of famines in Darfur from the eighteenth century to the 1970s. Based on the modern memory of these famines, and the ideologies analysed in Chapter 2, the Darfurian concept of famine is analysed. Several kinds of famine are identified; those that involve hunger, those that also involve destitution and social breakdown, and 'famines that kill'. This concept of famine is based upon the trinity of hunger, destitution, and death. Of these, destitution and its corollary of social breakdown are most important. Chapter 4 analyses indigenous understandings of drought, environmental crisis, and the causes of the famine of 1984/5. It includes a case study of how one group, the Zaghawa, responded to the chronic crisis that occurred in the fifteen years before the famine.

Chapters 5 to 8 develop stage three of the argument. They are concerned with hunger, destitution, and death—the three concepts that constitute 'famine' in Darfur—and with relief. 'Hunger' is something that one simply puts up with. Satisfying the pangs of hunger is not a major concern for famine-stricken families. Even during the worst of the famine, households spent only a fraction of their potential income on food. Their priority was instead to preserve their way of life, to avoid destitution. This is analysed in Chapter 6. Farmers strove to keep enough resources to be able to cultivate during the rainy season, and herders struggled to keep their animals alive. This involved great tenacity, skill at managing resources, and planned hardship. Even in a famine camp, where the extremes of hunger and destitution were to be seen, the aim of preserving the base of an acceptable future livelihood was evident.

Chapter 7 presents what is likely to be the most controversial evidence in this book. This is that, although some 100,000 people are estimated to have died due to the famine, these deaths were caused not by lack of food but by 'health crises'. These health crises consisted in localized outbreaks of disease, particularly measles and the diarrhoeas, which were precipitated by population movements and by lack of sanitation and clean water. It is commonly argued that diseases become more prevalent during famines because people are undernourished and so weak and more susceptible to disease. I am arguing that this is false, at least in the case of Darfur. Darfurian people have a fatalistic attitude towards death, which is that it is something you can do nothing about. This is shown to have some validity, if only fortuitously.

In Chapter 8 I discuss the relief programmes. Relief followed several distinct ideologies. Indigenous relief was given according to 'Sudanic' and 'Islamic' ideologies. Though the amounts given were small, they were often very effective. Much government relief was targeted to certain groups to whom the government felt special obligations, such as its own employees and townspeople. The international relief agencies followed a fourth distinct pattern, attempting to give to those in 'greatest need'. In many ways, this aid was misconceived. The givers of aid thought that they were giving to save literally millions from starving to death. This was based on a very biased picture of the famine. Millions did not starve to death, not because of international relief, but because of the survival skills of rural people. There is in fact no evidence that the 3 million sacks of relief grain distributed saved any lives. Following the analysis of mortality, I argue that if Darfur had been provided with clean water, better sanitation, and measles vaccination, most or even all of the the famine deaths could have been prevented, even without food aid. Food aid did help rural people avoid impoverishment, to a certain degree, but other sorts of intervention would have been more effective. These interventions include buying up animals at guaranteed prices, 'fodder aid', and employment schemes.

The final stage of the argument is developed in Chapter 9. Here, the analysis turns to two 'other famines' that struck Darfur during 1984/5. One occurred on the western border, and was related to the presence of Chadian refugees. The second occurred on the southern border, among people with a very different social economy. For different reasons, the analysis developed in the central part of this book fails to work for these famines. This illustrates the limitations of the explanatory schema, and suggests the need for analyses of famine appropriate to the particular causes of the famine, and to the nature of the particular society in question. The conclusion of the book therefore takes the form of a challenge, not a set of answers.

1

'Famine' in English

What is Famine?

Question: Was there a famine after *Dan Muubi* [about 1953]?
Answer: Yes. No one died, but the price of millet rose. When
the sack of millet costs 6000 francs, isn't that a famine?
(Interview with Sahelian herder quoted by Diulde Laya, 1975,
p. 88).

Famine is a particularly virulent form of [starvation] causing
widespread death.
                    (Amartya Sen, *Poverty and Famines*, 1981, p. 40).

There is clearly a major problem here. What is famine? The tension
between conflicting understandings of famine is a central theme of
this book. The Sahelian herder's concept of famine—hinted at
here—is similar to those held by the people of Darfur, the subjects
of this book. This concept strikes Europeans as strange, at odds with
intuition. Yet I am going to argue that the herder's concept is
fundamentally more accurate when it comes to analysing the nature
of famine in this part of Africa.

Contrasts between the concepts of famine held by European and
American scholars and those held by the people who actually suffer
famines have been noticed elsewhere, by Bruce Currey:

In Bangladesh, the culture defines three types of famine: scarcity is *akal*
(when times are bad); famine is *durvicka* (when alms are scarce) and
nationwide famine is *mananthor* (when the epoch changes) . . . [he cites
some regional variations] . . . These subtle terms contrast with the
international definition accepted at the Swedish famine symposium:
'widespread food shortage leading to a significant regional rise in the death
rates.' (1978, p. 87).

In many ways the Bangladeshi idiom for understanding famine is
different from the most common African idioms, which are

discussed below. Some aspects of these so-called 'definitions' are however similar. In both Africa and Bangladesh the concepts grow out of actual experience of famine, and in neither case is there a positivistic criterion of measurable changes in food availability or death rates. Most importantly, neither of these concepts of famine use the presence of deaths from starvation as a criterion at all. Similar concepts are to be found in east Africa, where Crosse-Upcott reported that the Ngindo people of Tanganyika distinguish hungers that do and do not kill people (1958, p. 1), and in India, where Rangasami has written 'I hope to establish that mortality is not a necessary condition of famine' (1985, p. 6).

Nevertheless, academic approaches to famine continue to stress that 'famines imply starvation' (Sen 1981, p. 39). John Rivers and his colleagues have stated that: 'Starvation is a semantic prerequisite for the definition of famine' (1976, p. 355). Even critics of conventional approaches to famine have not challenged this. Bruce Currey's (1978) 'community syndrome' definition continued to presuppose deaths. Mohiuddin Alamgir followed a similar argument but concluded, in an avowedly uncontroversial manner, that for conceptual purposes 'focus on death seems to be very meaningful since it is the ultimate manifestation of famine' (1980, p. 6). Native English-speakers are very resistant to the idea that a famine could occur without people starving: 'it wouldn't be a famine' is the response. The verb 'to starve' originally meant 'to die'. When used in the context of famine, 'starvation' implies death as a consequence, if not its inevitability at least its likelihood.

The central role of mass starvation in the concept of famine is a relatively recent phenomenon. In the following section I argue that the modern English notion of famine is an aberration of intellectual history. The conception of famine as mass starvation unto death was an outcome of the Malthusian debate of the nineteenth century. In the population theories of Thomas Malthus, famine played a role as nature's 'court of last resort'. Famine was said to follow unchecked population growth outrunning food supplies, and to result in mass starvation reducing the population to a level consistent with the supplies of food.

One part of this Malthusian concept of famine already lies discredited. This is the conception of food shortage as a necessary and sufficient condition for famine, a view discredited by Amartya Sen in his seminal book *Poverty and Famines* (1981). Using case-studies of four famines, Sen showed that famines may occur without a significant decline in the availability of food in the affected area. Some of Sen's empirical contentions have been disputed, but his reconceptualization of the nature of famine is widely accepted: 'Famine is the characteristic of some people not *having* enough food to eat. It is not the characteristic of there not *being* enough food to eat' (p. 1). Thus 'food shortage' definitions of famine, such as the 'international definition accepted at the Swedish symposium' cited by Currey no longer occur in reputable literature. In some cases a ₁ood shortage may cause famine, but food shortage is not famine in itself.

Sen has therefore excised one part of the Malthusian concept of famine. He has left the other part, the concept of famine as mass death from starvation, intact; even strengthened. This concept retains such a stranglehold on our thinking that it is hard to reject it, yet the continuing experience of modern famines show that this is what we must do.

First it is necessary to look in more detail at the operation of the English concept of famine. Sen, reviewing definitions of famine, noted: 'The definitional exercise is more interesting in providing a pithy description of what happens in situations clearly diagnosed as one of famine than in helping us to do the diagnosis—the traditional role of definitions' (1981, p. 40, footnote). This is a very important point: the 'pithy description' form of 'definitions' of famine leads to a focus on extreme cases or (in Alamgir's words) 'the ultimate manifestation' of famine, which is of little help in marginal or borderline cases. Rather, the 'definitions' express the concept of famine, almost a mental image of famine. Unfortunately this insight was a footnote to Sen's argument, which was concerned with different issues. Sen attempted to side-step the definitional debate, by using the word in what he called its 'most common English sense', which he paraphrased: 'Famine is a particularly virulent form of [starvation] causing widespread death' (p. 40). But this was an improvement on what had gone before only in that it concentrated on the nature of famine and not its alleged causes. In Sen's hands the concept of famine became 'pithy description' or 'ultimate manifestation' once again. Sen illustrated what famine is:

Starvation is a normal feature in many parts of the world, but this phenomenon of 'regular' starvation has to be distinguished from violent outbursts of famines. It isn't just regular starvation that one sees in 436 BC, when thousands of starving Romans 'threw themselves into the Tiber'; or in Kashmir in AD 918, when 'one could scarcely see the water of Vitasta (Jhelum) entirely covered as the river was with corpses'; or in 1333–7 in China, when—we are told—four million people died in one region only . . . (p. 39).

But this was sleight of hand. In contrasting famine with 'regular starvation', these extreme examples make us lose sight of the need for a conception of famine that fits with all famines, not just the most severe ones. Sen was trying to conceive of famine by picturing its most horrible manifestations, and then seeing how closely an event approximated to these. I have criticized Sen not because he was the worst offender on this count, but because his book is clear and to the point. Other English speakers share the error, because it is an error that lies in the 'most common English sense' of 'famine'.

In many poor societies in the third world, the concept of famine arises from the ordinary operation of that society. Idioms of hunger and famine are often central idioms for the expression of social relations and experiences. In Africa, words for 'famine' are typically the same as words for 'hunger'. In Swahili it is *njaa*, in Amharic *rehab*, in Hausa *yunwa*, etc.: all are used for both 'hunger' and 'famine'. Arabic is the principal exception to this, but even here the word *ju'*, meaning hunger, is also used as a cognate of *maja'a*, famine. Throughout the continent words for eating and hunger are used to express many differing positive and negative aspects of life. People or communities which are prosperous, predatory, or powerful are 'eating', those who are poor or powerless are 'hungry', even if they actually have enough food. Words for eating are used to convey profit, sex, enjoyment, political power, reward, bribery, and many other things. For instance Chinua Achebe's fictional account of west African politics (1966) is pervaded by imagery of eating. He expressed the people's opinion of their leaders' activities in these words:

Let them eat. After all, when white men used to do all the eating did we commit suicide? Of course not. And where is the all-powerful white man today? He came, he ate, he went. The important thing is to stay alive . . . if you survive, who knows? it may be your turn to eat tomorrow. Your son may bring home your share (pp. 161–2).

Reference to many other idiomatic uses of food, eating and hunger to express different aspects of life will occur throughout this book. This is not peculiar to Africa either. Recent work on Melanesia has focused on the central symbolic use of 'hunger' to express many aspects of life other than failing to eat enough (Young 1986; Khan 1986). Hence it is scarcely surprising that periods of shortage, poverty, suffering, or powerlessness, without starvation, can be periods of 'hunger', and hence 'famine'. Even when a famine does kill, it does not follow that killing is the central experience of that famine: the focus need not be on death.

Hunger is in part an idiom. In part it is an experience: famines remain landmarks of suffering in the consciousness of peoples. The meaning of the word for 'famine' in any society is an outcome of the idiom of famine and hunger used, and the history of actual famines experienced by that society. In the following section I shall turn to the idiom and experience of famine in Britain.

The Most Common English Sense

Amartya Sen was correct when he claimed to be using the word 'famine' in its most common English sense. But the current common-sense English concept of famine is the outcome of a particular history of famines, and particular debates on the nature of society. There is in fact good evidence that until relatively recently 'famine' and its cognates were used in Britain in a way similar to that employed in today's third world countries.

The word 'famine' came to English from the vulgar Latin *famina*, which was derived in turn from *fames*, meaning 'hunger'. The first usage of 'famine' cited in the Oxford English Dictionary is in Langland's *Piers Plowman*, written in 1362: 'Famyn schal a-ryse, fruites schal fayle thorw flodes and foul weder.' Chaucer, writing the *Pardoner's Tale* twenty-four years later, used the word in a sense closer to today's 'hunger': 'And schold hir children sterve for famyn'. Modern dictionaries class these two 'meanings' of famine separately. This is with hindsight: it does not follow that 'famyn' then meant anything different from 'hunger'.

Famines occurred in England long before the word 'famyn' was introduced. The Venerable Bede, writing in Latin in the eighth century on the life of Bishop Wilfrid, reports a famine that struck Sussex in about 680:

For three years before his coming into the kingdom no rain had fallen in those parts, so that a most terrible famine [*fames aceruissima*] assailed the populace and pitilessly destroyed them. For example it is said that forty or fifty men, wasted with hunger, would go together to some precipice or to the sea shore where in their misery they would join hands and leap into the sea, perishing wretchedly either by the fall or by drowning (Bede ed. 1969, p. 373).

The story goes on to describe how when Wilfrid began to preach the Gospel, a 'gentle but ample rain fell, the earth revived, the fields became green and a happy and fruitful season followed' (p. 375).

Famines were certainly known in medieval England. But the evidence shows them to be in the nature of 'hungers' or 'dearths' and not demographic crises of mass starvation. This can be seen by looking at the famine of 1315–17, the most severe famine recorded in English history. The crisis was due to harvest failures and was compounded and prolonged by outbreaks of livestock diseases, making it 'a famine that in its duration, severity and extent far surpassed all earlier dearths' (Abel 1980, p. 38). It saw the worst grain price inflation in English history (Kershaw 1973, p. 13). The famine killed people. On the basis of records from Winchester, Kershaw concluded that the famine years, taken overall, saw a crude death rate of approaching 10 per cent (1973, p. 11). Most of this he attributed to disease. This excess mortality affected population trends for decades (Postan 1950; Hollingsworth 1969, p. 382).

The famine was no doubt terrible, but its demographic effects were insignificant compared with the Black Death, which occurred thirty years later. Historians have debated whether these years saw a demographic crisis at all. Reading the accounts of the famine one is struck by the fact that it was primarily an economic or agrarian crisis, and only secondarily (if at all) a crisis of starvation and population fall.

The famine of 1315 was far worse than its successors. There were dearths in England in every century up to the nineteenth. The worst of the fifteenth century was in 1438 (Abel 1980); and the second half of the sixteenth century saw a succession of severe scarcities. From 1480 to 1800 one quarter of the harvests in England were 'failures', one sixth 'really bad' (Hoskins 1964, 1968). Hoskins described the very worst years for the agrarian economy (1594–7) as 'amounting at times to a famine' (p. 32). Easily the worst years in terms of death rates were 1557–9, when rates peaked at 60 per cent and 124 per cent above normal (Wrigley and Schofield 1981). Otherwise, overall death rates reached maxima of 40–44 per cent above normal only three times. There were also numerous (and worse) famines in Scotland, notably in 1615–25 (Flinn 1977), variously described by contemporary sources as a 'great dearth' and a 'famyn' (p. 116). There were also localized dearths. But Appleby, in his study of dearths in north-west England (1978), was noticeably wary of using the word 'famine'. He asked of the worst crisis in his study period 'Should we call this a famine? Perhaps' (p. 137).

It is hard to tell precisely how the word 'famine' was used in those times, but it seems that until the eighteenth century 'famine' and 'hunger' were used interchangeably. Shakespeare in *Macbeth* used it thus: 'Upon the next tree thou shalt hang alive till famine cling thee.' Elsewhere the word was used in an identifiably modern sense, as a period of general shortage of food. Thomas Hobbes used it this way. This hints at the origins of the modern English notion of famine in social philosophy. The term 'starvation' did not exist. 'To starve' meant to suffer or die, whether from cold, hunger, thirst or any other cause (a sense it still retains in remoter parts of Britain). A word that was used interchangeably with 'famine' was 'dearth'. 'Dearth' is an older word than 'famine', with roots in Anglo-Saxon. It is now almost obsolete in this sense. 'Dearth' does not imply that people are dying as a result, and does not imply starvation. The sixteenth-century Elizabethan governments, which were the first in England to introduce systematic legislation against famines, used the term 'dearth' (Leonard 1900). Historians of this period have been careful to use 'dearth', and reserve 'famine', with caution, for the very worst years. Even the worst famine of all, 1315–17, does not fit well with modern English conceptions of 'famine'. The phenomenon of these 'famines', and the understanding of them, was closer to the notion of 'famine' as hunger and dearth than the modern notion of famine as mass starvation and death.

The concept of 'famine' began to take on its modern sense only at the end of the eighteenth century, and notably in the debate engendered by Thomas Malthus.

Why did this change occur? Could it be that there were new types of famine in early industrial England? The answer is no: bread riots in Paris during 1789 and in London during the 1790s certainly gave the ruling classes pause for thought on the subject of food shortages, but there were no famines on a scale greater than had gone before. The converse was true: improvements in public health prevented the outbreak of epidemic diseases that previously had followed famine, such as during the dearth years of 1816–17 (Post 1977, pp. 126–7). Could it be that English thinkers were exposed to Continental famines, which were phenomena of mass starvation, unlike ordinary English dearths? It is certain that famines in France, Germany, and Scandanavia were worse than in Britain, but accounts of mass starvation are exaggerated (Post 1977, p. 122). However, Malthus's discussion of 'checks to population' in these countries made virtually no reference to famines at all. The closest was the famine of 1799 in Sweden, which Malthus himself witnessed, and which he described only as a 'severe dearth' (ed. 1890, p. 161). Could it be that exposure to America, Africa, and Asia led to exposure to a different kind of famine, or misperception of these foreign famines as being much worse than they really were? This is a more plausible account. The word 'starvation' was apparently coined by Mr Dundas MP (later dubbed 'Starvation Dundas') who referred to possible 'starvation' in the New England colonies during 1775. But neither Malthus, Dundas nor others actually witnessed mass starvation. The available writings of travellers, missionaries and others on famine throughout the world were reviewed by Malthus in twelve chapters of his Sixth Edition of *Essay on the Principle of Population*. Malthus's empirical evidence did not call for a dramatic re-evaluation of 'famine'. Famines were the same, but the way of thinking about them was changing.

In Malthus's *Essay* there was a contradiction between two concepts of famine. This contradiction was present in the First Edition of 1798, and remained until the final, much revised Sixth Edition of 1826. These two concepts created the contrast made in the opening section of this chapter. The first was the old concept of famine as hunger and dearth.

In the First *Essay*, Malthus noted that 'The traces of the most destructive famines in China and Indostan, are by all accounts very soon obliterated [by population regeneration]' (ed. 1926, pp. 110–11). This same point has been made by Malthus's critics Watkins and Menken, who reviewed the available demographic evidence concerning historical famines and concluded that famines cannot account for dramatic falls in population (1985).

In the later editions, Malthus invoked much empirical evidence from around the world. The evidence he cited supported the old concept of famine. Malthus's own experience of famine in Scandanavia during 1799 has been noted. Discussing Syria, he described a famine created by forcible government requisition of farmers' grain, so that 'At Damascus, during the scarcity of 1784, the [towns-] people paid only one penny farthing for their bread, while the peasants in the villages were absolutely dying with hunger' (ed. 1890, pp. 102–3). Malthus went on to describe the checks to population in the region. The first three were plague, disorders consequent on plague, and other epidemic and endemic diseases. Then '(4) Famine. (5) And lastly, the sicknesses which always follow a famine and which occasion a much greater mortality' (p. 103). Malthus noted that starvation in Abyssinia and along the Nile followed destruction of crops by war, and described how insecurity and slaving would prevent population growth in west Africa, though the land could support many more people. Malthus also noted that though the ultimate check was starvation, it was rarely the immediate one, because increasing scarcity of food acts gradually over a long period to depress wages and undernourish people, thereby preventing population growth.

Yet the logic of Malthus's argument made it necessary to invoke a second concept of 'famine', as Nature's 'court of last resort': 'Famine seems to be the last, the most dreadful resource of nature. . . . [Following unchecked population growth] gigantic inevitable famine stalks in the rear, and with one mighty blow, levels the population with the food of the world (ed. 1926, p. 139–40). The constituents of this second concept of famine came not from the experience of famine but from the logic of Malthus's argument. This vision of apocalyptic Famine, gigantic and inevitable, waiting to level the population with a single blow, the court of last resort in population control, was what seized the imagination of people in England. Famine came to be defined simultaneously as a food shortage, and as mass death through starvation. A new concept of 'famine' became current. It is unusual for a word to adopt a new meaning in this way, but the publicity of the Malthusian debate was exceptional. It was this publicity rather than the originality of thought that made Malthus important (Smith 1951), and many people participated in the debate without having actually read Malthus's *Essay* (Bonar 1895).

The Malthusian debate also marked another shift in thinking about famine. Previously there had been famines, in the plural, which were what individuals and communities experienced. The

criterion for an event being a famine was that those suffering it
understood it to be so. Now there was to be 'famine', which is an
externally quantifiable change of state among a population. The
criterion of famine became instead a measurable increase in the
death rate of an aggregation of individuals, diagnosed by medical
professionals as being due to starvation, and causally related to a
measurable decrease in the availability of food. Demographers,
physicians, and agricultural statisticians were now needed to
diagnose famine. The tendency to treat famines as a technical
malfunction rather than a social experience has been with us ever
since.

   The Malthusian legacy is complex, but at its core is the simple
reconceptualizing of famine as a food shortage and as mass-
starvation deaths. Amartya Sen has shown that famines have no
necessary relation to food shortages. It is the persistence of the
concept of mass death through starvation that is important to this
argument. It was this notion, among others, that dictated British
policy to Ireland in the 1840s:

> Officially, it was declared that no deaths from starvation must be allowed to
> occur in Ireland, but in private the attitude was different. 'I have always felt
> a certain horror of political economists', said Benjamin Jowett, the
> celebrated Master of Balliol, 'since I heard one of them say that he feared the
> famine of 1848 in Ireland would not kill more than a million people, and that
> would scarcely be enough to do any good.' The political economist in
> question was Nassan Senior, one of the Government's advisors on economic
> affairs. (Woodham-Smith 1962, pp. 375–6).

In the English debate on the Irish famine both the Malthusian and
the anti-Malthusian positions used a notion of famine in which
starvation deaths were central. Woodham-Smith noted that British
relief policies in Ireland were aimed only at the prevention of deaths,
so much so that during most of the famine there was a 'Quarter Acre
Clause' which prevented people who owned more than a quarter of
an acre of land from obtaining relief (p. 363). The aim was to assist
only those on the point of death through starvation. The Malthusians saw famine as caused by population outrunning food and
consisting in mass starvation. The anti-Malthusians disagreed on the
causes of famine but agreed on its nature.

   British policy in India was at times geared to Malthusian concepts
of population, resources, and famine. But even when not, the notion

of famine as mass starvation was current, and the Famine Codes were devised with the restricted objective of preventing starvation deaths (Drèze 1988, p.34). This created a tension in the minds of those responsible for administering India, between what they saw of famines and what they believed 'famine' to be. This is well illustrated by Lovat Fraser in his adulatory account of *India under Curzon and After* (1911). In the following passage he used this contradiction to credit the British Raj with the conquest of a type of 'famine' which had probably never occurred:

No famine in modern times is comparable to the horrors recorded during such visitations under native rule. . . . Thus Sir Theodore Morison holds that the use of the term 'famine' in India is now 'an anachronism and a misnomer'. He says: 'The true meaning of the word "famine" (according to the Oxford English Dictionary) is "extreme and general scarcity of food"; this phenomenon has entirely passed away. Widespread death from starvation, which the word may also be held to connote, has also ceased. Death from starvation is extremely rare, even in those districts which are officially described as famine-stricken. "Famine" now means a prolonged period of unemployment, accompanied by dear food . . .' (p. 281).

Morison and Fraser were in effect arguing that 'famine' no longer existed. This demonstrates again that it was Malthus's vision of gigantic Famine, the great leveller, that gained currency, not the reality of famine as dearth and hunger. And Malthus's vision of gigantic Famine was just that: a vision. It was a logical necessity for his argument that famine should be the last sanction and check on population. But neither his critics nor his advocates have ever pointed to a famine in which population was levelled to food supply in one gigantic blow.

What is important about Malthus in this argument is not that people accepted his theories of population and the causes of famine. Many did not and still do not. The point is that he created the terms of the debate, in such a way that arguments concerning famine that carry no ostensible reference to Malthus are still using the concept of famine that he coined. An example is the Russian famine of 1891/2. This was interpreted variously by the political factions in Russia at the time, but all agreed that it was a crisis of a failure of food supplies and mass starvation. However, Simms has argued that there was no agrarian crisis at all: 'It is not the physical impact, that is the numbers of starving or the disruption of the economy, that makes the famine important. [Instead] it is the psychological impact, what men believed to be the truth' (1976, p. 346). The 'men' in question were intellectuals, including Marxists and Populists. None of them were ostensibly Malthusians, but all of them subscribed to a Malthusian notion of the nature of famine.

Disaster Tourism

A central claim of this book is that the current English notion of 'famine' as mass starvation unto death is inappropriate, and should be discarded. However, pointing out that the intellectual ancestry of the concept of 'famine' is less than legitimate is unlikely to persuade those who have seen television pictures of stick-thin children in the famine camps of Africa, or indeed those who have seen the same children in the flesh, as relief workers, journalists, or other visitors to relief camps or feeding shelters. This is partly because of the grip which the idea of 'famine' continues to have on our thinking. It is also partly because the way in which outsiders are exposed to famines reinforces that concept. Outsiders have biased perceptions of famine: their observations are highly subjective. To understand why this is so we must look at the phenomenon of 'disaster tourism'.

'Disaster tourism' is a variant of the phenomenon of 'rural development tourism' identified by Robert Chambers (1983). Rural development tourists are typically consultant professionals with international agencies, academics, bureaucrats, or dignitaries who are given brief and selective tours of rural development projects in poor countries. These people are professionally concerned with the amelioration of poverty. Yet they do not truly observe rural poverty. Rural development tourism creates a set of biases which work to make the realities of rural poverty largely invisible to such people. The true depths of rural poverty remain unperceived. It is worth listing these biases, because they might be expected to make not only poverty invisible, but famines as well.

Chambers first looks at 'spatial biases': urban, roadside and tarmac. The development tourist is likely to see only certain places. These are principally the towns and rural places close to roads, particularly tarmac roads. It is well documented that in third world countries these locations are almost always richer and more developed than the rural hinterland. Linked to this is a 'dry-season' bias: outsiders tend to visit poor countries when travel is easiest and the climate most pleasant. They thereby miss the wet season when rural people are usually less well nourished, poorer, harder working, and more exploited. It follows that outsiders simply do not see many poor people, and do not see them at their poorest.

The second bias is 'project bias'. The ousider is most likely to see development projects; partly because he (or, rarely, she) is most likely to have been invited to inspect, finance, evaluate, or merely be impressed by these projects. Development projects are examples of development, which means that poorer people who are not receiving development assistance are not seen in or near them. They are also likely to be in richer areas to start off with. Thirdly there are 'person biases'; the outsider is more likely to meet men rather than women, the élite rather than the underprivileged, people using a project rather than people not using it, well people rather than ill people, etc.. Fourthly, there are 'diplomatic biases'; outsiders will be restrained by courtesy and tact if not by a language barrier from asking awkward and embarrassing questions, especially in the presence of their hosts or guides. All these are factors which lead to the underperception of third world poverty.

Lastly Chambers discusses professional biases. Outsiders' professional interests in only one aspect of society or the environment leads them to miss the closely integrated and intermeshed nature of rural poverty. Soil scientists fail to see the part played by indebtedness, economists fail to see the seasonal fluctuations in nutritional level, but few (perhaps with the exception of social anthropologists) see all the many causes working together.

Chambers admits some tendencies contrary to his set of biases, for instance that academics are usually found in the third world during the summer long vacation, which is the wet and 'hungry' season in west Africa and much of south Asia. Nevertheless, there is a definite tendency for the poor to remain unseen, or when seen, not to be perceived as poor.

The disaster tourist is often a different person, with a different brief, but is exposed to a comparable set of biases. In this case, however, the biases serve not to hide poverty, but to exaggerate it. Disaster tourists are typically journalists in search of a story, relief workers trying to make an assessment of need, or politicians in search of an image that combines action and compassion. Such people are usually alerted to the fact that a 'famine' is occurring before they actually witness it themselves. They thus arrive in the famine area armed with a notion of what may be happening—a 'famine'. They may be sceptical as to whether what they have heard :s actually true, but if they see evidence of a famine, they know what it entails. What they see, of course, is subject to distortions. The main distortions are the biases outlined by Robert Chambers and the transformation in the famine area due to the famine and the people's responses to it.

One of the striking aspects of rural peoples' responses to famine in Africa is their seasonality. Another is the extent to which people migrate long distances, especially to towns. Because farmers need to plant their fields when the rains return, they look for alternative sources of income during the dry season. Most such sources are to be found in the towns, or by the roadsides. It is the poorer, rather than the richer, rural people who follow these strategies. Many people wander about searching for work, or beg. Local charitable committees set up feeding centres and clinics for the most destitute, and often specifically for malnourished children.

As a result, the biases which normally mean that rural poverty is invisible, now mean it is magnified. The outsider arrives in the dry season, and sees poor people (many of them women and children, many ill) at the roadsides and in the towns. They are not hidden by their work, but rather made prominent by their demands for work and charity. Less poor people who have remained in the rural areas are not seen. They are eating unappetizing foods such as berries and leaves: this is often seen by outsiders as the final sign of desperation, whereas in fact it is one of the first things famine victims do, as these foods are free, and often both plentiful and nutritious. Migration is thought of as a last resort in a similar way; in fact people often come to the towns when no work is possible in the villages due to the dry season, and then leave to replant their fields later on. The 'project bias' leads the disaster tourist to the clinics and feeding centres, where the worst cases of malnutrition and disease are to be found. Diplomacy and courtesy, not to mention human sympathy, make him or her listen to the descriptions of the horror before the feeding centre or clinic started. It is bad taste to challenge suffering people's accounts of having 'lost everything'.

The professional bias of a journalist is to search for a good story: the 'good famine story' is that of a family who have been forced to abandon their home, have lived off nuts and berries, whose children are starving or already dead, and whose only hope lies in the charity of a (preferably foreign) aid programme. This is not to say that journalists deliberately exaggerate the scale of the suffering that is going on (though sometimes they do); merely that their professional priorities lead them to characterize a famine situation in a certain manner. Aid agency officials are likewise sometimes guilty of deliberate scare-mongering, and in a sense they 'benefit' from a famine or similar crisis. They also have a horror of getting it wrong, and failing to foresee and relieve an emergency. But, as in the case of journalists, this is secondary: what is most important is a sincere but distorted perception.

In normal times, a rural development tourist makes an implicit inference from observed non-poverty to universal non-poverty. In the case of our disaster tourist the implicit inference is from seen hunger and destitution to universal hunger and destitution. A disaster tourist may start as a sceptic, but in virtually all cases the extreme poverty of many highly visible people during a famine will be enough to convince him or her that a famine is occuring. Famine may be difficult to define, but 'famine' is an easy diagnosis to make. Once the diagnosis is accepted, a train of assumptions is also all too easily accepted. For such an outsider, 'famine' implies starvation, a 'famine-affected population' implies a population under threat of death by starvation.

Hence, disaster tourists are drawn towards aspects of the famine that reinforce their prior conceptions of what famines are. They also lead to exaggerations of the severity of the famine. Failing to comprehend how rural people really survive, disaster tourists often predict that in the absence of external aid, millions will starve. Fortunately they are usually wrong (de Waal 1987*b*). This tendency to exaggerate the severity of famines coexists with the 'normal' tendency to overlook rural poverty. An outsider who is on a 'development mission', as a rural development tourist, and who therefore is not looking for a famine, may travel through a famine-stricken area without seeing the famine. An outsider on a 'famine mission' may travel through the same area and predict that thousands are about to starve. Outsiders' judgements on the severity of poverty and famine may veer to either extreme, depending on what the outsider is looking for, and what he or she is exposed to.

Recent Approaches to Understanding Famines

In the previous sections I have argued that the modern English notion of 'famine' is an aberration of intellectual history, and that this erroneous concept is buttressed by biased exposure to famines, through the phenomenon of disaster tourism. In the following chapters I shall show how how the famine of 1984/5 in Darfur can be understood better if we discard the English notion of 'famine', and instead adopt the concepts used by the people who have experience of suffering famines. In the meantime I shall show that recent events that we have labelled 'famines' have in fact been dramatically misunderstood.

This discussion has a second purpose. Earlier, I mentioned that a common response of English speakers to the suggestion that a famine might occur without people starving is 'it wouldn't be a famine'. The implication of this is that a better word might be 'dearth', that the problem is simply semantic, and that the history of the word 'famine' is beside the point. However, restricting the use of the word 'famine' to events that involved mass starvation unto death would effectively reduce the number of famines in the modern world to very few, if any. Almost all of the events we call 'famines' would have to be redefined as 'dearths'. The Sahelian famine of 1973, discussed below, is a case in point.

There are several instances when relief agencies and the mass media have diagnosed or predicted a 'famine' which was not going to occur. A striking example is the non-famine in Cambodia during 1979 (Shawcross 1984). More recently, after the Western world had been shocked by the apparent failure of governments and relief agencies to respond to the exceptionally severe famines in Ethiopia and Sudan during 1984/5, a spate of misdiagnosed famines occurred. These included events in South Sudan during 1986, in Somalia during 1986/7, and in northern Ethiopia during 1987/8. Even in the exceptionally severe 'famines that killed' of 1984/5, gross misunderstandings of what was happening were common (see Chapter 8 and de Waal 1987*b*). Scholars have yet to analyse these recent famines and non-famines, so it is only possible to discuss them in a limited way. However, the famines of the early 1970s in the Sahel and Ethiopia have been the subject of much research, most of which has manifested the conceptual errors and biased perceptions discussed above.

The Sahelian Famine of 1969–74

The Sahelian drought of the early 1970s is a prime example of a famine misrepresented. Franke and Chasin (1980), in their epic history of the origins of the crisis, cited authorities that call it 'The most serious and the most spectacular drought and famine in African history', the greatest disaster in two centuries, etc. (pp. 5–6). The immediate post-drought years saw a flood of papers and books concerned with the drought and its aftermath. This discussion will start with what is the most systematic and detailed, certainly the longest, study of this famine in its historical context: Michael Watts's *Silent Violence*, an examination of Hausaland in northern Nigeria (Watts 1983).

Watts's concern was to show that 'In the 19th century the Sokoto Caliphate exhibited a remarkable resiliency to climatic stress' (p. xxii) but that since the penetration of capitalism, during and after colonial rule, there has been 'A phaoroic [*sic*] sequence of famines' (p. 19), and that 'Famines were and are organically linked to the rupture of the balance between peasant subsistence and consumption precipitated by the development and intensification of commodity production' (p. xxii). The famines in question occurred during 1913/14, 1926/7, 1942/3 and 1973, the last being the 'Sahelian famine' as it affected the savannas of Nigerian Hausaland. Good data concerning these famines are lacking. There is convincing evidence for a disastrous and killing famine during 1913/14, but this was only at the very dawn of colonial rule, and no mortality data exist. Watts cited some death rates for 1926 and 1927 (pp. 307–8), but these look extremely unreliable, because the measured birth rate doubled between 1926 and 1927: a nearly impossible feat. With regard to the 1940s, the data consist only of head-counts and anecdotes. Concerning the famine of the 1970s, Watts wrote: 'Many thousands of herders and farmers died a slow and painful death' (p. 373), 'At the very least 100,000 people died [during 1973]' (p. 374), and 'Perhaps a quarter of a million people died [during 1970–4]' (p. 464).

Watts's argument is flawed. He used two notions of 'famine'—the Hausa concept of *yunwa* (best translated by 'hunger' or 'dearth') and the post-Malthusian English concept of 'famine', and implicitly equated them. He described with great care and detail how rural producers in Hausaland were impoverished by the colonial and post-colonial state. He presented oral and documentary evidence for 'famines' during various years. Having defined the years as 'famines', he inferred that people must have starved, and argued back to locate the cause of the starvation in the political–economic structures he had described. But the inference from *yunwa* to 'famine' is illegitimate. This is notably the case for the 1970s: the Nigerian government maintained that nobody died due to starvation, and the demographic evidence suggests they were right (see below). Watts was entitled to refer to 'famine', but only in the sense of *yunwa* (i.e. dearth, hunger), not in the sense he has used it: 'Famine is a food shortage leading to widespread death from starvation' (pp. 17–18). Similar reservations apply to 1926/7 and the 1940s. In the light of this, the 'phaoroic sequence' of famines becomes less impressive, and it is arguable that nineteenth-century famines in Hausaland are less well documented than recent ones not because they were localized and brief (p. 104), but because they happened long ago, before regular records were kept of such things. Polly Hill has shown greater awareness of the problems of the word 'famine', and arrived at opposite conclusions to Watts: 'It is the general opinion in Batagarawa [a village in Hausaland] that the advent of the long-distance lorry has greatly reduced the risk of *real* famine' (1972, p. 231, emphasis mine). Laya's interviewees suggested the same: 'People no longer die from famines since there are motor cars now' (1975, p. 60).

It is unfair to single out Watts. Sen also quoted the figure of 100,000 starvation deaths (1981, p. 116). Other academics have subscribed to similar accounts of the nature of the famine (Meillassoux 1974; Lofchie 1975; van Apeldoorn 1981), quite apart from the journalistic coverage.

In fact there is no evidence that the figure of 100,000 starvation deaths is anything except fiction. The origins of the figure appear to lie in a mortality survey by the Centre for Disease Control cited by Sheets and Morris (1974). The survey results were interpreted so as to provide an upper limit to mortality estimates, which the authors considered to have been exaggerated (p. 134). Using the most extreme data, the single highest spot mortality rate found, and generalizing that to the nomadic population, a figure of 101,000 deaths was arrived at. Note that they used one spot rate of 70 per thousand per year for this: among the 26 sampled 'clusters' of nomads in Mauritania there was a mean death rate of 26 per thousand, and in the 11 sites in Niger it was 54 per thousand. Moreover, they used very low estimates for pre-drought death rates in the Sahel (21–3 per thousand): later estimates for normal death rates have been in the upper 30s per thousand (Hill 1985; Caldwell 1975, pp. 6–9). The data could more legitimately have been used to show that there was *no* excess mortality during 1973. The authors did conclude there was no evidence for any excess deaths among the farming populations—which includes Hausaland. So what had been an extreme 'maximum' figure, for nomads, became adopted as a minimum figure, for the sedentary population as well.

Other studies have confirmed this picture. Greene (1974) found that malnutrition and death rates among nomads in Mauritania were high, but among sedentary people were normal. Seaman *et al.* (1973) found that the nutritional status of children in Upper Volta was not significantly different from normal. Caldwell (1977, p. 94) summed up the (scanty) statistics thus: 'Nutritional levels, although poor, were similar to those found before the drought in other parts of Africa. The only possible exception was among very young children', and turning to mortality, 'In fact one cannot certainly identify the existence of the drought in the vital statistics, and mortality fell slowly during the period'. Mortality *fell* during the famine! 1969–74 was clearly not a famine of mass starvation.

In fairness, some reservations to this viewpoint must be voiced. Statistics for the population of the Sahel are very poor. Faulkingham (1977) found that death rates doubled during 1974 in one village in central Niger. Kloth *et al.* (1976) found similarly raised death rates in Niger and Chad, though not in Upper Volta, again during 1974. These surveys referred to a period after that covered by the sources cited above, a period after the peak of the famine crisis. The excess deaths were attributed to outbreaks of diseases such as meningitis and measles. It is possible that although the peak of the famine was past, the excess deaths it brought (through epidemic diseases) were still to occur. However, the possible occurrence of these excess deaths does not detract from the central point: mass starvation deaths did not occur.

Some medical writers have observed that the drought may have seen fewer infections than normal, implying that it is even possible that fewer people died than normal during the famine. It appeared to be the case that pastoralists were less susceptible to malaria when undernourished than when well-fed on a diet of grain (Murray *et al.* 1975; Murray and Murray, 1977).

The Sahelian drought therefore provides a striking example of

how the English concept of 'famine' and the images of famine
provided by relief agencies and the mass media, in all sincerity, were
very far from the truth. Millions did not starve in the Sahel, with or
without relief. Having reviewed the demographic and nutritional
evidence, Caldwell noted how this contrasted with perceptions of the
famine: The evidence seems at odds with one's own observations of
miserably thin children with stick-thin legs and all-too-visible ribs in
the drought refugee camps and nomadic encampments of the Sahel.
Nevertheless . . . ' (1975, p. 11).

Should we continue to call this event a 'famine'? We have to
choose between redefining the word 'famine', and altering drastically
our usage of the word, so as not to apply it to events such as this. On
the grounds that usage is logically prior to definition, the current
usage of 'famine' should stay, and the definition should change. The
Sahel did suffer famine.

The Ethiopian Famine of 1973

In contrast to the Sahel famine of the early 1970s, there was
undoubtedly sharply increased mortality in Wollo province, Ethiopia, during 1973 (Caldwell 1977, p. 95). Seaman and Holt (1975)
found a cruel death rate of 82 per thousand in Wollo and
considered it possibly an underestimate. Raised death rates were
found among all age groups, not just children. All sources attest to
mass starvation. This was famine under any description.

However, even under these circumstances, the work of social
anthropologists in Wollo did not identify starvation as the most
important aspect of the famine for the victims. Perhaps the very
worst hit group were the Afar pastoralists of the lowlands. After
visiting the area at the start of the famine, Cossins surmised that: 'It
must be hard for the Afar, facing the overwhelming prospect of
famine and starvation, to see anything other than the immediate
provision of food as consequential now' (1972, p. 2). Nevertheless
this fits ill with other evidence. 'Many people die,' said one of
Cossin's informants. 'Disease is the first cause but the Issa (Somali)
are the second' (p. 51). The anthropologist Glynn Flood spent much
longer living among the Afar. His writing also had a different theme
(1976). The question he asked was not whether the Afar people
would die of starvation, but whether their pastoral way of life could
survive the profound changes of which the famine was just the most
striking manifestation. Similar themes emerge in other studies.

Mesfin Wolde Mariam has perhaps more experience of famine in Ethiopia than any other social scientist. He has discussed the reluctance of famine-stricken farmers and herders to part with their land and livestock in order to satisfy their hunger (1986, pp. 61–6). He suggested that hope for a future revival can outweigh the suffering of the present. Lundstrom compared the functioning of land rights systems and religious authorities in highland Wollo and Tigray during the famine (1976). The focus was not upon what caused starvation, but upon how social institutions changed in some ways and maintained continuity in others, under the pressures of famine.

This work should be seen in the context of other work which centred on starvation and the command over food of the starving, for example that of Sen (1981). The implication in Sen's work is that command over food is the overwhelming, even the only concern of famine victims. The implications of the anthropological studies are that even when people are dying from starvation, the 'conceptual centre' of famine, for both the victims and people studying it, may not necessarily be that same starvation. The experience of a threat to a way of life may be more real than the experience of the threat of starvation.

This dilemma of what terms to use faced the editor of a major collection of papers on drought and famine in Ethiopia, covering not only Wollo but other areas as well: he solved the problem by affixing the word *rehab*, Amharic for both 'hunger' and 'famine', to the title (Hussein 1976). This is what we must do to understand famines in Ethiopia, and in the rest of Africa too.

Who Cries 'Famine'?

The issue of definitions, conceptions, and perceptions is a minefield. There is another potentially disabling explosion in it. Paul Richards asked to know 'the kind of ideological representation built into reports of famine. Who cries "famine" and for what purpose?' (1983, p. 44). I have mentioned Simms's (1976) conclusions that the importance of the Russian famine of the 1890s lay not in its impact on the rural people, but its presence on the political agendas of various groups. Megan Vaughan (1987) in her study of the famine that struck Malawi in 1949/50 has gone further and shown how different meanings were given to the famine not only by the different elements within the colonial government, but also by the people of Malawi who suffered it. In particular the famine was ascribed different meanings by men and women.

The gulf between the understandings of people in Africa who suffer famines and of those who avowedly try to help them is now greater than ever before. It has been widened by the advent of the mass media and by the phenomenon of disaster tourism. The exaggerated perceived severity of the famine and the inert semantics of 'emergency' (an 'emergency' is not expected to have ways of dealing with itself) become reasons for panic and for ignoring the opinions of local people. The event is defined by foreigners, who create a perceived moral imperative for external intervention. The famine victims live (or die) under an alien definition. Another strand of this is the 'famine industry' of the specialized agencies, who see famine in terms of technical issues such as 'early-warning systems', 'food security', logistics, and 'nutritional surveillance'. A closer analysis of just one example will show how an apparently beneficent (or at least innocuous) technical measure can lead to outsiders arrogating to themselves the power to 'cry famine', at the expense of the local people who are suffering.

'Nutritional surveillance' generally refers to the systematic measurement of the weight, height, and mid-upper-arm circumference of children, so as to assess their 'malnutrition'. Properly speaking, this is anthropometric surveillance, measuring thinness. The proportion of children of various degrees of thinness is then taken as an indicator of how vulnerable a population is to famine, or how severely it is actually suffering from famine. A variant is the use of similar techniques to identify individual children in a relief camp in need of special feeding: this variant will not be discussed here. The underlying rationale is simple. Thin children have become so because of failure to consume food, and so a population with many thin children is suffering a 'nutritional deficit'. The logic leads directly to the provision of food relief as a remedy.

Few nutritionists would subscribe to this simple logic. Thinness is actually the outcome of many factors, including disease, which is related to environmental conditions such as water quality. Unless very extreme, a child's thinness is a poor predictor of the risk of that child dying (Martorell and Ho 1984). In most situations, providing food alone is of little use in overcoming thinness (Koopman *et al.* 1981; Tomkins 1986*b*). Anthropometric surveillance as a way of identifying the need for food relief or the vulnerability to famine is almost useless. Nutritionists doing surveys take care to include investigations of local water supplies, general socio-economic conditions, and other relevant factors. Yet it is the gross percentages of 'malnourished' that are extracted from field reports and transmitted to agency headquarters and donor organizations. The argument is that these figures are 'objective'. They are also spurious.

The problems with nutritional surveillance and related techniques, and their inappropriate imposition on poor countries, are increasingly recognized (Shoham 1987; Nabarro and Chinnock 1988). However, the figure of 'percentage malnourished' retains a powerful grip on the perceptions of famine by international agencies. This leads to a narrow conception of the problem as a 'nutritional deficit'. An extreme manifestation of this trend is the tendency to define famine as 'nutritional emergency'. 'Nutritional deficit' may even take precedence over excess deaths as a criterion of famine. For instance, during 1974 in the Ethiopian Ogaden, investigators found high levels of excess child mortality but near-normal levels of nutrition, and decided that there was currently no famine (Relief and Rehabilitation Commission 1974). More recently, a monitoring programme in Chad has considered nutritional status to be more than twice as valuable an indicator of vulnerability to famine as the level of mortality (Autier 1988). As we shall see, people in Darfur see 'nutritional deficit' as the least of their problems during famine. Such clashes of conceptions result in outsiders 'imposing aid' inappropriately on people (Harrell-Bond 1986).

The development of techniques such as nutritional surveillance creates a 'citadel of expertise' (often inappropriate expertise) which prevents dialogue with lay people, including the famine victims. It also reinforces the 'otherness' of famine, and its isolation from ordinary life (Hewitt 1983). 'Famine' has become a technical malfunction, not a human experience. This is another legacy of the nineteenth century.

However, even under the burden of imposed aid, those who suffer famine struggle to define the event as they see appropriate. This is usually not recognized by outsiders. The Mursi of south-west Ethiopia were a rare case on whom aid was not imposed, and outsiders were present who recognized the benefits of this. The Turtons have written:

The 1970s was probably the most disastrous decade experienced by the Mursi since the human and animal pandemics that ravaged East Africa during the 1890s. The fact that they came through this experience with their social and economic institutions intact and an undiminished sense of their cultural identity must be partly attributed to the failure of aid agencies to come to their assistance. . . . It was this 'failure' that left the way open for the Mursi to respond to the crisis in their own way and towards the end of the decade set up their own 'agricultural settlement scheme' in the Mago valley (1984, p. 179).

The theme is familiar: emergency relief, like development aid, is only truly effective if the recipients have the power to determine what it is and how it is used. Georg Simmel, in a classic sociological analysis of relief to the poor (ed. 1971) captured the problem. He identified the *de facto* (European) definition of 'the poor' as those to whom we give assistance, avowedly to correct their position, but in fact to prevent them from correcting their position for themselves. The concept of poverty is bound in to what we (the non-poor) can do to alleviate it, rather than what they (the poor) can do for themselves. Likewise the contemporary English concept of 'famine' is bound in to what relief agencies can do to alleviate it. The point of this is not to pronounce upon the ethics of the aid business, but to place famine relief in the context of power relations between rich and poor countries.

All the English definitions of famine cited leave the affected people as agents out of the causal scheme altogether: they imply that either food shortage or failure of entitlement to food directly causes people to die of starvation. These are essentially conceptions we could only apply to other peoples' societies: if a famine were to strike our own, it would be conceptualized in a different way, probably as a time of dearth, but also as a heroic struggle against the destruction of our way of life. For instance, this is how the famine in the Netherlands during 1944/5 is remembered.

The starting point for an analysis of famine should therefore lie with the understandings of those who suffer famine themselves. The following three chapters examine how famine is conceived of in Darfur, and the remainder of the book interprets the events of 1984/5 in the light of that.

2

Darfur

Landscapes

Darfur is huge. It covers an area as large as France, and more than
half the size of Kenya. Sudan, the largest country in Africa, is often
thought to consist of two parts, 'north' and 'south'. Darfur and its
neighbouring region Kordofan deserve a separate classification: the
'west'. The western border of Darfur is equidistant between Port
Sudan on the Red Sea, and the coast of west Africa in Cameroon.
Darfur's position relative to the rest of Sudan can be seen in Fig. 2.1.
During its history, Darfur has been part of empires based as far
apart as the Nile and the Nigerian savannas. Darfur has ruled its
own empire: at the height of its powers the Sultanate of Dar Fur
ruled an area as large as many modern African states. The modern
region of Darfur borders on three countries: Libya, Chad, and the
Central African Republic, and itself straddles the frontier between the
Sahara desert and the cultivable savannas of tropical Africa (Fig. 2.2).

The landscapes of Darfur are drawn on a vast scale. In the north
the overwhelming impression is of a dry and inhospitable world, 'ill
provided with any such thing that is necessary for the sustenance of
man or beast', in the words of the eighteenth-century traveller W. G.
Browne (1806, p. 285). More recently, the northern district of Dar
Zaghawa has been described in these words:

The normal aspect is one of vast sandy stretches from which rise occasional
picturesque bare sandstone outlines or small rusty-coloured granite hills
broken by erosion into boulders equally bare, and casually piled on top of
one another. There might be pastures of dry standing fodder, fields of wild
grasses with thorn trees covered in foliage, occasional millet fields that have
been harvested or failed to ripen. The beds of the clay basins look peeled,
without a single blade of grass, baked in the sun like bricks, and with the
tracks of animals' hooves imprinted in them. The wadi beds spread out
beneath huge shady trees, drinking troughs and occasional irrigated
gardens. The horizon is never bare, whether there rises from it a long ridge
of angular rocks like the bent spine of some prehistoric monster, or a sharp
peak pointing skywards like a finger (Tubiana and Tubiana 1977, pp. 3–4).

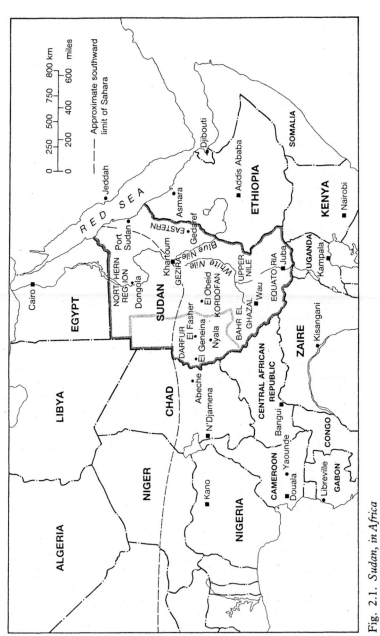

Fig. 2.1. *Sudan, in Africa*

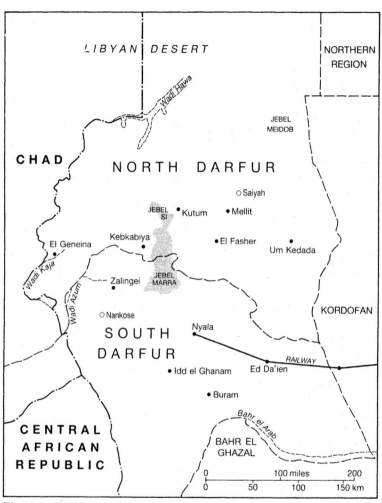

Fig. 2.2. *Darfur*

This passage introduces the four basic features of the physical landscape, which are sharply distinct. The first feature is sand. There are plains and low hills of sandy soils, known as *goz*, and sandstone hills. The whole eastern half of Darfur is covered with *goz*, often unbroken by any other feature. In many places it is waterless and can only be inhabited where there are reservoirs or deep bore-holes. *Goz* may be dry but is often fertile, providing rich pasture and arable land. In the north the *goz* gives way to the wind-blown sand sheets of the Sahara. Secondly there are seasonal watercourses, known as *wadis*. These range from small rivulets that flood a few times every wet season, to the great watercourses that cut through western Darfur and flow hundreds of miles to Lake Chad, which are in flood for most of the rains. Many *wadis* have large pans of alluvial soil. This soil is rich but hard to break with a hoe and cultivate. The third feature is basement rock, sometimes bare, sometimes covered with a thin layer of sandy soil. Much of western Darfur consists of basement complexes, too infertile to be cultivated, but with intermittent forest cover providing grazing and browse for animals. Finally there are the mountains formed by prehistoric volcanic activity. In Dar Zaghawa and neighbouring areas there are heat-hardened volcanic plugs, reaching up like spires. In central Darfur the massif of Jebel Marra rises 10,000 feet to its peak at the Deriba crater, creating a small area of temperate climate, high rainfall and permanent springs.

The landscapes are transformed every year. From June to September is the rainy season (*kharif*). During the first weeks of the rains, dry and dusty landscapes become a vibrant green. *Goz* hills look bare and brown in May, as though nothing could ever grow. By August they may be a carpet of green. By November they may stand with millet, golden, head-high to the horizon, reverting to brown as the harvest is gathered and animals eat the stalks. Rain is of course critical. In the far north none falls for years at a time, and the land remains dry, though only a single shower is needed to bring forth a growth of luxuriant grasses. In the far south annual rainfall averages over 700 millimetres, and many trees remain green throughout the year.

Darfur is home to about 3.2 million people (Fig. 2.3).

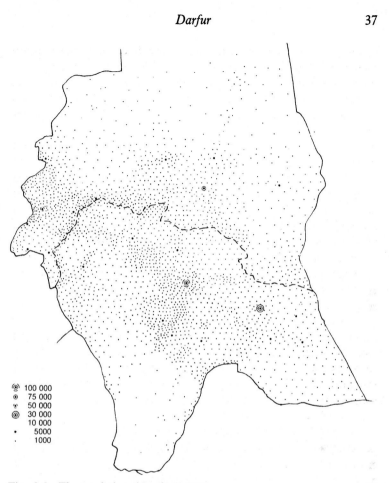

100 000
75 000
50 000
30 000
10 000
5000
1000

Fig. 2.3. *The population of Darfur in 1983*

Impressions of a Disaster Tourist

Darfur is a large area with virtually no all-weather roads. Most outsiders, particularly the important and busy outsiders who make decisions on international 'aid' to Darfur, cannot hope to see very much of it. Their visits are a form of 'rural development tourism' (Chambers 1983). In Darfur at present they differ from most development tourism in that the majority of aid projects are

conceived with the premiss that Darfur is threatened with environmental bankruptcy and economic collapse. The members of aid
missions arrive imbued with the sombre responsibility of knowing
that a 'rescue package' is needed. They want to see the true horrors
for themselves. Such visitors are better thought of as 'disaster
tourists'.

It takes several days to drive to Darfur from Khartoum, assuming
you do not get lost in the myriad of tracks across the *goz* plains of
northern Kordofan. Disaster tourists prefer to fly direct to the
regional capital, El Fasher. Over one hundred years ago the traveller
Gustav Nachtigal described the environs of El Fasher as 'extra-
ordinarily devoid of trees' (ed. 1971, p. 257). Time has not
improved things. During the dry season, when disaster tourism is at
its peak, El Fasher sits in the centre of a sea of bare sand. As the
aeroplane comes in to land the visitor is presented with the
compelling image of an apparently man-made desert surrounding
the city (Fig 2.4).

Disaster tourists cannot leave Darfur having only spoken to
government officials and expatriate experts: a field trip is necessary.
The visitor cannot go too far, because of limited time, and nor can he
or she be taken to a village that is clearly a satellite of the town. The
most well-driven route for disaster tourists is north-east, to villages
near to Mellit. This trip can be made in a single day if necessary, but
if an overnight stop is wanted there are agreeable and picturesque
villages on the route. This area is inhabited by Berti people, who are
millet farmers, but on a good day the visitor might see some
Zayadiya 'nomads' with herds of camels.

Saiyah is one village frequented by disaster tourists. It lies two
hours' drive north from Mellit, on the western edge of the *goz* plain
that stretches from there to the Nile. *Goz* plains are renowned for the
monotony of their landscape, and also the monotony of their farming
possibilities. Irrigation is not possible on *goz*, so only wet-season
crops (millet, sorghum, groundnuts, sesame) can be grown. On low-
rainfall *goz*, such as the environs of Saiyah, there is only millet.
However Saiyah is fortunate in lying close to the Tagabo Hills, a
spectacular chain of sandstone cliffs and pinnacles which stand along
the horizon to the north and west (Fig. 2.5). The local farming
potential is also made more interesting by a *wadi* that runs from
these hills, along which irrigated gardening is possible.

Experts such as Fuad Ibrahim (1984) consider that millet farming

Fig. 2.4. *El Fasher, from a sketch by the author*

on *goz* cannot be sustained where there is less than 300 millimetres of rain per year, without causing irreversible environmental damage. Annual rainfall north of Mellit is currently less than 200 millimetres. The environs of Saiyah present the horrors of desertification in full. Every field is full of dried millet stalks with nothing but bare earth in

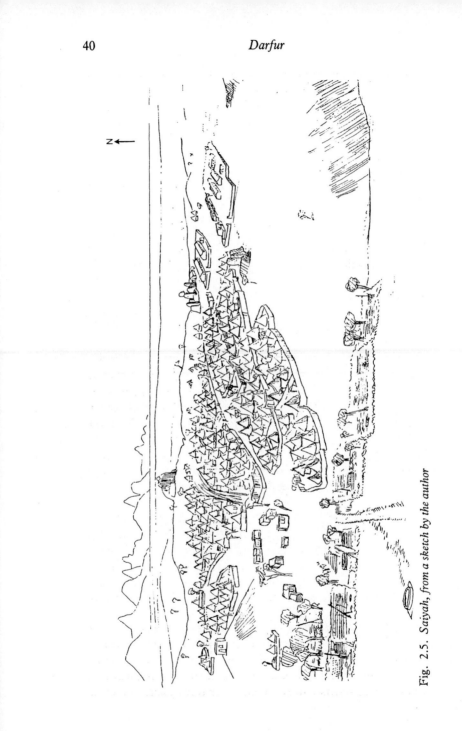

Fig. 2.5. *Saiyah, from a sketch by the author*

between them. There are no fields lying fallow. With every gust of wind more of the topsoil is taken from the fields and deposited in the lee of the thornbush fences that surround each field, building up little sand dunes. Larger sand dunes are accumulating to the north of the village, as if to march on the houses themselves. In the *wadi* herds of goats, sheep, and camels from the surrounding area congregate to be watered, but there is hardly a blade of dry grass in sight from which they could feed. Instead they can be seen pulling at foliage on the last remaining trees.

The people of Saiyah are Berti. The Berti farmers have systems of farming and social organization which are relatively simple to explain (Holy 1974). After the first rains farmers plant millet by hand, using a digging stick, over a large area of cleared ground. The Berti ideology emphasizes the value of farming, and the uncertainties of the climate encourage the farmer to plant a large area, in case yields should be poor or locally variable. After a few weeks of rain there is a tremendous growth of weeds, and the millet seedlings have to compete for sunlight and moisture. To obtain the maximum yield it is essential that all the weeds be removed, and removed again a second or third time as they grow back. Weeding is an arduous task and involves all the family's labour over a period of a month or more. The traditional *nafir* or communal work party, paid in millet beer, is notorious for its inefficiency and is now rarely found (Holy 1987). The amount of land that can be cultivated depends mainly on the amount that can be successfully weeded. In a fully weeded field nothing grows except the stands of millet, a foot or more apart. The land around Saiyah has been fully weeded and fully grazed for a generation. It looks like a beach.

The people of Saiyah supplement their farming income with animal husbandry, *wadi* gardens, and casual and migrant labour. The visitor will notice the animals being watered. The irrigated gardens along the *wadi* bed provide a stretch of welcome green. Though there is hardly a tree or a blade of grass to be seen, women can be seen bringing firewood and fodder into the village: they have clearly walked for miles.

Saiyah is headed by a senior sheikh, known either by his traditional Darfur title of *shartai* or the 'modern' title of *omda*, introduced by the Anglo-Egyptian government. *Shartai* Adam Ahmad Billahi of Saiyah is a man who emanates dignity and wisdom. He is hospitable, but not to the point of extravagance. While he serves his guests with tea and a meal, he will attend to the villagers who constantly arrive at his compound with disputes to be settled. Some of these concern tax assessments, because in his capacity as *omda*, this is *Shartai* Adam's responsibility. Others concern matters such as bride-wealth or inheritance. The majority concern land. The visitor will learn more about the land-rights system of the Berti from listening to an hour's disputation in the *shartai's* court than from the bland labels of 'communal ownership' and 'usufructuary rights' that the guide or expert will provide.

Village sheikhs are responsible for allocating land-use rights within their villages. The *shartai* not only allocates land for Saiyah village but adjudicates disputes between rival villages. Two cases that were heard on 8 January 1987 illustrate this. One concerned a man who had surreptitiously extended his farmed area onto someone else's land. His defence was that the land was not in use. The wronged farmer argued that he had failed to plant the area through shortage of seed in 1986: the land had not been truly abandoned. What swung the case his way was that the offender had already been warned several times for expanding his fields without permission and had also blocked a path to a well. Though he won the case, the wronged farmer will not dare leave his fields fallow or empty again. The second case concerned a new hamlet that had been spawned to the east. The land in a parent village was overworked and too many people had claims to its use, so a group had left to form a new hamlet. These farmers now wanted their own village sheikh, because the sheikhs of nearby older villages were interfering in their use of land, trying to keep it as a reserve for their own villagers. The following day *Shartai* Adam left for Mellit to follow up the procedure of appointing a new sheikh. Both these cases show a social system that cannot contain a relentless pressure to expand cultivation, which destroys fallowing, pasture, and forest, and undermines the ecological foundations for its existence.

Saiyah makes the visitor sad and pessimistic. Old men in the village speak of the time when the *wadi* was lined with palm trees (they all died), when the forest was so thick on the road south that a person who travelled on top of a lorry would arrive in Mellit with his clothes torn, and when a normal harvest would yield enough to feed a family for two years or more. Holy (1974) has confirmed the wealth and optimism of this area during the 1960s. The villagers now seem locked into a downward spiral of impoverishment and environmental destruction. Unwilling or unable to change, every response they know serves only to destroy the environment they depend on. As their cows die they turn to goats, which eat their way through the few trees hardy enough to survive the droughts of the 1980s. As millet yields fall and the population grows they cultivate ever larger areas and weed ever more thoroughly, degrading the *goz* still further. Even the weather seems particularly cruel here. In 1985 and 1986, as other parts of Darfur received good rains, the rains in Saiyah were no better than the worst drought years. The disaster tourist will leave with (at best) an impression of a peasantry engaged in a valiant but futile struggle against the elements or (at worst) a picture of a way of life that is not changing but instead is slowly committing suicide. He or she will leave with the belief that without external help Saiyah will die; all the worst expectations will have been confirmed.

This sketch of Saiyah is superficial but closer study shows that it is essentially correct. The impressions of the disaster tourist are right. This may be one reason why Saiyah and the surrounding area are so often visited by foreign officials. Fortunately, Saiyah is not typical of Darfur. The reasons why this is so will be discussed in detail later. Here it suffices to say that for social and historical reasons the Berti areas of north-east Darfur are one of the few places that are not making huge changes to their way of life. Saiyah is a bad place to start understanding Darfur.

The remainder of this chapter will take a village in south-west Darfur as a case-study to illustrate the workings of Darfur society. This village is called Nankose. Its outward appearance is no more typical of Darfur than Saiyah. But the processes of dynamism and change found in Nankose are a much better guide to the society and economy of Darfur than the stagnation of Saiyah.

Nankose Village

South-western Darfur looks very different to the northern areas just described. The landscape consists of rolling basement hills, often thickly forested, with stretches of upland *goz*. There are none of the bare distant horizons common to north Darfur. There is an occasional vista to one of the broad alluvial valleys which cut through the hills; a swathe of dark green foliage even at the height of the dry season. Along this system of *wadis* are the richest soils in Darfur.

Each *wadi* is thickly settled and intensively farmed. Nankose is a village of about 300 households that lies on a small *wadi*, tributary to Wadi Debarei.

This area is wet. During the rains, travel is impossible because the *wadis* are in flood. During the dry season the waters retract to become strings of stagnant pools, which slowly dry up. Water remains just below the surface however, as can be seen by the greenery of the trees and the *wadi* gardens. Rainfall at Garsila, which is close by, was an average of 825 millimetres during the decade 1946–55, 686 and 607 millimetres respectively over the succeeding two decades and 558 millimetres during the years 1976–85.

Nankose is built on a shallow slope overlooking the *wadi* where most of the arable land lies. From the hillside the village appears as a dense cluster of houses with conical straw roofs (Figs 2.6). Looking closer one can see that these are grouped into compounds, each containing between one and four houses. Each compound is enclosed by a fence and also usually contains a *rakuba* shelter in which to entertain guests, a grain store and a yard in which animals can be tethered at night. It is divided up into parts for men and women. The compounds crowd together in the centre of the village, with winding paths between the high grass walls, and two wider streets forming a cross. There is a mosque, a clinic, several small shops, and a Koranic school. At the foot of the slope, under a group of big shade trees, is a market area with several lines of *rakubas* that serve as stalls on market-day. The village well also lies at the foot of the slope. Beyond the market-place are a few compounds, more scattered, belonging to recent arrivals to Nankose, some artisans, and some tents belonging to a group of cattle-herders who are living nearby. The main languages spoken in Nankose are Arabic and Fur.

Farmers and Citizens

The people of Nankose are mostly farmers. They have a complex farming system which a short discussion can only outline. It is based on three categories of cultivable land. The best land is heavy cracking clay, known as *tiin*. This lies close to the bed of the *wadi* itself. It can be cultivated in the wet season for grain crops, either sorghum or millet, or the two intercropped. In the dry season irrigated vegetable-growing is possible, and much of the *tiin* area is fenced off into enclosures, each with its own *shadouf* for raising

Fig. 2.6. *Nankose, from a sketch by the author*

water and little irrigation ditches. Onions, tomatoes, and okra are some of the vegetables grown. Chewing tobacco (*tombac*) can be grown on *tiin* and in the sand of the *wadi* bed itself during the dry season. The problems with *tiin* are that it is labour-intensive to plant (less so if a camel plough is hired) and to weed, and there is a danger of floods and waterlogging. The next best land is a lighter alluvium

known as *tartura*, which yields well though rather less than *tiin*. Both
tiin and *tartura* are usually farmed without fallow, with only a slow
decline in yield. This is partly because it is possible to pasture
animals on the fields after harvest time, so the fields can be manured.
Finally there is *goz* land, out of the valley bottom altogether, which
is infertile by comparison, and which must be fallowed regularly.
Tartura and *goz* cannot be irrigated for cultivation during the dry
season.

These different micro-environments mean that a variety of crops
can be planted. Farmers can grow long-season and quick-maturing
grains, and low-risk millets and higher-risk sorghums. They can also
obtain two crops a year from the *tiin* soil.

Nankose is a stratified community, and the most important factor
in this is differential access to land, especially *tiin*. There are no
commercial farmers as such, but the richest quarter of the farmers
cultivate over half of the land and rent out still more. These farmers
produce grain, vegetables, and *tombac* for the market, and hire
labour to do so. Inequality based on landholdings has developed due
to changes during the last thirty years.

One change concerns labour. Earlier observers of this area noted
that little wage-labour was available apart from what itinerant west
Africans, known as Fellata, could supply (Barbour 1950, pp. 123–4;
Barth 1967a, p. 26). Since the drought of 1969 many more people
from northern Darfur have come south to Nankose each season to
obtain work. As yet there is no class of landless labourers in Darfur,
but there are plenty of poor farmers needing to make good a chronic
shortfall in grain production. Apart from the migrants, the poorest
quarter of Nankose's people farm only 8 per cent of the land, much
of it rented. A second change concerns marketing. Until the 1960s
there were also few channels for marketing produce. Since then the
growth of the towns, notably Nyala, has created a demand for
produce, including grain. Roads have been improved. One villager,
Mohammed *Gatar* ('Train', on account of his inexhaustible energy)
bought a truck in 1969, one of two now owned in Nankose. The
extensive cultivation of *tombac* and large-scale grain sales date from
this period.

Before these developments occurred the opportunities for profit
from farming were few, and richer villagers prefered to invest in
cattle (Haaland 1972). Recently there has been a switch towards
agriculture. This has had important reverberations through the

fabric of life in Nankose. Because land is so important, these reverberations are seen best in the system of rights to land.

A tradition of usufructuary land tenure exists, under which membership of a community entitles a farmer to an allocation of land from the sheikh. Nankose actually has two sheikhs. Sheikh Abdel Rahim is an aspiring politician of the Umma party, and controls the land to the south and west of the village. Sheikh Issa, who is less influential, controls the land to the east. If a farmer wants to obtain a large allocation of land, it is important to carry influence with one of the sheikhs. This has become increasingly important as pressure on land has increased, and any farmer who increases his holdings is likely to be challenged by another. Usufruct rights to a field persist as long as there is physical evidence of the farmer's labour to be seen on the land. While the land is cleared or planted, or while irrigation ditches can be identified, rights persist. If the land is returning to bush, to the extent that wild trees have grown up and borne fruit, the rights lapse (this is usually taken to be three years). However, now that alluvial fields are in constant use, the usufruct is an effective freehold. Usufruct rights to particular fields are heritable. Islamic legal injunctions over inheritance are espoused but rarely if ever practised, except occasionally when disputes come to court. A father will distribute most of his land between his sons before he dies, pre-empting inheritance laws. Inheritance or gift from one's parents is the most common origin of claim to land. None of the land is formally registered under Sudanese law as individual tenancies.

The tightening of land rights presents a problem to poor households who need to expand their landholdings. Under the usufructuary system, households expanded and contracted their farmland as they moved through the demographic cycle. Households with large holdings can now farm them using hired labour, or rent land out, and so no longer need to release the land when they are not farming it themselves. Free land is now scarce. Hence the expansion part of the cycle is increasingly difficult. Nankose has not reached the stage, evident close to Nyala, where people are even fencing pasture and claiming individual freehold (Behnke 1985).

Newcomers are the other losers in this tightening of land rights. Usufructuary rights were based on membership of the community. In Fur areas such as Nankose, 'membership of a community' is a complex notion. The ideal case is descent in the male line from the man who first cut the trees and cultivated the land in the vicinity.

However, for many people in a village such as Nankose this ancestry is adopted or fictive; newcomers have been assimilated into the community as *de facto* kin. Islam demands giving hospitality and refuge to strangers. Beaton (1948) described how newcomers lived on the fringes of Fur villages for a year before choosing either to move on or stay and become full members of the community. In Darfur there is a tradition of ethnic adoption. In the oral tradition this is exemplified by several 'wise strangers' who came to Darfur, became Fur (or Zaghawa, Masalit, etc.), and became leaders. Ahmad al Bornawi was one such stranger who is said to have brought rain-making powers (Beaton 1939). Ahmad el Magrur, who built the first mosque in Darfur, is remembered as 'an Arab who became a Fur'; he married the Tunjur Princess Keira and thereby founded the 'royal family' of the Fur sultanate. There are many others too, such as the story of the abandoned Arab baby boy found by a stream who became the leader of the Fur of Dar Enga. 'I tell you this story', explained El Haj Sanusi Mohammed, 'to show that the people of one tribe [*gabila*] do not have one ancestor [*jidd*].' These are familiar themes in Sudanese ethnography (Buxton 1963).

The Fur state was itself founded on the principle of ethnic assimilation. Communities 'became Fur', by adopting the Fur language and customs, and by putting themselves under the patronage of the Fur state (Beaton 1948; Baring 1969; O'Fahey 1982). This process was most pronounced in the south and west, but even in the Fur heartland around Jebel Si there are 'Tunjur-Fur' (Dar Furnung), 'Arab-Fur' (Jebel Si), 'Zaghawa-Fur' (Kaitinga), 'Turra-Fur' (Turra Ja'ami) and others. MacMichael (1920) commented on this, and the issue of ethnicity provokes involved discussion in this area even today. The main Fur grouping is called Kunjara, whose meaning is glossed as 'gathered together'. Historical sources suggest that 'Dar Kunjara' was synonymous with 'Dar Fur' until the eighteenth century at least (Burckhardt 1819, p. 485; Nachtigal 1971, pp. 348–9). The fact that observers have had difficulty in categorizing the Fur language (Beaton 1948; Jernudd 1968) suggests that it may have been a colonizing language with hybrid or pidgin origins.

Hence an ethnic label represents a 'citizenship' rather than common ancestry. Rights to land are not based on elaborate reconstructions of genealogy but on the current fact of acceptance as a member of the community.

The Anglo-Egyptian Condominium Government tried, with limited success, to prevent the processes of ethnic change in areas dominated by the Fur. For instance, they became worried about the 'detribalization' of small groups such as the cattle-herding Beni Hussein, and gave them their own sheikhs and *dar* (homeland) (Civsec 66/4/32). Nevertheless, a contingent of the Beni Hussein assimilated to Fur and formed a new clan, known as Madinga. But recent arrivals in Nankose have not assimilated. They retain their prior ethnic identities, and most of them live on the peripheries of the village. The block to recent assimilation appears to be the difficulty of obtaining land, and thereby fully joining the community.

Women in more conservative areas of Darfur own land in their own right, and enjoy sole access to its produce (Barth 1967a). These rights are stronger in customary law than Islam. In Nankose the more 'modern' or Arab notion of joint household management of resources is current. Household division of labour often means that the husband makes most of the decisions and the wife does most of the manual work. But the position of women remains much better than in eastern parts of Darfur (including Saiyah) and central areas of Sudan.

In some ways, the growth of private ownership of land is a return to an older tradition of land tenure that existed until the overthrow of the Fur Sultanate in 1916. This was a system of land charters issued by the sultans, known as *hakuras*. In many cases these were freehold grants of land to individuals and their descendants (O'Fahey and Abu Salim 1983). The freeholdings could be estates worked by slave or client labour, or fiefdoms from which rent and tribute were exacted. Land was therefore a valuable commodity, and *hakura* owners were wealthy and prestigious. In 1916 the Condominium Government abolished this system and effected what it called 'the release of Sudanese servants'. Land and labour were no longer commodities. While the ideology of land persisted, its economic basis had been destroyed (the anomaly between ideology and economic reality in the 1960s was noticed with puzzlement by Haaland (1972) and Holy (1974)). The recent switch towards investment in farming, away from investment in livestock, is therefore in reality a switch *back* to farming. In Nankose the *hakura* approximated to a slightly different pattern, which is common in less central areas of Darfur. Here a *hakura* is a grant of land jurisdiction over a certain area (Holy 1974, p. 95), in this case given to the 'seventh grandfather' of *Shartai* Arbab Rizek Sabi of Dileij.

Fur el Baggara

The term *Fur el Baggara* strikes a strange note. The Baggara are a confederation of groups of cattle-herding Arabs who inhabit much of southern Darfur. Strictly speaking the term *baggara* means 'cattle-people' in Arabic; there is a complementary term *abbala* for the camel-herders who inhabit the desert edge. The Baggara have a reputation for constantly being in conflict with the local farmers, including the Fur. *Fur el Baggara* translates as 'cattle-herding Fur'.

In Darfur ideology there are 'nomads' and 'farmers'. In practice the distinction is blurred. First, there are no true nomads in Darfur. Most of the people who are described in that way are in fact seminomadic or transhumant. Many of them have farms, and they divide their families into two parts, one that stays to cultivate and one that moves with the animals. Even those that do not farm usually move along regular routes as the seasons progress, returning to the same pastures every year. Second, most of the animals are owned by people who are principally farmers. Most of the farmers of Nankose own livestock, sheep, goats, cattle, and in a few cases camels. After farming, livestock-rearing is the main form of production. Farmers also keep donkeys for transport. In the middle years of this century, buying animals was the only channel that a farmer had for investment. This reached such an extent that some rich Fur farmers owned as many cattle as the Baggara pastoralists themselves. Sheikh Issa, for instance, is said to have owned 200 cattle. At this point the grazing in the vicinity of the village became insufficient to sustain the animals through the dry season, and it became necessary for Sheikh Issa to entrust his cattle to a transhumant Arab herder, who took the herd south to find grazing and water. Other local Fur became seminomadic themselves, and left farming (Haaland 1972). They were known as *Fur el Sayyara* ('Migratory Fur') or *Fur el Baggara*. In doing so they became 'professional colleagues' of the Arab pastoralists, and 'became *Baggara*'. However, they did not aspire to 'become Arab' or to join one of the Arab groups such as Beni Halba.

The Baggara Arabs around Nankose are mostly Salamat. Most of them have small farms as well as herds. Because dry-season water is available in Nankose, and dry-season pasture is to be had on harvested millet fields, these pastoralists have a short-distance migratory cycle every year. During the dry season they are found in the valleys, and during the wet season in the nearby hills. Some of them have few animals and depend mainly on farming, but they can always be distinguished from the Fur villagers because they continue to live in tents. Sometimes, though increasingly rarely, they are joined by a *Fur el Baggari*. A second group of herders arrives during the dry season. These are camel pastoralists from northern Darfur, being Mahamid Rizeigat. Some of their members have millet farms on the *goz* of northern Darfur; they do not farm in Nankose. They have a long transhumance, moving several hundreds of miles from the valleys of south-west Darfur during the dry season to the Zaghawa plateau during the rains. Though these two groups specialize in cattle and camels respectively, both herd goats and sheep as well. This is partly because having a mixed herd spreads the risks involved in herding; it is less likely that the entire herd will be decimated by a single outbreak of disease. It is also because these smaller animals can be readily sold when a small amount of cash is needed, or slaughtered to provide a meal for a guest.

Pastoralists in Darfur have a hard-headed attitude to their animals. They regard herding as an economic venture rather than a cultural imperative. Their staple food is grain, not meat, blood, and milk. Most do not grow enough grain to feed themselves, and so they buy it from the market with the money obtained from selling animals, or occasionally from selling milk. A herder's livelihood therefore depends on the state of the market and the wider economy, as well as the health of his animals. His main aim is to be able to sell a few animals each year in order to buy grain and other necessities, but at the same time not endanger the prospects for his herd by doing so. The farmer who keeps animals follows similar thinking; livestock are kept so that they can be sold to meet cash needs. Both aim at the 'sustainable off-take rate': the proportion of the herd that can be sold annually to provide a cash income, without depleting the herd or distorting its composition.

On the basis of the 'sustainable off-take rate', and data on the fertility, mortality, and relative prices of animals, and herd composition, it is possible to construct an 'economic livestock unit' (ELSU). This represents the value of livestock to the owner if he follows this strategy. More formally, it is the number of animals of a given type which are needed to provide income to buy enough grain to sustain a person for one year. The ELSU is not found in the literature. It differs from the Tropical Livestock Unit, which is used primarily for assessing the impact of an animal population on range and pasture, and the Productive Livestock Unit, which is based on milk production. The ELSU varies with both economic and ecological conditions. For the 'average' year (derived from data for the years 1970–83) the following figures emerge:

$$1 \text{ ELSU} = 1.5 \text{ cows} = 1.4 \text{ camels} = 5 \text{ sheep} = 6 \text{ goats}$$

However, herders do not bank on every year being a normal year. Herders recognize the fluctuations in the economic productivity of their animals. If we revise the assumptions about fertility, mortality, and prices to account for a poor (but not disastrous) year, such as 1973–4, the ELSUs change, and the minimum stable herd size needed to sustain a person is much larger:

$$1 \text{ ELSU (poor year)} = 3.6 \text{ camels} = 19 \text{ sheep} = 19 \text{ goats}$$

As can be seen, goats and camels fare better than sheep in poor years. All fare better than cattle; under these assumptions *all* the calves are needed to replenish the herd, so that none can be sold without depleting the herd size. The ELSU value of cattle during a drought year is zero. This means that herders who depend upon cattle alone must expect their herd sizes to decline during drought years, no matter how many cattle they have; there is no equilibrium cattle-herd during a poor year. These relative differences between types of animal became very important in the dry years of the 1980s.

The Arab pastoralists and Fur farmers have complementary ways of life. For the most part they coexist peacefully, though each complains about the other. 'The Arabs have no "roads" [*turug*]' said one farmer, implying that they also have no religious principles. The Fur commonly label them *Umshushu*, meaning 'savages'. The Arabs for their part call the Fur *Zurga*, 'blacks'. Minor disputes are frequent, and the Salamat leader (they have no sheikh here) Abdel Aziz meets with Sheikh Issa to settle the matter, agree on fines, etc.. Relations between the Fur and the northern Rizeigat are more strained and unpredictable.

The Market-Place

Rural Darfur has a galaxy of large periodic markets. Nankose itself has only a small twice-weekly market. Here most of the trading is local; the butchers buy several cows to slaughter for meat, there are some sheep and goats for sale, and market women sell vegetables, spices, and products such as mats, baskets, and pots. A few itinerant retailers set up stalls selling cloth, soap, and cheap consumer goods. Farmers may be selling small measurements of grain; this is bought up by a cartel of middlemen who gradually fill up several sacks to deliver to Haj Adam, the main merchant and second lorry-owner of Nankose.

There are also three large periodic markets that the villagers of Nankose can visit, and return from on the same day. The nearest is at Dileij. Here the market has a square of brick-built shops and stores. On market-day there are a dozen trucks present. These trucks arrive early. Haj Adam brings sugar and consumer goods from Nyala. He also brings passengers: men returning from several years working on the Gezira scheme, young boys wandering over Darfur to study at Koranic schools. He takes grain and vegetables to Nyala. Mohammed Gatar hires his truck out, most often to Zaghawa merchants. These may arrive from northern Darfur to buy *tombac* for the El Fasher market. They bring imports from Libya, and people: Chadians looking for casual work on their way to *Dar Sabah* ('Land of the Sunrise', Central Sudan), seasonal labourers from the north. The major transactions are all determined in advance. The wholesale traders and truck-drivers have longstanding arrangements with the local retailers who buy their goods and the local middlemen who obtain the produce they come to buy. This is a social and commercial institution, not an arena of free competition. The traders have travelled hundreds of miles and cannot afford the risk of an incomplete sale, or the time needed to find, assess, barter, buy, and rebag each kilo of grain or bundle of *tombac* leaves. *Shartai* Arbab and the market committee hold court in a restaurant. They hear disputes over ownership of market stalls and payment of dues. If grain is short they may negotiate with the traders to withhold from buying grain in bulk, or even consider a ban on non-residents buying grain.

Porters load the lorries as the mechanics and spanner-boys make the constant repairs that are needed, as many of the trucks are decades old, and the roads are rough. In one part of the market, livestock are bought and sold, with a market clerk observing and collecting the market dues on each transaction. In another part, blacksmiths and tinsmiths are at work; nearby are tanners, saddlemakers, and shoemakers. There are matmakers, basketmakers, ropemakers, potters. There are carpenters and tailors working in the shops. There are small restaurants, supplied by butchers, firewood-gatherers, charcoal-burners, and water-carriers with donkeys. Behind the shops are women brewing beer. There may be dried fish brought from Chad or Bahr el Ghazal, rock-salt from the desert, garlic from the heights of Jebel Marra. *Fakis* are writing amulets, bone-setters treating wounds. The poorest are selling fodder for animals or wild foods for people, or simply begging. Foot- and donkey-traders set up stalls selling imported fabrics. Labourers ask where farm work can be had. Herders exchange information about cattle prices in markets a hundred miles away. Richer farmers examine varieties of seed newly imported or provided by the Jebel Marra Project, and discuss experimenting with them.

Few of the people selling in the market depend solely on trade or craft for their livelihood. Most combine these activities with farming and keeping animals. Most of the households in Nankose have opportunities for earning an income outside agriculture. Poorer households have one or more dry-season income-generating activities, even if it is only building fences or gathering firewood and fodder. The richer households hire out camels for ploughing, or own shops in the village, and two villagers own lorries. Rich and poor alike sell agricultural produce: grain, vegetables, peppers, *tombac*. There is also a group of artisans. Artisans, especially weavers, have suffered from competition with cheap imported manufactures. But now the main problem facing artisans and those dependent on low-status trades is their vulnerability to short-term economic changes. They are doubly at risk. They are dealing either in non-essentials, or at least in goods which people can postpone buying when times get hard: tailors, carpenters, and shoemakers may find they have a temporary but devastating fall-off in trade. Many work in activities where the market is likely to be flooded by poor farmers if there is a crop failure (e.g. firewood- and fodder-gatherers, beggars, labourers of all kinds). The second aspect of their vulnerability is that these people usually rely on buying much of their food needs from the market, rather than growing it themselves, and so find themselves in trouble when food prices rise.

Search for the Subsistent Tribal Peasant

The economy of rural Darfur has been described as 'tribal' (Holy 1980). Elsewhere it has been characterized as having separate 'subsistence' and 'cash' spheres (Barth 1967*b*). These descriptions are hard to reconcile with the picture of Nankose just presented. Ethnicity is 'citizenship' not 'common ancestry'. The market-place is a central social and economic institution for all sections of society. It is true that Darfur is a varied region and Nankose exemplifies a rich part of it, but later case-studies will show that the search for a 'subsistent tribal peasantry' is futile. There have been changes since Barth and Holy did their fieldwork, but even older sources attest to the place of commerce in Darfur's history (see Chapter 3). Much of the trade was and remains controlled by indigenous merchants. Nevertheless, both these descriptions contain a germ of truth, and this is a truth that relates to the ideology of the household in Darfur. The 'subsistent tribal peasant' does not exist in Darfur, but rural people often talk as though he or she ought to. It is a normative concept.

'Subsistence' must be interpreted so that it is not the opposite of 'market-oriented'. It should be taken to mean 'living at a standard which satisfies minimum needs'. So a subsistent pastoralist is one who satisfies minimum needs by exchanging livestock for grain through the market. While many people in Darfur remain less than subsistent, this notion is clearly an important one, and is certainly one that informs the thinking and planning of rural people. One category of 'poor' people (*miskin*) is thought to consist in those who can support themselves throughout the year only with a struggle.

Subsistence is 'normative', in three senses. One sense is that it is a measure of sustainable income and production. Producers should not have to deplete their assets in order to fulfil minimum needs. The second is that the income is evaluated with respect to a 'normal year'. Few farmers expect to grow enough grain in a drought year, let alone a year such as 1984, and so farmers should not be regarded as below normative subsistence because production in these years is not adequate for them. Similar considerations apply to herders. The idea of a 'normal year' holds itself up to scorn: such years rarely if ever occur. What is real, both statistically and psychologically, is a 'normal' spread of some good and some bad years. The third sense is that minimum needs should be met by socially acceptable means. This is the most interesting stipulation. By examining what is and what is not acceptable, we discover how the economics of subsistence are inseparable from the social values of community life.

One category of unacceptable activities includes the 'despised trades', such as pottery (for women) and blacksmithing (for men). The extreme case of this is Zaghawa potters and blacksmiths, who form a separate caste, live in their own villages, and are unable to intermarry freely with ordinary villagers. Their status has undertones of servility, which is often ascribed to their alleged past special relationship with the aristocratic class of the Zaghawa, for whom they made weapons. In villages such as Nankose they live apart from the main body of the village, and in the markets they have their own, separated area. Often they have no land. They are not considered as fully participating in the village community. Their ostracism is related to the implications of the activities they do, which involve tampering with the basic elements of existence, especially fire, leading to 'polluted' status (Douglas 1966). They are also often specialists in hunting and gathering, activities associated with the wilderness, the non-social sphere. They may satisfy their minimum needs, but are not normatively subsistent.

Related problems of exclusion affect poor people who earn money in some of the most common ways, such as firing bricks and burning charcoal, or who obtain food by gathering in the wilds. Others are affected in less extreme ways. Those who earn their living by casual labour or by selling firewood or fodder, live in the 'interstices' of society. They have to travel from place to place, or spend time outside the community altogether, in the wild. Though not ostracized, they are socially marginal. They lack the material means to participate fully in the community, not having grain to participate in communal work parties, or animals to pay as bride-wealth for the sons of the house.

Another powerful set of attitudes relates to wage-labour. Agricultural wage-labour is considered shameful, so much so that people often travel to neighbouring villages where they are less well known in order to seek to do it. Historical accounts of Darfur contain many descriptions of local people being too proud to do it, so that the only labourers were strangers to the community. Attitudes to farm labour are slowly changing, but in another respect opinion has not altered at all: the people of Darfur almost unanimously refuse to share-crop.

Share-cropping is well understood in Darfur (southern Sudanese or west Africans are employed) and not excessively exploitative (typically the harvest is divided into equal halves). The reason for the refusal is that share-cropping involves the same farm-level distribution of tasks and rewards as farm slavery used to do, until its legal abolition in 1916. Servile status is, like ostracism, a polar opposite to subsistence. Slavery had two main implications. One was exclusion from being a full member of the community; slaves were typically described in the idiom of being non-kin, as was common in Africa (Lovejoy 1981; Miers and Kopytoff 1977). The other was loss of autonomy, dependence on others for providing a source of income, and being unable to make one's own productive decisions.

In less extreme form, this loss of autonomy is seen among wage-labourers and people in the low-status income-generating trades. The stigma remains: these are shameful activities, and should be done only out of dire need.

Therefore, though normative subsistence has strong economic implications of wealth and poverty, it is in fact built upon two axes that are principally social. One axis is membership of the community, as opposed to marginal or excluded status. The second is autonomy in making productive decisions, as opposed to dependence or servility. The ideal community is a kinship group of autonomous producers, none of whom are compelled to work for the others, and none of whom have to take on demeaning or ostracized trades. This is the ideal of the subsistent tribal peasantry. Closer analysis has shown that the tribal or kinship community is a myth, albeit a powerful one. Kinship is an idiom used to express membership of a community. Investigation has also shown that the subsistent producer is not one who does not participate in the market, but rather one who does not participate in the market in a demeaning way. Finally, though there are 'nomad' and 'farming' variants of this ideology, in fact almost all households fall along a spectrum in between these extremes.

The notion of 'belonging' has another important implication. Only those who 'belong' to a community enjoy the rights that follow from being recognized as a fully social being. One of these rights is assistance in times of hardship. If a visitor to Nankose asks to be taken to see the poor people of the village, he or she will typically be shown an old or disabled person living alone, or supported by a relative, or a family with many orphans. These people are certainly poor in a material sense (they are thought of as 'very poor', *fagiir*) but in a social sense they 'belong'. The visitor will not be taken to see the family of an unemployed artisan, a seller of wild foods, and certainly not a drought-migrant from the north encamped on the margins of the village. These people are also materially poor, but they do not 'belong'. In a similar way to that in which the poor of Elizabethan England were divided into 'deserving' and 'undeserving' on supposedly moral grounds, the poor in and around a Darfur village will be divided into the 'belonging' and 'non-belonging' poor.

John Iliffe, in his recent epic history of the African poor (1987), has made a related point for the Moslem savanna societies of west Africa, noting the 'identification of destitution with lack of normal social relations, and hence lack of support (other than charity) when incapacitated' (p. 42). However, Iliffe's analysis, while of great value, has not captured this 'belonging/non-belonging' distinction, because his central concern is with the 'very poor', and because he relies on documentary sources. Most of such sources are produced by those who are non-poor and who have a greater or lesser responsibility for assisting those whom they see as poor. This is the familiar problem of 'the poor' being defined by the non-poor (Simmel ed. 1971). It is likely that people who live in the interstices of society, and who do not present an acute threat to overwhelm the social order, will not appear in the archives at all, either because they are not deemed worthy of relief, or because they are not considered poor at all. Hence Iliffe concluded that 'The poor . . . were the handicapped and unfortunate individuals who lacked family care, supplemented periodically by victims of political or climatic insecurity' (p. 47). The latter group ('conjunctural poor') appear only briefly in the accounts, at the peaks of crises, not in the context of their longer-term struggle for subsistence and belonging. The analysis of ideologies of poverty and relief will be taken up again in Chapter 8.

3

The History and Concept of Famine

The famine of 1984/5 was an event of historical significance in Darfur. It is now widely accepted that a social scientist studying a famine should place it in a historical context (Anderson and Johnson 1988). That is not all, however. The victims of the 1984/5 famine themselves also put the drought and famine in a historical context: for instance they commonly compared it to the great famine of 1913/ 14. The question as to which famine was the worse provoked much debate. This is partly a matter of a current representation of that famine. Throughout much of Darfur 1913/14 was known as *Julu*, meaning 'Wandering', and people discussed whether 1984/5 was likewise a famine of 'wandering'. But it is also a matter of a genuine historical consciousness. In some villages of Jebel Si the famine of 1984/5 was actually named after 1913/14: it was given the name *Kadisa*, meaning 'Cat'. Some informants even suggested that the 'cat' famine of 1913/14 was itself named after a famine of the 1820s (see below). Historical awareness is also shown by the way in which texts such as those of the nineteenth-century merchant el Tunisi (1854) are read, discussed, and criticized by rural people. If modern texts such as that of O'Fahey (1980) were available in Arabic they would be subjected to similar critical scrutiny.

Much of the social history of Darfur remains to be researched and written, and what follows is merely an outline. It is derived from oral sources, from the unpublished work of local historians such as Sabil Adam Yagoub, Abu Hamed Hasaballah, Ibrahim Yahya Adam, and others, and from published and archival material. The documentary sources and the local historians deal largely with matters such as warfare, administration, and land. Their evidence is at its scantiest and least reliable when dealing with phenomena such as poverty and famines, and at times is seriously at odds with oral accounts. One example is the famine *Julu* which is entirely overlooked in some written accounts of the last years of Ali Dinar. The discussion of famines therefore relies heavily on oral histories, with documentary material providing secondary evidence only.

The *Ancien Régime*

The history of Darfur before the seventeenth century is largely conjectural. It seems clear that a succession of empires was based in what is now Darfur: Zaghawa, Daju, and Tunjur. The Tunjur empire ruled much of what is now Chad. There is a direct link between the last Tunjur sultan, Shau Dorshid, whose castle stands at the summit of a mountain at Ein Fara, near Kutum, and the first of the sultans of Dar Fur. Starting with Sultan Suleiman Soloni, Dar Fur rose to become a prominent power in Sudanic Africa. During the early nineteenth century Dar Fur ruled as far as the Nile in the east, and controlled Wadai as a vassal state in the west. This was a state as large as many modern African states in terms of land area and possibly population. The history of the Dar Fur state, its predecessors, origins, conquests and court intrigues has been documented by Lampen (1950), Arkell (1951a, 1951b, 1952a, 1952b), O'Fahey (1980), Sabil Adam Yagoub (unpublished manuscripts), and others. During the nineteenth century the sultanate came under pressure from the expanding Turco-Egyptian empire and its advance guard, the Khartoum traders. By the time of its fall in 1874 Dar Fur had contracted to its modern boundaries.

The internal workings of the sultanate are best thought of as a series of three concentric circles. The innermost circle surrounded the capital. Until the late eighteenth century the court, known as *fashir*, was mobile, mostly in the Kebkabiya area, until a permanent capital was set up at Rahad Tendelti, soon renamed El Fasher. By the nineteenth century, most of the land in the vicinity was given out as *hakura* land grants to followers of the court (O'Fahey and Abu Salim 1983). This area was closely administered, and probably heavily taxed. The second circle consisted of consolidated Fur dominions. This area was ruled by an administrative hierarchy of *shartais*. Nankose lay in this area, where indigenous non-Fur people on the southern frontier of Fur hegemony were gradually consolidated under Fur rule. People here paid tribute grain and labour to the state (Beaton 1948). The third circle included client states, military provinces, slave-raiding domains, and semi-nomadic tribes on the borders of Darfur. These were only intermittently controlled, and el Tunisi (1854) commented that the Rizeigat Arabs were wont to send the severed head of the tax-collector to El Fasher in place of the tribute that was demanded.

The evidence for famines in this period is scanty. A great famine said to have happened in the reign of Sultan Teyrab (1752–87) is known as *Karo Tindel*, Fur for 'Eating Bones [from carcasses]'. Nicholson (1979) has given evidence for a severe Sahelian drought during the 1750s, and Browne (1806, p. 320) reported that 'seven years' before his arrival in Darfur, which was in 1793, the rains failed and 'the agricultors were reduced to great distress, and it happened that many people were obliged to eat the young branches of a tree pounded in a mortar'. A migration of Berti people southwards to Korma district can be dated to about this time. It is likely that a famine whose memory survives two centuries on took a toll on human life, or at least changed peoples' ways of life markedly. Another famine that is recalled is *Buz*, which is said to have occurred during the reign of Sultan Mohammed el Fadl (1802–38), which may have been caused by the Sahelian drought of 1828–9, inferring from low levels in Lake Chad (Nicholson 1979). The name *Buz* in Fur means 'everyplace', perhaps referring to the wide extent of the famine.

It has sometimes been argued that traditional African social systems were well adapted to the threat of drought, and consequently that great famines are a twentieth-century phenomenon (e.g. Watts 1983; Raynaut 1977). This was not the case in Darfur. It is true that the chronology of famines is denser in recent years, but that is due to the fact that all but the most severe famines are forgotten after a couple of generations. There is little in the social system of Darfur's *ancien régime* that would have prevented or ameliorated famines. The sultans were frequently fighting wars, displacing people, and requisitioning their produce. Taxation could be heavy. While the *shartais* and *hakura* holders have subsequently evolved into village sheikhs, they were historically tax-collectors and administrators, whose loyalty did not necessarily lie with the villagers. This is illustrated by the tax assessments that they made when re-employed by the Anglo-Egyptian Government in the years after 1916: on occasions the assessment of crops was 'so ridiculously high that in many cases the *ushur* [one tenth tax] assessment must have been in excess of the total crop' (Civsec 122/1/1). There were also classes of people who were dependent on the pleasure and prosperity of their overlords, for instance tenants on *hakura* estates and slaves. These would be the first to suffer in a famine. Grain might be stored in communal *zaka* stores in anticipation of a poor

year, but famines occurred, then as now, precisely when a succession
of poor years depleted stores of grain. In Nankose, old men who had
experienced the last pre-colonial famine (1913/14) were scornful of
the suggestion that the social system might have been more resilient
or equitable. They recalled: 'No-one helped another person, except
sometimes his own brother or father', and 'No help was offered to
the people'.

'A Heap of Ruins': 1874–1916

The forty years after 1874 witnessed an appalling succession of
famines in Darfur. During this time the human population was
probably halved, and turmoil affected every part of the region.
Today's human geography of Darfur is to a great extent the outcome
of the disruption of these years. The era stands as a landmark of
suffering in the consciousness of people in Darfur, a backdrop
against which subsequent events are seen.

In 1874 Zubeir Rahma Pasha, indirect and somewhat unwilling
agent of the Ottoman empire, conquered Darfur. He defeated Sultan
Ibrahim Garad at the battle of Menawashei, and fought loyal Fur
elements throughout the following year, creating much devastation
in rural areas. Harvests were also poor in 1873: Lake Chad was low,
indicating drought conditions, and Gustav Nachtigal in September
of that year described being served *'Makhet*, which is usually
substituted only in an emergency for corn, of which the people,
therefore, seemed not to possess very much' (ed. 1971, p. 194). A
major famine followed, *Karo Fata* ('White Bone'): it is remembered
as a 'famine that killed'.

Zubeir did not stay long in Darfur. He was soon recalled to Cairo
by the Khedive, and the Turco-Egyptian empire absorbed Darfur.
Not peacefully: not only did elements loyal to the Fur sultans
continue fighting throughout the eight years of the *Turkiyya*, but
Zubeir Pasha's lieutenants, notably Rabih Fadlallah, continued free-
lance slaving and pillaging along the western frontiers of Darfur and
in Wadai. Rabih is remembered in Dar al-Kuti (south-west of
Darfur) as having 'eaten all the land where he passed, he took all'
(Cordell 1985, p. 55), and for having unleashed thirty years of
unparalleled bloodshed. In Darfur itself the *Turkiyya* did not last
long. During 1882 the Mahdists began to take control of southern

Darfur. The Khalifa Abdullahi, second in command to the Mahdi, was a Baggara Arab from the Ta'aisha of Darfur. Many among the Baggara federation of Arab tribes were among the first and most loyal Mahdists. By the end of 1883 the Mahdist armies controlled Darfur, and by 1885 they controlled Sudan.

Only a few months after the Mahdi was victorious, he died of an illness and was succeeded by the Khalifa Abdullahi. The Khalifa may have come from Darfur, but he did not command the support of all the Ta'aisha, let alone other groups such as the Fur. During 1885–8 there was a series of revolts against Mahdist rule, first by the Rizeigat and then by the Fur (Holt 1958).

The disruption caused by these wars is not documented or remembered: it was to be overshadowed by a great 'famine that kills'. This was the famine of 1888–92, which was possibly the worst ever. Unlike the situation in Ethiopia, which suffered the Great Famine at the same time, and in riverain Sudan, drought was not a cause. There was certainly a plague of locusts, probably in 1889. The major cause was fighting between the Mahdist forces under the governor of Darfur, Osman Jano and a rebel army under the religiously inspired leadership of Abu Jumeiza. It was only the time of the Khalifa's policy of forced migration, *tahjir*, to Omdurman. His message to his own kinsmen of the Ta'aisha in 1889, when they were reluctant to move, suggests the mood of the times: 'You have the choice of treading the path of the garden or the path of the fire' (quoted in Holt 1958, p. 145). It was also a time of drought and severe food shortages in riverain Sudan. The Mahdist forces had several aims: to crush the rebellion, to punish the Darfurians unwilling to move to Omdurman, and to requisition the grain in western Darfur to feed themselves (Pankhurst and Johnson 1988). At one point there were more than 36,000 Mahdist troops in El Fasher, and when on campaign they 'ate, drank, wore or stole' everything there was (Kapteijns 1982, p. 77). In western Darfur the armies are remembered as having 'eaten' the villages. Many people, including those of Nankose, fled westwards towards Chad. In El Fasher, it is said that 'the strong ate the weak'; presumably this is also an idiomatic usage. This famine is usually known as *Sanat Sita* ('Year Six') because it started in the Islamic year A.H. 1306, though it was actually said to be worst in the years seven and eight.

During the next decade there were further famines, caused mainly by fighting and some plagues of locusts. The Sahel as a whole also

suffered low rainfall during 1894 (Nicholson 1979). All areas of
Darfur suffered. The destruction of the years 1888–92 had left the
rural population scattered, impoverished, and vulnerable. In the
south-east the Rizeigat herders recall being so destitute after *Sanat
Sita* that they were reduced to gathering wild foods anyway and the
succeeding famines passed them by.

Ali Dinar was a prominent Fur loyalist with ambitions to be
sultan, but he was compelled by the Khalifa to join him in
Omdurman. Ali Dinar told his own story:

> I remained with the Mahdists until [British] Government troops captured
> Omdurman [in 1898] and then I collected my men and came to Dar Fur. On
> my arrival I found that the country was in a pitiful state of ruin and
> devastation. It was all barren and there were no camels, no cattle, no goats
> and not even one single donkey (Civsec 112/2/6).

Ali concluded by summing up Darfur in 1898 as 'a heap of ruins'.
He appointed himself Sultan, intending to restore the *ancien régime*.

Allowing for Ali Dinar's exaggeration, Darfur had suffered. The
first decade of the restored Fur Sultanate saw further suffering. Ali
Dinar attempted to reimpose his rule on the southern Arabs. In 1900
he sent a general named Salim to fight the Beni Halba: the
subsequent famine is remembered as 'Salim's famine'. In the same
year Ali Dinar expressed his views on the Ma'aliya Arabs: 'I consider
their extermination necessary' (quoted in Theobald 1965, p. 46). A
Mahdist garrison also remained in the heart of Dar Fur, at
Kebkabiya, under *Faki* Siniin. It was only in 1909 that Ali Dinar
managed to starve Kebkabiya into a state such that Siniin could be
defeated.

Other areas of Darfur were heavily taxed during the years 1899–
1901 as a result, and north-east Darfur saw huge expropriations of
land for slave-worked estates owned by the sultan. At least one
famine is reported for this period in north-east Darfur. The years
after 1902 were more peaceful, with miltary activities fewer and only
on the borders of Darfur, and taxation was less onerous. A locust
infestation and cattle plague during 1908 are attested to by both oral
tradition and Condominium government intelligence sources (Civsec
112/2/5; Darfur 1/33/169). In the climatic history of the Sahel this
was also a dry phase, which culminated in 1908 (Schove 1977,
p. 43).

Dar Masalit escaped the worst ravages of these years until 1909, when a French invasion was repulsed by the Masalit armies under Sultan Taj el Din, who unfortunately died on the battlefield and so was unable to prevent a French punitive expedition the following year reducing the country to a famine which has no recalled name.

More was still to come. The third region-wide 'famine that killed' of this period, and the only one whose major cause was a drought, occurred during 1913/14. There was exceptionally low rainfall in 1913. This was exacerbated in south-eastern Darfur by fighting between the Rizeigat and the forces of Ali Dinar. Musa Madibu, *nazir* of the Rizeigat, wrote in late 1913: 'our land has now become a desert, without inhabitants other than the birds and beasts. We exist on the trees for food, and our cattle are dying for lack of food.' In a later letter he elaborated: 'There is not a single house that is not burned down by [the Fur armies]' (Intel 2/1/6).

The drought and famine of 1913/14 contributed to the instability that finally toppled Ali Dinar's regime. Government military intelligence reports, Ali Dinar's correspondence, and oral history all attest to breakdown of local government, raiding for food, and enormous famine migrations. From Nankose people left again towards Chad. Zayadiya Arabs left for Kordofan. Many Berti moved southwards, away from drought-stricken areas. Much of eastern Darfur was first settled by the Berti at this time. Zaghawa came down as far as southern Darfur. In El Fasher, grain prices reached the equivalent of six Egyptian pounds per *ardeb* (128 kg.), twenty times the price of 1908, three times the highest famine prices obtaining in Omdurman, and a price not exceeded until the famine of 1949 (Intel 6/8/24, p. 238). The famine was so severe that after touring his southern districts in mid–1914 Ali Dinar was moved to suspend taxes for a period. 'Many people died for want of food', he wrote (Civsec 112/2/7).

This 'famine that kills' is known most commonly as *Julu* ('Wandering'); other names are *Um Sudur* ('Mother of the Chest'), *Dulen Dor* ('Sun Famine', on account of the cloudless skies), and numerous other local names. This 'year of commotion and blood-shed' was followed by 'plague and disease on a large scale, such as we have never seen or heard of before' (Ali Dinar, Civsec 112/2/6).

The memories of those years of hardship still remain in Darfur. A Ta'aishi sheikh described how one group of Ta'aisha, returning destitute from Omdurman after the defeat of the Khalifa, hid the few seeds they had for planting in cleft sticks, so they would not be robbed and killed for them. MacMichael (1915) in an intelligence report for the government in Khartoum just before the invasion of Darfur, described the land of the Ta'aisha and other western Baggara Arabs as 'almost denuded of Arabs' (p. 3) and the Ta'aisha themselves as 'a mere remnant of a once powerful tribe' (p. 26). Those Arabs that remained had few animals and were forced to cultivate. Many of the Fur were scattered, mainly westwards, and came back in much smaller numbers to reoccupy their villages. Some came back as late as the 1920s. Their small numbers can be gauged from the fact that they lost territory to the much-depleted Arabs.

Ali Dinar refused to pay the tribute demanded by the Condominium Government in 1914, claiming that he had no money. This was only partly true: he was at that time busily coining his own money (Arkell 1940). He did send 200 bulls, as 'assistance' to the government, but then wrote rescinding this and saying that instead they were a wedding present for his friend, Rudolph von Slatin. The Khartoum Government was not impressed. Ali Dinar was encouraged in his ambitions for complete independence by the outbreak of the First World War, which he saw as God's punishment on Britain and France for plotting against him. He had strong millenarian tendencies in these times. By 1916 he was addressing his correspondence to 'The Governor of Hell in Kordofan and the Inspector of Flames in en Nahud' (quoted in Theobald 1965, p. 175). During that year the Condominium Government sent an expeditionary force to Darfur, and Ali Dinar was overthrown and killed. Loyal elements fought on into 1917, causing yet another famine in south-west Darfur.

Closed Districts: Darfur after 1916

The invading Anglo-Egyptian army of 1916 found Darfur disrupted by four decades of 'commotion and bloodshed'. Whole areas were hugely depopulated and had been recolonized by wild animals. Near Kebkabiya, where Nachtigal in 1874 had noted a 'remarkable scarcity of wild animals' (ed. 1971, p. 250), the British expedition of 1916 reported 'some thirty or forty elephant were seen, and there were also said to be Lion, and when the inhabitants were asked what the latter lived on, laconically replied *Nas* (people)' (Civsec 122/1/3).

Darfur was in a highly unusual state. Unfortunately, observers of Darfur have often written as though the years immediately after 1916 were a norm or baseline with which to compare subsequent developments, rather than an aberration. Thus Ibrahim (1984) began his history of pressure on natural resources with this period. Statistical history started in Darfur in 1916 with the first systematic measurement of rainfall, and the first official estimate of population a few years later, so the reasons for this are easy to see. Most of those who have written descriptions of rural life have tended to assume that contemporary developments consisted of novel external intrusions on age-old rural tranquillity. R. Davies, Resident in Dar Masalit during the 1920s, wrote:

For four years money has been gradually filtering into the country . . . it is now practically true that nothing can be bought except for cash . . . those who formerly wore homespun now call for Manchester goods. Tea, coffee and other goods are craved for by people who had barely tasted any of them a few years ago (quoted in Kapteijns 1982, pp. 254–5).

What he says may be strictly true, but what was western Darfur like fifty years before? Compare el Tunisi's description of Kebkabiya in 1803:

The environs of which reminded me of the country places in Egypt; but the town is better built, richer, and more lively. Many foreigners are seen there. The natives are, for the most part, wealthy merchants, having a great number of slaves, with which they trade (1854, p. 23).

Burckhardt (1819) noted that Dar Fur merchants were among the richest in Cairo. What the early British observers saw was not a 'moral economy' but a shattered economy.

The changes instituted by the Condominium Government hampered the reintegration of the economy. The main concern of the government was to prevent a resurgence of Mahdism. This required the creation of a stable social order. Tribal *dars* ('homelands') were created, with a structure of administration, based on 'traditional leaders'. This 'native administration' was supposed to provide control that was both firm and locally legitimate. These developments served to dampen the processes of ethnic change and assimilation. The fiefdom and estate systems were abolished and slavery was made illegal. These moves served to make land and labour into non-commodities, and thereby stifle the possibilities for

large-scale farming. This was the cause of the switch away from
farming and the drive for farmers to invest in livestock, noted in
Chapter 2. Under the Sultanate, people had aspired to assimilate to
the Fur for political reasons, now Fur aspired to assimilate to the
Baggara for economic reasons. Urban populations were small, and
trading licences hard to obtain under the Closed Districts Ordnance.
Tax burdens were low: the administrators feared the disruptive
effects of high taxes. Apart from the brief uprisings of religious men
claiming to be the *nabi Issa* in the 1920s, Darfur remained at peace.

Otherwise, Darfur was neglected, as is illustrated by a letter from
the Civil Secretary in Khartoum to the Director of Agriculture and
Forests. This was written in 1945, at a time of increased interest in
the productive possibilities of Britain's overseas territories.

> I understand that practically nothing has been done in the way of an
> agricultural survey [in Darfur]. . . . It is I think axiomatic that in Darfur all
> we can really aim at is to improve the local standards of living by increased
> productivity and increased local exchange of products (Civsec 64/2/11).

'A little gum, honey, etc.' are the only exports he mentions. To be
fair, the production and export of livestock was encouraged. It
remains the case that facilities for cattle at Nyala and Ed Da'ien
railway stations are better than facilities for human passengers, and
it is likely that they travel in more comfort as well.

This mixture of imposed changes and neglect made for stagnation
in Darfur. Rural people were obliged to migrate to central Sudan or
sell animals to earn a cash income. How did this affect rural
vulnerability to famine? There were years of famine in 1926/7, 1930/
1, 1937, 1939, 1941/2, 1945, 1949/50, 1955, 1959, 1969, and 1973.
This appears to be a terrible sequence. However, according to oral
histories, none of these famines killed people, and only the worst of
them (1949/50) left people destitute. The main cause of these
famines was drought (1926, 1941, 1949, 1959, 1969, and 1973), but
in comparison with the decades before 1916 and since 1969, the
weather was favourable. During the early period, locust infestations
were a problem (1930, 1937, and 1939). Later, locust control
programmes became effective. Veterinary services controlled most
cattle diseases after the 1920s (Wilson 1979). During the years up to
about 1970 rural smallholders probably enjoyed the greatest freedom
from state demands for money or produce, and were best able to
follow pure 'subsistence' agriculture. War, the main cause of famine

up to 1916, was no longer a problem. In 1926 an epidemic of relapsing fever killed tens of thousands of people in western Darfur and Jebel Marra (Maurice 1932; Hartwig 1978). Thereafter, though famines characteristically brought with them outbreaks of infectious diseases, notably meningitis and measles, human epidemic diseases were largely brought under control (Bayoumi 1979).

This probably meant that farmers were less exposed to the risk of a grain shortfall than during any other period. However, the complementary aspect to this benefit is that when a deficit occurred, there were few opportunities to gain an alternative source of income. Little wage-labour existed in Darfur, and Gezira was too distant for seasonal migrant labour to be possible. There was only a small and poorly developed market in grain for those with cash from having sold animals, tobacco, or gum.

The two decades straddling national independence in 1956 saw the beginnings of modern economic development in Darfur. This involved the introduction and encouragement of ground-nut farming, the drilling of deep-bore wells in *goz* areas and the extension of the railway line to Ed Da'ien and Nyala in 1958–60. Land was beginning to be a commodity again. From this time south-east Darfur, close to the railway, became the most economically advanced part of the region, more similar to neighbouring Kordofan than to the rest of Darfur.

It has been argued that the expansion of commercial farming leads to a rural population being more vulnerable to famine. In Darfur this did not occur. The commercial farms are relatively small; few are more than 100 hectares. These were areas newly opened up for cultivation, not land taken from smallholders or pastoralists. It is true that there was a bloody dispute between the ground-nut farmers and herders of south-east Darfur during the 1960s, but the herders actually won. There is no class of people totally dependent on the agricultural wage-labour market for their livelihood; the growth of a labour market has in fact made small farmers more secure as there are more fall-back opportunities in the case of crop failure. This is attested to by the fact that in the south-east of Darfur the famine of 1949 was relatively mild, while those of 1959, 1969, and 1973 did not affect the area at all. The people of Darfur are sceptical of the idea that the growth of what Watts (1983) called 'commoditisation' has increased vulnerability to famine. On the contrary, they credit their ability to withstand famine to the very same factors. Rather than a balance being ruptured in the rural economy, a balance was returning.

Unlike in the west African Sahel, no-one cried 'famine' in western Sudan in 1973. Most writers (O'Brien 1985; Shepherd 1984) have assumed that this was because the Sahel suffered famine whereas Sudan did not. This shows misplaced faith in outsiders' diagnoses of famine. The Sudanese authorities were certainly concerned about 'the west'. In 1973 the rainfall in Darfur was the lowest on record, comparable to that in the Sahel. The Sudan Council of Churches considered that 85 per cent of the population of Darfur, or 1.9 million people, were 'drought affected' (SCC 1974). The 'affected population' were more stoical. Only people in the north-west and Dar Masalit considered this year to be a (mild) famine. Elsewhere, people did not deign to give it a name. The Census of 1973 showed relatively high child death rates in Kordofan and Darfur (Farah and Preston 1982, p. 367), probably attributable to the drought. Social scientists have spilt much ink chasing this particular set of shadows. The alleged reasons why Darfur allegedly escaped the alleged Sahelian famine are wrong, or irrelevant.

One alleged reason was the development of mechanized grain production in eastern Sudan (O'Brien 1985). It is true that grain production in eastern Sudan expanded greatly during the 1960s and early 1970s. Grain production in Gedaref in 1973 was 1,973,000 tonnes, above the average for 1961–80. Most of this grain was grown for the internal market in Sudan; massive grain exports were yet to occur. But, as economists have pointed out, national grain availability does not of itself prevent famine (Sen 1981). Keen (1986) has shown that the price of grain in Nyala during 1973 was more than twice the price in Gedaref: this shows that the people of Darfur had to pay a premium for any grain from the 'national market' that reached them.

Another way in which the boom in Gedaref could supposedly have helped is through the flow of remittances back to Darfur from eastern Sudan. However, while it is true that the good production in Gedaref during 1973 certainly helped the Darfurians who were living and working there, it does not follow that it helped their kin back in Darfur. *Dar Sabah* is too far away for seasonal migration. Those who were there tended to re-create the conditions of smallholder farming by taking up tenancies in Gezira or starting small sorghum farms near the Ethiopian border. Remittances back to Darfur were at best sporadic.

A third alleged reason for the non-famine is that people could migrate southwards in Sudan without national frontiers to cross, whereas they could not do so in the Sahel (Adams 1975, p. 278). In fact the reverse is true. A Hausa from Niger was more likely to find employment and sustenance among the Hausa of northern Nigeria than a Baggara Arab from Darfur was among the Dinka of southern Sudan, especially as 1973 marked the close of seventeen years of civil war in south Sudan. Moreover, in 1973 there was net immigration to Darfur, consisting of an estimated 200,000 Chadian refugees (al Bashir 1978).

The main reasons why there was no famine in Darfur during 1973 were that the drought was not as severe as it was to be a decade later, and commodity production was flourishing. Animals did not die in significant numbers; the effect of the drought was to restructure herds. Crop failures were neither total, widespread, nor repeated. It was a time when the production of and income from cash crops was slowly increasing, and the local labour market remained strong.

All Manners of Suffering

Many famines are remembered in Darfur (see Table 3.1). They form part of the historical narrative, playing a role in the fall of

Table 3.1. *Famines recalled in Darfur 1885–1985*

Year	Districts	Examples of names	Cause
1885			
	All Darfur[a]	*Sanat Sita, Jano,*	War, forced
1890	All Darfur[a]	*Ab Jildai*, etc.	migration, locusts, cattle disease
1900	South-west Darfur[b]	*Salim, Alabas*	War etc.
	Mellit	*Um Mukheita*	Drought
	Kebkabiya[b]	*Siniin*	War
1910	Dar Masalit[b]	(no name)	War
	All Darfur[a]	*Julu, Um Sudur, Dulendor*	Drought, war
	South-west Darfur	*Um Sider*	War

Table 3.1. (*cont.*):

Year	Districts	Examples of names	Cause
1920			
	Western Darfur	*Kuburu, Ab Tokolai*	Locusts
	Dar Masalit	*Bedawita*	Suppression of revolt
	Northern Darfur	*Ab Malwa*	Drought
1930			
	Northern Darfur	*Kadis Dakhal, Sei Kiri*	Locusts
	Eastern Darfur	*Um Rotel*	Locusts
	Northern Darfur	*Ab Habaya*	Locusts
1940			
	Northern Darfur	*Ab Tokolai, Um Goldi*	Drought
	North and West Darfur[b]	*Khafaltina, Um Regeba, Um Mukheita, Abu Arobain*	Drought
1950			
	Dar Masalit	*Rujal Jafal*	Epidemic disease
1960	Um Kedada	*Meliss*	Drought
	Kutum-Kebkabiya	*Abu Arba*	Drought
1970			
	North and West Darfur	*Ab Sotir, Sanat Kruul*	Drought and Chadian refugees
1980			
	All Darfur[a]	*Sanat Ju', Reagan*	Drought

[a] Famines that kill
[b] Other severe famines.

governments, the migrations of people, and religious uprisings. The concept of famine is also closely bound in with central ideologies in Darfur society. This can be understood by looking at how the words for famine are used, and the meanings behind the names given to past famines.

In Darfur Arabic, in common with other African languages, 'eating' is used idiomatically to mean enjoying money, power, sex, and other good things. Likewise, 'hunger' is used for all manners of suffering. Arabic is unusual among African languages in that the word for 'hunger' (*ju'*) is not identical with the word for 'famine' (*maja'a*). However, the two words do have the same root, and *ju'* is often substituted for *maja'a*. The other concepts involved in *maja'a* are destitution and death. When we map out the conceptual geography of *maja'a*, important differences in comparison with English appear.

Famine names fall into distinct categories. One category consists of names referring to shortage of grain. Many of these refer to small measurements of grain, those being the units whereby grain was sold in markets or distributed by community leaders from *zaka* stores. These names include: *Ab Malwa* ('Father of the Malwa'), *Ab Tokolai*, *Um Rotel*, *Abu Arba*, *Um Goldi* (after the 'Goldi' cigarette packet), and others. Some names refer to the high price of grain, e.g. *Abu Arobain*, 'Father of Forty (Piastres)', that having been the price of a measure of grain. Others refer to the places where people had to travel to obtain grain, such as *Saafar Mellit* ('Journey to Mellit'), *Sanat Konsi* ('Year at Konsi'), and a whole succession of other places too numerous to mention. In some cases these refer to people organizing camel caravans to go and buy grain, more often they refer to the population migrating to the area. Lastly there is the lone case of a name that refers to the problems of maintaining order at grain stores: *Ab Sotir*, 'Father of the Whip'.

When did these famines occur and what is remembered about them? These names are most commonly used to refer to the following years: 1926/7, 1930, 1937, 1939, 1941/2, 1949/50, 1969, and 1973. On rare occasions they are used to refer to 1888–92 and 1913/14. In their main usage they refer to famines that were comparatively mild, or to areas only marginally affected by more severe famines. They do not refer to 'famines that kill'. Some of these famines were described as merely periods of hunger when people were not even threatened with destitution. Reference to grain shortage implies hunger; it need not imply anything else.

The people of Darfur have a simple and sanguine attitude towards hunger. Hunger is something you put up with. Islam does not make a virtue of abstinence; in the fasting month of Ramadan people are not enjoined to eat less than at normal times, but merely to fast during daylight hours. Hunger has no religious resonances, it is merely one manner of suffering. People often bind their stomachs in order to lessen the pangs of hunger.

A second category of names includes those that refer to wild foods

that are eaten during times of dearth. These include *Um Mukheita*
('Mother of *Mukheit*'), *Ab Direisai* ('Father of *Direisa*') and many
others. These wild-food names tend to refer to the same years of
famine as the 'shortage of grain' names, except that they are used
rarely for the mildest, and more frequently for the more severe
famines. Hence they refer mostly to famines that did not kill people.
Like reference to grain shortage, reference to wild foods implies
hunger. They also have another implication. Collecting wild foods is
stigmatized; it is something that the poorest do during normal times,
and it involves becoming marginal to the community. In times of
dearth people who are not destitute may collect wild foods, thus
taking a socially marginal role for a short time. They are briefly
destitute, and then regain subsistence; they are briefly marginal, and
then 'belong' again. These famine names imply temporary poverty
and exclusion, but not long-term destitution.

The names in a third category do imply destitution in a more
serious or long-term way, as well as implying hunger. The concept of
subsistence, and its converse, destitution, is tied in with participation in a functioning social order. As people become completely
destitute they are unable to participate in society; they become
outcast, they violate the conventions of society, and they become
dependent. The names in this category refer to this mass destitution
and social breakdown in a number of ways. The great eighteenth-
century famine is known as *Karo Tindel*, meaning 'Eating Bones
[from carcasses]'. The great famines of 1888–92 and 1913/14 are
both sometimes known as *Ab Jildai*, 'Father of the Skins'. Both
these names refer to people breaking the injunction to eat only the
flesh of an animal that has been slaughtered in the correct way. A
famine that occurred in south-west Darfur during the reign of Ali
Dinar is referred to as *Alabas*, which has the meaning of eating
selfishly, not sharing food. The famine of 1913/14 is most commonly
known as *Julu*, meaning 'Wandering' (alone, in search of food, as a
chicken does when it scours the ground for grains). Another name
given to this famine is *Nitlaaga*, 'We'll Meet Again': this is what
people said before setting off on their wanderings. This recalls the
complementary aspect to the social breakdown and 'mass-stranger-
hood' of that famine: the re-creation of communities that is expected
to occur afterwards. Community is suspended, and later reinte-
grated. 1913/14 is also known as *Um Sudur*, 'Mother of the Chest'.
This is variously explained as 'striking people in the chest' and

'people crawled upon their chests', the latter being symbolic of subjection and dependence. In western Darfur the year 1949 is sometimes referred to as *Um Regeba*, 'Mother of the Knees', with similar symbolism. Sometimes 1984/5 is known as *Ifza'una*, 'Save Us'. All these names are powerfully symbolic of the breakdown of society, of being outcast, solitary, or dependent: all opposites to the ideals of belonging, community, and autonomy. From the history of Darfur we know that the famine names in this category refer to severe famines: famines that render people destitute and on occasions kill them.

When a famine kills people, people will often append the phrase 'famine that kills' (*maja'a al gatala*) to the name of the famine. There is no category of famine names which themselves refer to death. That is, when a famine kills it qualifies for a separate label, rather than another subcategory of names which would form an extension of this hierarchy of names of increasing severity. This suggests two possibilities. One is that 'famines that kill' cross an important barrier, where naming breaks down. The second is that even when a famine causes deaths, the destitution and social breakdown it causes are more significant for the sufferers.

The distinction drawn between famines that do and do not kill could be interpreted as implying that rural people have an idea of what is a normal and what an abnormal mortality rate. But this approach is sterile. It is hard enough to derive a normal mortality rate for Darfur which is acceptable for statistical purposes (de Waal 1989), without the extra question of whether it is recognized as such by rural people. In a community such as Nankose one person can be expected to die every fortnight; during a famine that kills perhaps one will die every week. In a small village the frequencies are lower. The frequencies fluctuate according to season and many other factors. An increased death rate would often be difficult to notice. Moreover, what is normal for one generation is not necessarily normal for the next. With death rates dropping, a level of mortality equivalent to the 'normal' of a century ago would be very abnormal today. In fact, rural people in Darfur do not think in terms of a death *rate* at all. It is a notion that presupposes a statistical mode of thinking that is not generally found. Rural people do not think of the populace as an anonymous aggregate population, but as a moral community. They do not think of *excess* deaths as a discrepancy from what is average or normal. Rather, *early* deaths are a violation of what ought to be the case, which is people living to their natural life span.

The concept of a 'famine that kills' could be elucidated by investigating the demography of historical famines that kill. However, these occurred between 1874 and 1916 and the required analysis is impossible. The population history of Sudan in this period is a fraught subject. Some writers (e.g. Balamoan 1977) have taken extreme positions and argued for a catastrophic population fall during the Mahdiya, but reliable evidence is lacking. Nachtigal's estimate for the population in 1874 was 3.5 million people, but this was no more than a guess (ed. 1971, pp. 356–7). Early Condominium population estimates ranged from 300,000 to 525,000 and were also very dubious. The French in Chad considered that the famine of 1913/14 alone killed 300,000 people in Wadai and, together with epidemics, more than halved the population (Decalo 1977, pp. 212–13). The latter claim is frankly unbelievable.

The best approach to understanding the thinking behind 'famine that kills' is to consider that what is important is not how many people die, but the evident reason why they are dying: famine. As we have seen, 'famine' means, in Darfur, not merely starvation but also hunger (that is, all manners of suffering), destitution, and social breakdown. When people are dying, manifestly because of the hardship and disorder associated with a famine, it is a 'famine that kills'.

The very worst famine in remembered history, *Sanat Sita*, 'Year Six', in 1888–92, seems to have surpassed the capacity for being given a descriptive name. There is also the poorly documented famine that decimated Dar Masalit in 1909/10, after the area was ravaged by the French. This famine has no recalled name, and some informants recall it as a famine that killed.

There are assorted other famine names, that usually tell us about the causes of the famine in question, rather than its effects. Some names refer to drought: *Dulen Dor* ('Sun Famine', 1913/14); *Khafaltina* ('It [the rain] Betrayed Us', 1949); *Meliss* ('No Harvest', 1959), and others. Many names refer to locusts, usually the type of locust responsible. Some names refer to people, usually people held responsible for starting a war that caused a famine, such as *Jano*, *Salim*, and *Siniin*. There is also *Reagan*, held to be responsible for the food relief of 1985. One name refers to the skeletons of dead animals, *Karo Fata* ('White Bone': 1874). A number of names refer to cats, for little apparent reason. It may be a translation problem: a famine in the first half of the nineteenth century was known as *Buz*, Fur for 'every place'; *Buz* is also Darfur Arabic for (female) cat (*Kadisa*). The famine of 1930/1 is known as *Kadis Dakhal* ('The Cat Entered'), ostensibly because of the silent approach of the famine (caused by locusts). This may be correct: the Fur name is *Sei Kiri* ('Without any Noise'), and the government was also caught by surprise. Some famines are named after previous famines which they are said to resemble: in one Fur area near Jebel Si the famine of 1984/5 was named *Buz* (or *Kadisa*), after 1913/14, which was itself possibly named after the *Buz* famine of the nineteenth century. The famine of 1917 in Nankose was called *Um Sider* ('Mother of the Little Chest'), coming as it did only three years after *Um Sudur*, the (big) chest famine.

It is clear that the notions of 'hunger', 'destitution', and 'death' are three constituent concepts of *maja'a*. In English, an event must include all three to be a 'famine', with starvation deaths being the ultimate criterion. In Darfur, the concepts work differently: there are different kinds, corresponding to different severities, of *maja'a* (which I shall continue to translate loosely as 'famine', though it is better translated as 'famine and/or dearth'). There are two major distinctions. One is between famines that kill, and famines that do not. The second is between famines that consist only of hunger and famines that consist of destitution and social breakdown too. The power and importance of the symbolism of destitution and exclusion suggests that the concept of *maja'a* has a focus on destitution. All instances of *maja'a* are instances of hunger. This trinity of hunger, destitution, and death will become the broad framework for analysing the famine of 1984/5 in later chapters.

4

Drought

Darfur was stricken by drought in the early 1980s. The drought was the most obvious and immediate cause of the famine. This was not merely a one or two years' failure of the rains. In many parts of Darfur, the drought has been unremitting for a decade and more. At the same time, Darfur has suffered ecological degradation: the bare *goz* that rings El Fasher town, and the bleakness of Saiyah. In the years after 1978, Sudan was also plunged into a huge economic crisis. The commercial, monetized economy which had advanced into Darfur over the preceding decades was suddenly crippled and forced into retreat.

This chapter analyses the causes of the famine of 1984/5. It looks at the different elements of drought and ecological and economic crises, and analyses local and outside interpretations of these.

A Shortage of Rain

People in Darfur typically gave accounts of the origins of the famine in a moral idiom. Thus certain things happened because God was 'punishing' people, or because things were 'wrong' or 'out of place'. This moral idiom included different levels of explanation, from the cosmological to the local and particular. At one extreme there were millenarian or apocalyptic accounts, at the other extreme blame was put on certain groups such as nomads or charcoal-burners. People also refered to facts such as poor rainfall or soil erosion in highly empirical ways. The way people disputed the extent, importance, and relationships between these phenomena suggested a 'scientific' way of thinking, subsumed within the general 'moral' framework.

The famine was caused by drought. This was the overwhelming opinion. This global, simple explanation in fact consists of a number of contributory explanations. One question is: why is there a drought? The second is: what does a drought consist of? Just as famine is not (or is not just) mass starvation, drought is not just a shortage of rainfall.

Why Was there Drought?

Opinions on this matter were unanimous. The drought was suffering sent from God. Though some people refused to speculate about God's motives, most interpreted the drought as a retribution for wrongdoing. In the survey of 1986, 763 rural people were asked if God had sent the drought as a punishment: 88 per cent agreed, and a further 9 per cent said it was sent by God, but that people should not presume to understand why.

It is useful to visualize the diversity of Darfur in order to appreciate what kinds of different experiences of drought underlay peoples' accounts. In the far north there stand huge forests of dead trees, many uprooted by the wind, with sand drifts forming in their lee. One elderly man in Dar Zaghawa explained that this drought was to be found described in the Koran (he had been told this by an itinerant *faki*), and was a sign of the end of the world. Rain had not been 'normal' in this area for twenty years. As he talked a dust storm was blowing through the withered millet stalks on his field. His village was surrounded by a forest of trees, mostly dead. For that particular way of life, it *was* the end of the world. By contrast, in Nankose, the drought was only a two-year shortfall in rain. This required much less ambitious explanations, for instance God's displeasure at merchants continuing to extract usury, or at peoples' failure to fast during Ramadan over recent years on the excuse that it had fallen in the planting and weeding season.

Millenarian tendencies have a long history in Sudanic Africa. Mahdism and *Nabi Issa* uprisings have been mentioned in the previous chapter. Ali Dinar interpreted the 1913/14 drought and famine in apocalyptic terms. During the 1920s a drought of the severity of the 1980s might have been similarly interpreted. But the few *fakis* who preached this interpretation in 1984/5 did not gain a large following. In general, explanations were 'global' in the sense that they encompassed all of society, including powerful and remote bits of it such as the national government in Khartoum, but not 'cosmic' in that they were not millenarian. When searching for droughts and famines to compare the recent one with, people overwhelmingly refered back to *Julu* (1913/14). Very occasionally *Sanat Sita* (1888–92) was invoked. *Julu* was similar to 1984/5 in that it was caused by drought, and in that it contributed to the fall of a government. The most common and most considered explanations for God's punishment were at this level of importance: the drought

was of national and generational significance, but not the end of the
world or the change of an epoch, as was *Sanat Sita*. At the most
precise, one man explained that the drought had begun in May 1969
and broken in April 1985. These two dates correspond with the
beginning and end of the Nimeiri regime. The dates do also fit
remarkably well with the rainfall data, collected by what one hopes
to be politically neutral climatologists. Bad, evil, or corrupt
government was the explanation expressed with most vigour. It was
also the most popular choice in the survey of 1986, with 64 per cent
of the people who had an opinion mentioning it. Other people who
were unwilling to give an opinion on political matters also said that
the drought had begun in 1969, sending discreet signals of their
beliefs. While the government was an obvious target for blame,
people also put responsibility on Darfur society. The guilty parts of
society tended to be 'other people': townspeople, nomads, 'Chadians'. The sins being punished were general evildoing, laziness,
concern with money, greed, sexual immorality, disrespect for
parents, failure to pray or give alms, or fast during Ramadan.

.The fall of the Nimeiri Government in April 1985 created
optimism, but people still anxiously performed rituals that might
influence God to be merciful. These included observing Ramadan
with great strictness and also giving *sadaga* alms during that month,
and performing the rain prayer *istisgha*. It was often explained that
although performing the *istisgha* served to move God to provide good
rain, it was not the failure to follow this ritual in previous years that
had caused drought. Thus the influences on drought were generally
located outside the community, but potential influences for good
rains were located partly within the community. This articulation of
explanations in terms of community relations is important and will
recur in the discussion.

What Does Drought Consist of?

The explanations for the causes of drought were global. In contrast,
the explanations for the constituent parts of the drought were much
more particular. God causes everything, but at the same time some
of the things He causes may in turn cause other things. Informants
were prepared to discuss 'particular' causal links, but only on the
understanding that God was also causing the phenomena in
question.

Old people compared the recent drought with *Julu*. One man commented that *Julu* had been worse, because types of trees had died then that had survived the recent drought. This opinion was unusual; most informants thought that the climate was deteriorating in unprecedented ways. While people recognize the occurrence of droughts in history, all droughts are not the same. Droughts are not just more or less long or severe. Each drought, like each famine, has a different character. They recur, but not in a mechanical or repetitive way, at least not within a span of generations. The recurrence of the *Buz/Kadisa* names for famines induced by drought in Jebel Si is a rare exception to this. Thus, thinking about 'drought' in general is not useful, it is better to consider 'the drought', as a discrete historical development. Moreover, people in Darfur do not regard 'drought' and 'desertification' as separate phenomena. Instead they see desertification as part of the manifestation of drought.

Declining Rainfall

In Darfur it is widely believed that the climate is getting drier. The rainfall statistics show that this is true. Anne Clift-Hill (1986) has analysed the available data from every rainfall station in Darfur. These data go back to 1916 for El Fasher and to more recent dates elsewhere. Unfortunately there are no records for most stations in north Darfur for the drought years of the early 1980s, because the government neglected to pay the people responsible for collecting the data. All but one of the twenty-eight stations showed declining rainfall, sixteen of them statistically significant at the level of 99 per cent probability. The exception, Kebkabiya, had records that stopped in 1977. Figs. 4.1 and 4.2 illustrate this. Since records began it has rained less by on average three millimetres in Nyala, 2.1 millimetres in El Fasher, and 3.7 millimetres in El Geneina every year.

Rural people prefer to see the worsening climate not as a falling average yearly rainfall, but as a changing pattern of good and bad years: good years are becoming scarcer. This was universally claimed in northern Darfur, but sometimes disputed in southern Darfur. In 1985 in northern Darfur I tried to get opinions on what the numerical ratio of good and bad years had been in the past, but answers were vague: 'we had rain here [in the north] like they now

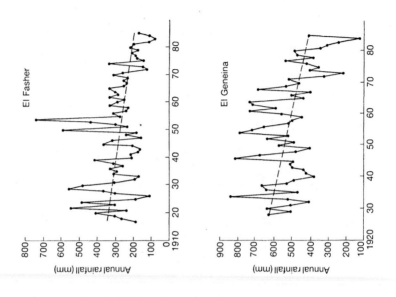

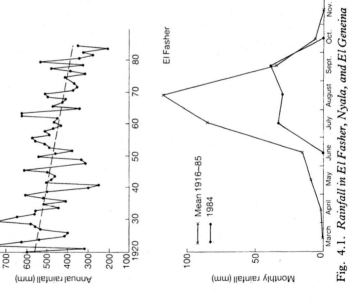

Fig. 4.1. *Rainfall in El Fasher, Nyala, and El Geneina*

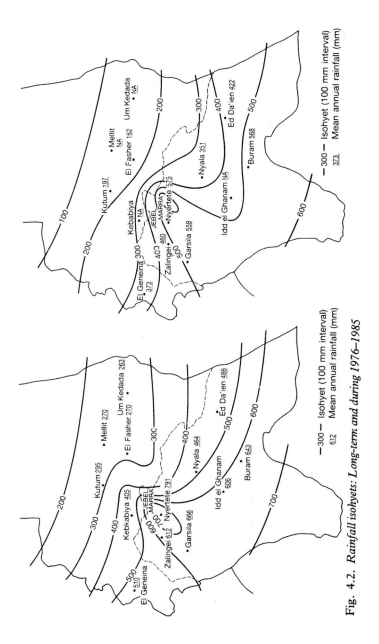

Fig. 4.2. *Rainfall isohyets: Long-term and during 1976–1985*

do over there [in the south]', or 'more were good than bad'. However, it was possible to obtain numerical answers for the number of good and bad years 'these days', so this question was asked in the survey of 1986. Answers to this question showed considerable awareness of the weather.

The difference between the chronic drought of northern Darfur and the shorter failure of rainfall in southern Darfur is clearly seen in Table 4.1.

Table 4.1 *Mean ratio of good to bad years as estimated by respondents*

Site	Location	No. of respondents	Good : bad	Rain 1976–85 (mm.)[a]
Angabo	South	64	1.7 : 1	422
Nankose	South	92	1.2 : 1	558
Legediba and Sabola	South	45	1 : 1	500 (est.)
Arara	West	69	1 : 1.7	400 (est.)
Jebel Si	North	74	1 : 3.6	250 (est.)
El Fasher	North	118	1 : 4.1	162
Saiyah	North	53	1 : 5.8	125 (est.)
Furawiya	North	51	1 : 6.3	100 (est.)

[a] This column shows the mean annual rainfall in millimetres from 1976 to 1985 from the nearest rainfall station, if nearby, or an estimate derived from the isohyet map (Fig. 4.2).

This 'good years versus bad' approach is a useful way to analyse climatic change. There appear to be phases when good years predominate, and other phases when bad years do. For instance the two decades before 1916 were a time of exceptional dryness right across the Sahel culminating in the drought of 1913 (Grove 1973), when the River Nile reached its lowest level for probably two centuries (Hurst 1923). Rainfall statistics, by starting in 1916, miss this period and so exaggerate the rate of decline. Dry years predominated in the 1940s, and again after 1969. But it is also the case that good years are becoming less wet, and poor years are becoming drier. Climatologists have agreed that since the start of the nineteenth century each half century has on average been drier than the preceding one (Grove 1973; Schove 1977).

People in Darfur saw the change in the rainfall as more complex than just a changed pattern of good and bad years. Within a single wet season, the pattern changed too. The wet season had shortened and become more unreliable. There were more heavy thunderstorms, and longer gaps between showers. These gaps could cause growing plants to wither and die. People pointed to phenomena that had never occurred before, such as the clouds gathering, and a curtain of dust blowing, but then no rain falling. These were often explained in terms of the winds being wrong: the north desert wind continued when the rain-bearing south wind should have come. These observations corroborate what the rainfall statistics show. As the overall amount of rain has declined, the pattern of rainfall has changed. Instead of the 'savanna pattern' of frequent lighter showers it has moved towards the 'desert pattern' of infrequent but very heavy storms.

'Sons and Daughters of Drought'

Most people, especially in the north, considered that drought was the whole 'family' of lack of rain, deforestation, degradation of pasture, and declining yields. Asked to explain the relationships between them, one man said the latter were all the 'sons and daughters of drought'.

Creep of the Desert

Everyone in the north was aware of places turning into desert. This was ascribed to lack of rain above all, though other important attributed causes were 'winds blowing sand from the desert', 'cutting trees', and 'farming all the land'. Stated baldly in this way, the accounts sound rather like the explanations environmental scientists might give. There are important similarities, notably the empirical observation of what kind of ecological degradation was happening where, and what local conditions might have been important in causing it. Opinions in this empirical idiom were collected in the survey of 1986. The responses showed that most people thought cutting trees was an important cause of the creep of the desert (55 per cent of a sample of 672). After that the causes most popularly ascribed were winds blowing sand (41 per cent), lack of rain only (31 per cent), overcultivation and oversettlement (21 per cent) and lastly—minimally—overgrazing by animals (7 per cent, with only 0.3 per cent putting it as the 'most important'). There was a strong statistical link between the two explanations of 'wind blowing sand' and 'cutting trees': fully 21 per cent of respondents gave an explanation of 'lack of rain' and these two factors.

These figures show that perceptions concerning the causes of desertification varied. Some of the variation reflected local differences: the contrast between Saiyah and Nankose is a case in point. Some variation reflected differences in individual opinions. The figures do not show what these perceptions meant to people.

As in the case of rainfall failure the understanding of desertification was articulated in a moral idiom. In this case, it was less global and more particular. In Saiyah the blame for the cutting of trees fell mostly on nomads and immigrant farmers. In Nankose, it fell on nomads, charcoal-burners, and 'Chadians'. The people of Saiyah would admit to cutting trees, but they held that a certain number of trees had to be cut, and the nomads and immigrants had gone beyond that limit. Worse, they were cutting the wrong trees, or cutting them for sale. Similarly, overfarming was often ascribed to immigrants farming too much, and creating pressure on land so that the villagers could not give their own farmland a rest from cultivation. This was a superficial moralizing, an articulation of pressure on resources in terms of community politics.

These perceptions differed from 'expert' opinion in important ways. Darfur people were unanimous that declining rainfall is the underlying problem. This not only destroys the environment in itself, but forces rural people, against their better judgement, into non-sustainable land-use practices. Many disaster tourists, by contrast, appear to hold that farmers are destroying their environment through carelessness and ignorance, and the declining rainfall is irrelevant or secondary. More sophisticated accounts recognize farmers' ecological knowledge, and identify social and economic pressures on farmers as contributors to destructive land-use practices. The discussion of Saiyah in Chapter 2 and the work of Mustafa Babiker (1988) in western Kordofan show that this has some truth. Fuad Ibrahim (1984) identified deforestation and overfarming as major causes of stabilized *goz* degenerating into wind-blown sand sheets. Thus he agreed on two points with rural people, but he disagreed in seeing wind-blown sand as a consequence rather than a cause of desertification. However, the major disagreement concerns animals. In the 1970s experts considered south Darfur to be stocked to the carrying capacity of the rangelands (Wilson and Clarke 1975; HTS 1977), and northern Darfur to be seriously overstocked (Ibrahim 1984). The owners of the animals clearly think otherwise. On one issue all are united. There may be disputes about the precise nature and causes of ecological deterioration but none that it is happening.

Violations of the Moral Landscape

There is a deeper moral idiom used in describing the creep of the desert. This is exemplified by a Jaluli sheikh near Kutum. Sheikh Hilal described the wind blowing off the desert, taking sand from the hillsides and leaving it in the *wadi* beds, so that when it rained the water failed to run along the proper watercourses and instead wandered in the *goz*. In the mountains, meanwhile, the water had not stayed on the terraced farms but rushed down to the *wadi* and caused a flood which had taken away gardens at Fata Borno. Sheikh Hilal might have added, as other informants did, that the water was also eating *khors* (gullies) out of fields. The theme was that order is disturbed, and things are in the wrong places. Sand that ought to be on hillsides was in *wadis*, water that ought to flow in the *wadis* was flowing instead in the fields, water that should be feeding the gardens was taking them away.

As well as this 'moral landscape', Darfur has a wider 'moral geography'. Nankose can provide an example (Fig. 4.3). Cultivated areas and villages are the *dar* or *balad*, the sown, the domestic. Fur people are associated with this area: they are farmers, and 'belong'. To the east and west are broadly similar farming people; other Fur, Berti, Masalit. Hills and forests count as *khalla*, that is wilderness, but 'useful' wilderness providing bush fallow, pasture, wild foods, firewood, and potential farmland. *Khalla* is found mainly to the north and south of the *dar*. Associated with the *khalla* are the semi-nomadic herders; slightly disreputable, but also useful. The Salamat cattle-herders belong to the southern *khalla*, the Mahamid camel-herders and Zaghawa to the northern *khalla*. Further to the south are the Fertit. 'Fertit' was a name given by the Fur overlords to their pagan southern neighbours whom they considered potential slaves. As Fertit communities 'became Fur' and became Moslem, they lost

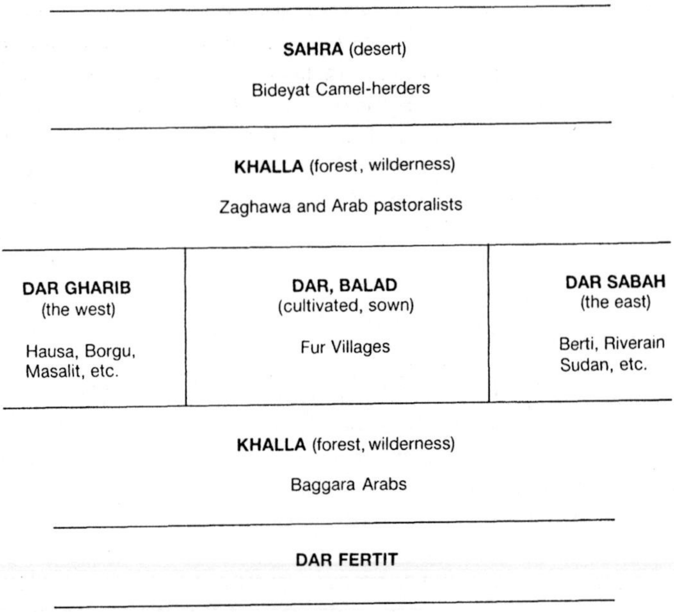

SAHRA (desert)

Bideyat Camel-herders

KHALLA (forest, wilderness)

Zaghawa and Arab pastoralists

DAR GHARIB (the west)	**DAR, BALAD** (cultivated, sown)	**DAR SABAH** (the east)
Hausa, Borgu, Masalit, etc.	Fur Villages	Berti, Riverain Sudan, etc.

KHALLA (forest, wilderness)

Baggara Arabs

DAR FERTIT

Fig. 4.3. *Moral geography of Darfur: Fur villagers*

their Fertit label. They stayed stationary, and the frontier with Dar Fertit moved southwards. Dar Fertit was and is not so much a place as a moral category (O'Fahey 1982, pp. 82–3). To the extreme north is the deathly wilderness of the *sahra*, the desert. Here we find the Bideyat: the archetypal desert people. MacMichael (1915, p. 50), having noted the fearsome reputation of the Zaghawa, went on to describe the Bedeyat as 'an exaggerated form of Zaghawa. They are darker, wilder, bigger thieves, more independent, more treacherous and live further north than the latter'. He might have added that they are commonly held to be pagans. MacMichael had not visited Darfur and was reporting on a commonly held image, which persists today.

In Saiyah, the comparable moral geography is under threat. The destruction of the forests has brought the frontier of the desert right up to the villages, an actual and symbolic violation of the order of the landscape. The creep of the desert is a symbol of the awful power of the encroachment of all that is wild and hostile to life, the desert, into all that is homely and supportive of life, the sown. This was to be seen and heard most clearly in a nearby village, Khibabesh. The villagers described how the drought had killed the forests and brought with it a strong, persistent, and new wind from the north-east. 'Before, the trees protected us [from the wind]' it was explained. The wind brought sand from its proper place in the desert, and left it in the village, even right inside the houses. 'We are eating the desert' complained one woman. Literally true (her cooking pots had sand in them), and also a symbolic contradiction which summed up the threat to the whole moral order created by the drought and its 'sons and daughters'.

With the desert have come the people of the desert; feared Bideyat camelmen and others come south and prey on settled communities, and pastoralists bring their animals to cultivated places. They have penetrated further south than physical evidence of the desert. With ecological change has come an insecurity of community identity and relations.

The Arab herders have a different moral geography (Fig. 4.4). For them, the cultivated–forest distinction does not correspond to the home–wilderness opposition. They are also mobile. They see themselves as opposite, complementary, and equal or superior to the farmers. Their moral geography resembles a chessboard, with one set of squares being places inhabited by farmers (Fur, Berti, etc.) and the complementary set being the domain they can themselves inhabit. These areas extend up into the desert and down into

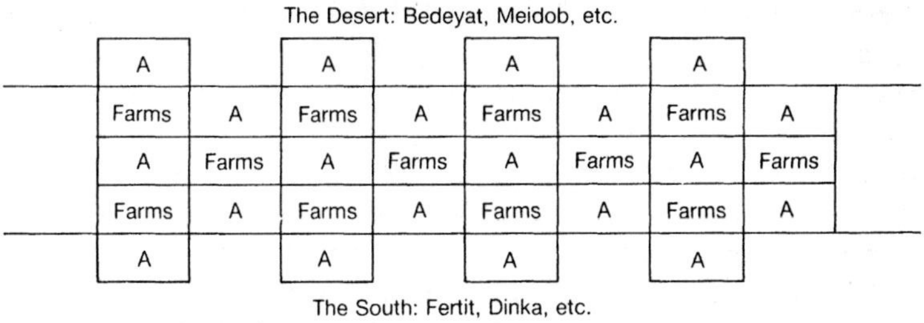

The Desert: Bedeyat, Meidob, etc.

A		A		A		A	
Farms	A	Farms	A	Farms	A	Farms	A
A	Farms	A	Farms	A	Farms	A	Farms
Farms	A	Farms	A	Farms	A	Farms	A
A		A		A		A	

The South: Fertit, Dinka, etc.

Fig. 4.4. *Moral geography of Darfur: Arab herders (Note*: areas marked 'A' are actually or potentially inhabited by transhumant Arab pastoralists.)

southern Sudan, where they live alongside non-Arab herders. For Arab pastoralists, drought and desertification do not present such a long-term threat to the moral order: they are accustomed to moving (most of their fixed *dars* were creations of the Condominium period). The movements do however present many hazards, which will be examined in Chapter 6.

Declining Yields

In southern Darfur there is no sign of the desert as such. Some people in Nankose refused to comment on desert creep: 'it is far away from here and we have no experience of it.' What they were all aware of, however, was a slow but inexorable decline in yields from their farms. People were emphatic that they are obtaining fewer sacks of millet from each *mukhamas* of land than their parents used to. The agricultural statistics agree (Ibrahim 1984). Explanations for this were conducted in a specific and empirical idiom, which reflected local farming realities. These included water 'eating' the soil into gullies and failure to observe fallow. In Saiyah, where wind erosion is a problem, farmers complained of the wind bringing agriculturally useless loose sand and taking fertile compact *goz*. Some talked of parasitic weeds and pests such as millet-head worm, locusts, and birds, but most did not think these had become more of a problem recently. All mentioned lack of rain.

A theme of moral degeneration was popular among older farmers, and a few younger ones. This recalls the evildoings that account for God withholding rain. They argued that today's farmers were lazier or less intelligent than their parents, or had failed to take their elders' advice. In this case, the ecological change was articulated in terms of conflict between generations within a community. It also implied conflict between the (elderly) sheikhs and the younger people who do most of the farming. This conflict was seen in a discussion of the community politics of migration out of villages in Dar Zaghawa, northern Darfur, to start farms in the south: the older generation considered the abandonment of northern farms and migration to be a moral failing among the young. The counterclaim by the young was that their fathers had failed to provide for them, for instance by selling animals which the sons had hoped to inherit.

The understanding of desertification and declining yields was therefore expressed in a double idiom. Issues were cast in moral terms, and often in terms of very specific conflicts between communities or parts of a community. At the same time empirical facts were noted, studied, and disputed carefully, particularly where the specifics of farming were concerned.

The Zaghawa: Social Transformation in the Face of Drought

Chapter 2 opened with a description of the stark landscapes of Dar Zaghawa, with rocky horizons 'like the bent spine of some prehistoric monster'. This section is a case-study of the inhabitants of this remote area, the Zaghawa. The case-study starts in the desert-edge community of Furawiya, where people are pastoralists. Here it is even drier than in Saiyah. However, while the drought of the 1970s sent Saiyah into a seemingly irreversible decline that has continued during the 1980s, the same experience inoculated Furawiya against what was to come, by triggering a socio-economic transformation. This included mass emigration. The second part of the case-study is Angabo village, in south-east Darfur. This is an area of Zaghawa diaspora; many came here in the 1960s and 1970s to settle, herding animals but chiefly cultivating millet and ground-nuts. Angabo is rich, but no longer growing richer. Some people are already leaving, and new settlers are looking elsewhere for potential new farms. The third part of the case-study is Legediba, a new village lying right on the frontier of expanding southward culti-vation. The Zaghawa are here too, 500 miles south of Furawiya, making even more radical changes to their livelihood and society (see Fig. 4.5).

The Desert Edge: Dar Zaghawa

The earliest written description of Furawiya comes from the Route Reports of the British Army's Northern Patrol, written by P. V. Kelly in January 1917: 'Furawiya. Altitude 2780 feet. Excellent shade and grazing and a plentiful supply of water all year round from *gosar* wells (1.5 *rajils* [1.5 "men", i.e. about 8 feet]) in *khor* bed' (Civsec 122/1/3).

In 1984/5 and again in 1987/8 the wells almost ran dry, and water could only be had at a depth of about twenty-five feet. In 1917, permanent settlements stretched well to the north of Furawiya; now

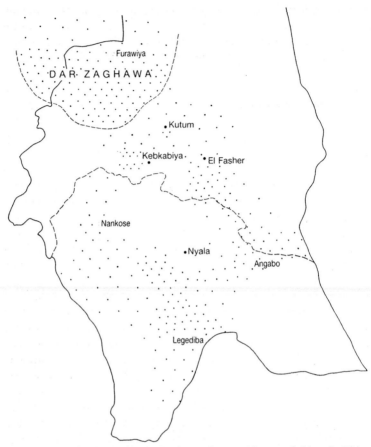

Fig. 4.5. *Dar Zaghawa and the Zaghawa diaspora (Sources*: fieldwork. This should only be regarded as a rough indication of the location of Zaghawa populations.)

the village is one of the most northerly permanent villages in Darfur. There are few rainfall statistics for this area; we know that Umboro, a few miles to the south, received a mean of 284 millimetres during the years 1958–66 (Tubiana and Tubiana 1977, p. 33). Now the area receives about 100 millimetres a year.

Marie-José and Joseph Tubiana, having lived intermittently among the Zaghawa between 1956 and 1970, described them as 'chiefly breeders of cattle, sheep and goats, next come camels.' (1977, pp. 40–1). Cattle predominated in southern and western areas of Dar Zaghawa, where they were herded in migratory transhumant style southwards. Camels and small stock were kept mainly in north-east Dar Zaghawa, where they were herded northwards to the desert pastures of Wadi Hawa and the expanses of the succulent *jizu* grass after the rains. Furawiya lay midway between the two zones.

Zaghawa women cultivated fields of millet on *goz*, particularly in the valleys where run-off water from the hills collects. Even in the wet 1950s and 60s, the Tubianas wrote: 'the cultivation of bulrush millet is a gamble verging on the absurd' (p. 6). They were probably exaggerating; the altitude of the Zaghawa plateau and the careful selection of sites for fields makes cultivation possible, even though rainfall may be well under 200 millimetres. Zaghawa ideology plays down the role of farming, and the land-rights system in use is of the simplest usufructuary kind. Most Zaghawa households have some cultivated land; in Furawiya only 12 out of 151 had no land at all and were purely herders, though others did not plant every year. This combination of an usufructuary land tenure system and an ideology that plays down cultivation, makes it possible for a Zaghawa to leave without worrying about failing to find land on his or her return.

The gathering of wild grains was and is of great importance. This is witnessed by the systematic manner in which wild grains are harvested, threshed, and stored. Animals are kept off the fields of wild grain, as they are kept off millet fields, until harvesting is complete. Particular villages often have prior rights to certain areas of wild grain, though attempts by individuals to enclose fields of the wild grain *difra* for private ownership were stopped by a meeting of Zaghawa sheikhs in 1980, who decided that wild foods were a free resource for the whole community. Finally, the Zaghawa include a despised caste of blacksmiths and potters (men and women respectively). Outside Furawiya they have a separate village.

Since 1969 a combination of drought, desertification, and economic changes have transformed Zaghawa society. There were droughts in 1968–70, 1972–3 (the famine *Sanat Kruul*; 'Kruul' is a rendering of the sound made by luggage creaking against the ribs of a camel, as households migrated), and 1976. The pasture is seriously degraded. Many wells are dry. From 1979 to 1984 Wadi Hawa flowed only once, and the *jizu* pastures never bloomed. The Zaghawa reject the notion that their land was overpopulated or overstocked. 'The rain cheated us', is their complaint. Nevertheless during the fifteen years to 1984 the Zaghawa effectively adapted to a changing environment. When the famine of 1984/5 struck, they were well prepared.

One important change has been a shift from herding cattle to herding camels and goats (Fig. 4.6). The Zaghawa responded to the drought of the 1970s by restructuring herds. By putting the Tubianas' data from 1965 and 1970 (p. 43) together with recent survey data (Buckley 1987), the trend can be clearly seen. During the late 1960s, numbers of cattle were falling, while sheep and camel numbers grew, and goat numbers doubled. In 1970 cattle still outnumbered camels by three to one, but by 1986 camels outnumbered cattle nine to one in the east and thirty to one in the west of Dar Zaghawa. In Furawiya, cattle numbers fell from over 300 in 1980 to four in 1986. The remaining cattle owners were thought 'vain'. Cows are now an expensive luxury; the environment is more suited to camels and small stock. The figure shows that similar restructuring was occurring elsewhere in Darfur (data from Holy 1980, p. 65; Wilson and Clarke 1976; Wilson 1976a, 1976b; de Waal 1987a, pp. 93–4, 98–9). This change is not only purely economic, but has had implications for many more aspects of Zaghawa society. For instance, cows used to be the means of payment of bride-wealth and blood money. Cash, not other animals, has taken their place.

Even more dramatic was the change that occurred in the human population of Dar Zaghawa. Most people left, and many changed their way of life entirely. The Zaghawa diaspora changed not only Dar Zaghawa but the whole of Darfur. Before the 1960s few Zaghawa were found outside Dar Zaghawa except during drought years such as 1913/14 and 1949. Immediately after the first of the recent droughts, in 1970, there were estimated to be 250,000 Zaghawa in Darfur, of whom 150,000 were in Dar Zaghawa. From the Census of 1983 we can estimate that 82,000 were remaining in Dar Zaghawa. Less than a third of the Zaghawa were actually living in their *dar*. Near Furawiya there are several sites of villages, now entirely abandoned, marked only by stones and clay granaries from around which the wood and straw huts have disappeared. In some villages the abandoned compounds outnumber the lived-in. Many of these people moved south. In Nankose, ten resident Zaghawa families were interviewed, and many more were found in Angabo, Legediba, and El Fasher. There has also been a restructuring of population within Dar Zaghawa itself. This is because wells in small villages have dried up, and the people have moved to larger villages

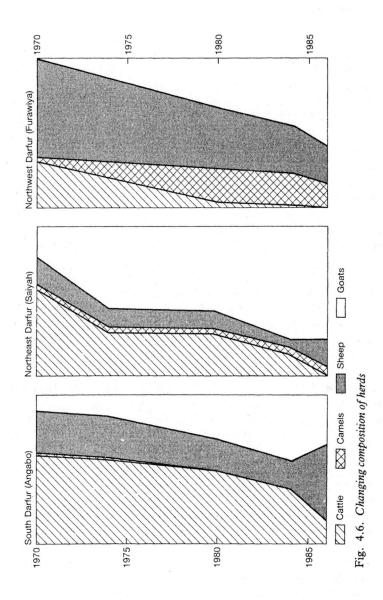

Fig. 4.6. *Changing composition of herds*

with permanent water. Furawiya itself is one such village, which is actually growing.

The Zaghawa who have left in this migration have changed their modes of livelihood and forms of community. The effect on those who remain behind is not just a lessening of pressure on resources. The northern Zaghawa now have greater flexibility in how they respond to the unremitting stresses of living on the Zaghawa plateau. Their livelihood increasingly depends on being able to use a range of diverse ecological and economic niches. This means being mobile over large areas, and maintaining links with farmers, traders, and townspeople.

Zaghawa communities in the north and south maintain links. Some of these links are through extended families. However, creating family links across the region is difficult. There is an Islamic preference for marrying first cousins whenever possible. This tends to consolidate power and property within a fairly small span of kinship, and limits the options for making family alliances through marriage. Strategic dynastic marriages are found mainly among the Zaghawa aristocracy and the more powerful merchants. Family-level links are limited to a minority of families where brothers or first cousins are split between north and south Darfur, where the southern farming kin may play host to the northern herders in times of drought. There are also certain groups who move between the north and south almost every year. One such group is the poor, including potters and blacksmiths, who depend on seasonal wage-labour in southern areas to make good their production shortfall in the north. The depopulation of Dar Zaghawa has deprived this group of much of their local market, so they have become semi-nomadic. The other group are rich migratory herders, who may move several hundred miles in search of pasture, and may stay several years continuously in south Darfur if the grazing in the north is poor.

The most important north–south links are mediated through the political authority of the senior Zaghawa sheikhs. The Zaghawa are a hierarchical society, consisting of aristocrats, commoners, and an artisan class. The transformations of the 1970s were often encouraged by the aristocracy, who extended their power and wealth as a result. Aristocrats who remain resident in the north (such as Sultan Dosa of Tina), wield power through their representatives (*mandubs*) in the south and the towns. The *mandubs* are in most cases close relatives, and they are mostly merchants. They dispense patronage (employment, land, credit) to the Zaghawa from the north. The fact that senior Zaghawa leaders can command the loyalty of people even though they are hundreds of miles away means that they do not try to prevent migration, in fact they are critical in facilitating it. More junior local leaders, such as village sheikhs, may oppose migration as they thereby lose people and consequently authority. These tensions were clear in a discussion of migration held in Abu Gamra, south of Furawiya. The majority of younger household heads were prepared to move south if the drought continued, but older people, including the sheikh, accused them of moral failings and were against the move. They were, however, powerless to prevent it.

While ecological change made the Zaghawa diaspora necessary, it was the systems of land tenure and political authority, and the broad horizons of their moral geography, that made it possible. The Zaghawa do not subscribe to either the 'Fur-type' or 'Arab-type' schemas of moral geography. In fact it is difficult to find a schema to which they do subscribe, apart from the notion that people and their *dars* can move. Their *dar* includes desert, forest, and cultivation; their livelihood depends on being able to straddle all these categories, none of which is central. Once outside the Zaghawa plateau, the Zaghawa have no conceptual frontiers to cross.

Angabo: A Staging Post

The Zaghawa may be ready to migrate anywhere, but they can only settle where local people will accept them, or where there are no local people. Consequently they are to be found in the interstices of the moral geography of the remainder of Darfur: in the towns, on the margins of other ethnic groups' *dars*, and in newly colonized areas in the far south.

Angabo lies in Goz Ma'aliya, near Ed Da'ien in south-east Darfur. It was one of the first areas of southern Darfur to receive Zaghawa settlers. The landscape here is flat *goz*, unbroken by any other physical feature. In contrast to Nankose, only wet-season crops such as millet, sorghum, ground-nuts, and sesame can be grown. It contrasts with Saiyah only in so far as it is far less degraded, and wetter. Ed Da'ien received a mean of 586 millimetres of rain during 1946–55 and 422 millimetres during 1976–85. There are still large forested areas, many gum arabic trees, known as *hashab*, and fields left for bush fallow. This is reminiscent of old descriptions of Saiyah, and Saiyah provides a grim vision of what ecological deterioration may yet do to Angabo.

In Angabo we can see the growth and stagnation of a village based on the limits of a system of land use. Goz Ma'aliya is basically waterless. The Ma'aliya Arabs used most of the land for pasturing camels, and also collected *hashab*. Villages existed only in a few places, such as Girnai, in the north-west corner, where a reservoir had been built. From the late 1940s, the government drilled bore-holes in Goz Ma'aliya, thereby opening up new areas for cultivation. In 1963 a bore-hole was drilled near Girnai, at Angabo, so the local people and their sheikh, Hamed Fadlallah, moved there. A man named Ahmad Mustafa owned the majority of the *hashab* trees in the vicinity; he thereby effectively owned the land, and he became a second village sheikh. This was the time of the ground-nut boom in Darfur. The railway had recently arrived. The Ma'aliya were losers in a bloody land dispute with their southern Rizeigat neighbours, and were compensated in cash, not cattle. The cash was invested in farming. Cultivation spread out from the newly settled village of Angabo in concentric circles. The land started as forest or *hashab*. It was cleared and cultivated, yielding best in the second or third year of cultivation, with a slow decline in yield that was partly offset by fallowing. After a decade or so, farmland was abandoned and thorn-bushes and gum-trees took root. The land nearest the bore-hole was cultivated first and now lies abandoned. Moving outwards from the village there are rings of long-farmed land, some fallow, recently cleared land, and forest. The most productive farmland is now some distance from the village. This pattern is most clearly seen in Landsat imagery (Scott-Villiers 1984). It is shown in condensed form in Fig. 4.7. Offspring villages have grown up nearer the frontier of expanding cultivation, some twenty miles to the south. Angabo, the parent village, is beginning to contract as a centre of production. Fewer farmers hire labour, and more seek to do it. Increasingly the local importance of Angabo lies in the services it provides: water, the market, the clinic, and the school.

Angabo was attractive to Zaghawa settlers for several reasons. Goz Ma'aliya was the area of greatest economic dynamism in Darfur during the 1960s. Credit for establishing cash-cropping was available, and markets were nearby. Angabo is also on the margins of the Ma'aliya *dar*, so settling and acquiring land were relatively easy.

Fig. 4.7. *Angabo, from a sketch by the author*

Gum-trees are owned privately. The '*hashab* sheikh' of Angabo sold trees and thereby dispensed the land on which they grew. Settlers with cash could buy land, freehold. The sheikhs of Angabo demand only nominal payments from villagers, in their capacity as 'first settlers'; no other allegiance or assimilation is required. Zaghawa authority structures could remain intact. In central Dar Ma'aliya this would have been politically difficult.

A total of a dozen ethnic groups are represented in Angabo. There is little formal hierarchy in the village. Inequalities are marked: one quarter of the farmers own two-thirds of the farmland, and the poorest quarter farms a meagre 3 per cent.

Angabo village may be beginning to stagnate, but the community is not. Over one third of the households had arrived in the years 1974–85. Some had moved only locally; most came from the north. Increasingly, Zaghawa immigrants were using Angabo as a 'staging post' or 'landing area'. These people came to Angabo from the north, either direct from Dar Zaghawa or in several stages (Fig. 4.8). Typically they would use ties with Zaghawa patrons or relatives to rent some land and obtain some wage-labour, before moving again, further south. This kind of spontaneous resettlement is lengthy, expensive, and risky. Most settlers had small landholdings and few animals. Local people also use Angabo in a cycle of movement. There are more opportunities for earning money from petty trading and other income-generating activities in Angabo than in the offspring villages. Poorer people can rent farms and supplement their production from these sources, before moving out to one of the newer local villages where farming is more profitable.

Angabo is partly a stable community of farmers. These people have adapted to the stresses of drought by restructuring their herds away from cattle towards sheep, and by growing more drought-resistant millets and less sorghum and ground-nuts (de Waal 1987*a*, pp. 99–102). Angabo is also part of a process of change in the Darfur economy, a crucial mid-point between the declining north and the dynamic southern frontier. It is Legediba village, in the far south, that completes the case-study.

Legediba: The Southern Frontier

Legediba lies in Goz Dango. Like Goz Ma'aliya, this used to be a featureless waterless forest. Rainfall is higher (Buram, to the north, averaged 568 millimetres in 1976–85), and the forest is thicker. It was used only by hunters, and *baggara* herders (Fellata, Habbaniya) who trekked their cattle south along its fringes after the rains. The water-holes that supplied these stock routes were the focus of the first small settled communities. Habbaniya farmers began to settle

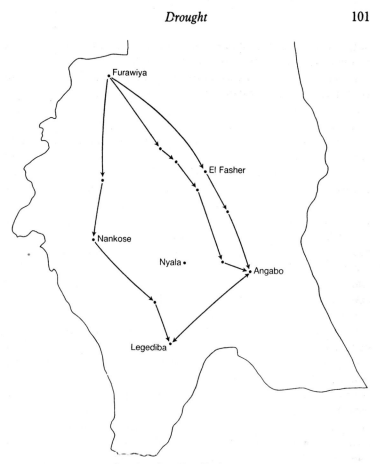

Fig. 4.8. *Illustrative migrations from Dar Zaghawa*

Goz Dango during the 1950s, and during the years 1958–72 there was a ninefold increase in cultivated area (Mohammed el Hassan 1980). Zaghawa pioneers began to arrive in the late 1960s, as groups of young men, touring the area, often in the company of Fellata herders who acted as guides. The pioneers would choose an area and demarcate it by felling or barking trees, and then await the coming of their relatives, gripped by what Mohammed el Hassan calls 'the fever of holding land' (p. 2). In 1973, when a bore-hole was drilled, Legediba itself began to be significant.

Legediba is a settler village. It is multi-ethnic, though dominated by Zaghawa, and amongst the Zaghawa, not by sheikhs but by merchants. It is as stratified as Angabo. The pattern of a community with little formal structure but marked stratification, which was found in Angabo, is found in a more extreme version in Legediba.

Who owns Legediba is a matter of acrimonious dispute. The Habbaniya claim that the land comes under the jurisdiction of their *omda*, who lives several villages to the north, basing their claim on prior use of the pasture in this area. The Zaghawa sheikh of Legediba claims an autonomous right to the land, based on a contentious interpretation of a government land grant. If the Habbaniya position prevails, the Zaghawa sheikh will legally fall under the land-centred authority of the Habbaniya *omda*, and no longer under the far-reaching patronage of the Zaghawa *mandubs*. Similar disputes have dogged the nearby planned settlement of El Amud el Akhdar, which has a majority of Zaghawa farmers (Mohammed el Hassan 1983*a*, 1983*b*). *De facto* no one owns the land at the frontier of cultivation in Goz Dango, because no individuals have farmed it before, and so no individuals have any direct claim on it. It is still possible just to go and cut the trees and start a farm, and this is what people do. It is claims to land jurisdiction that are politically sensitive.

The settlement of Zaghawa here started in 1969 and gathered pace after 1973. It was the final destination of people who had earlier abandoned the north due to the chronic decline. Most came here from intermediate areas such as Angabo. The first settlers were relatively rich and dynamic. There was nothing to fall back on if they failed: no wage-labour, no low-status trades. The labour market remains fragile, but it is now easier for a poor settler to subsidize the first few years of farming, before self-sufficiency is achieved. There was a steady trickle in throughout the 1970s, with a sudden big increase in the early 1980s (Fig. 4.9). Thirty-five per cent of the sampled households came during 1981 and 1982, when areas such as Angabo were beginning to stagnate, but before the famine. The main factor in this surge was an increase in commercial farming by Zaghawa merchants in Legediba. This strengthened the labour market, easing the hardships of settlement. During the famine years and immediately afterwards, when both would-be settlers and would-be employers were poorer, resettlement virtually stopped: only 8 per cent came during 1984–6. The famine itself did not witness increased southward resettlement.

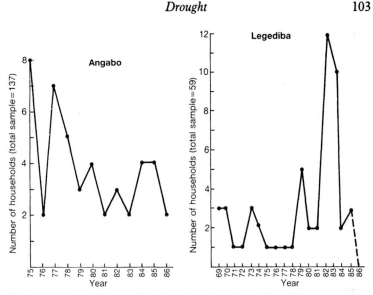

Fig. 4.9. *Sampled households migrating to Angabo and Legediba*

Legediba has a fast developing cash-crop economy, dominated by Zaghawa patronage. Landholdings are concentrated in a few hands: excluding the commercial farms owned by merchants from Buram, the top 5 per cent of villagers own over forty hectares each. These are mostly Zaghawa. Many of the poorer farmers depend on credit. Six traders control the market. They are Zaghawa, linked to the Zaghawa aristocracy by kinship, and the Legediba sheikh and farmers by patronage. The extremes of oligopoly are found. A cartel of middlemen under contract to the traders buy all the ground-nuts in advance. The costs involved in operating in this market are high. Legediba is sixteen hours by truck from the nearest central market in Nyala. (Angabo by contrast is less than two hours from Ed Da'ien.)

The growth of Legediba may ultimately be the outcome of an imbalance between population and resources in the north. The settlers do not make such a simple equation. The problems are seen as those of access to resources. First there is the community politics of land rights. Second is the absence of necessary technology. Without bore-holes *goz* areas remain uninhabited and without tractors the *naga'a* clays cannot be farmed. Thirdly, without marketing infrastructure and demand for labour it is not possible for people to move southwards to where land is available.

Legediba is an area of dynamism and growth in Darfur. But it is not as rich as more long-established areas, and it is more vulnerable. Grain production in 1980 was at little more than subsistence levels. The wet climate is a problem as well as an opportunity; there are crop infestations and strong weed growth. Here declining rainfall has actually made cultivation easier. Ground-nut production is concentrated in a few hands, and Legediba market is among the first to be cut from the traders' circuits when fuel is scarce or production poor. Livestock numbers are low; there are stock diseases and tsetse flies. Wateryards in this area have a reputation for breaking down. These risks can be borne because Legediba is not alone, it is linked to Zaghawa communities in Angabo, Furawiya, and other parts of Darfur: in times of famine, the people of Legediba move northwards. The odds against successful resettlement in Goz Dango are long. The Zaghawa merchants make their clients bear much of the cost and risk of the venture. Nevertheless, Legediba survives, and grows, as a credit to Zaghawa adaptability and tenacity.

Causes of the Famine

Shepherd wrote that the drought of 1968–74 in Sudan 'turned the screw a few threads further into peasant and pastoral society' (1984, p. 77). The discussion of the Zaghawa shows that for them at least, the truth is more complex. In may ways they were better prepared to withstand drought in 1984 than they had been fifteen years earlier. This hints at another conflict between local and external interpretations.

The most common model for explaining African famines employed by political scientists can be caricatured in this way: rural economies are traditionally well-adapted to withstand drought, but under the burdens of domination and distortion by external forces, they become rotten, and succumb to famine when subjected to the unexceptional stress of drought. Drought is merely the last straw for people whom political and economic processes have already rendered marginal and insecure. Most poor people in Darfur have a different model for the causes of the famine. Theirs depicts the rural economy as sound, the national economy as largely irrelevant, and the drought as a phenomenon of exceptional severity, capable of causing famine under any circumstances. By 'the drought' they mean not only the shortfall in rain during the seasons of 1983 and 1984, but the long-term decline in rainfall, and its corollaries of desertification and declining yields.

People often made a telling comparison with *Julu* (1913/14). *Julu* followed a comparable drought. It was the only other famine this century in which food could be had nowhere in Darfur. The only advantage that people had in *Julu* compared to today was that then they could sell their children. People complained of a shortage of work in 1984/5, but admitted that in *Julu* there was none at all. Cash incomes from *hashab* and ground-nuts were poor in the early 1980s, but better than the nothing of seventy years earlier.

The differences between the view in rural Darfur and the interpretations of political economists are partly substantive. It is also partly a question of types of evidence. Rural people have experience of selling firewood and eating wild foods, and of how these activities contributed to their survival. Outsiders have statistics for production and prices, generated at a national level, and correlations between these and reports of famine. Both have the tendency to explain an event by the limited evidence they have. In the remainder of this section I shall begin to show how an explanation of the causes of the famine should contain elements of both the accounts.

Factors of Non Production

The years after 1978 saw economic crisis and mismanagement in Sudan on a record-breaking scale. Sudan's foreign debt mounted so quickly that each published estimate was out of date by the time the figures were public; it was also rescheduled a record number of times. Exports fell by almost half between 1981 and 1982 alone: imports fell by an equivalent proportion but still cost far more than the exports could pay for. Public funds were embezzled, trading licences sold, and state farms and other enterprises privatized in ways that plumbed new depths of corruption, such that corruption itself came to be recognized as 'the fifth factor of production' in Sudan (Kameir and Karsany 1985). Many goods, from diesel to sugar, could often only be had on the black market, at hugely inflated prices. This was disastrous for the urban, trading, and cash-crop economies of Darfur, but it does not follow that vulnerability to famine was comparably increased.

Darfur's independence from the 'national' grain market has already been mentioned: this did not change. Darfur had no significant mechanized farms. The role of migrant labour in short-term prosperity is also marginal. Livestock numbers were steady or increasing, as were their prices relative to the price of grain (see below Fig. 6.5). Darfur's suffering in this period was largely confined to the realm of cash crops, and the implications of this for labour markets and general prosperity.

Ground-nuts are the major cash crop in Darfur, and their history over this period is indicative of the sad decline of the cash-cropping economy after the promise of the mid 1970s. Declining yields certainly played an important part, but problems with inputs, price instability, ineffective marketing structures, and accelerating trans-port costs were at least as important. In addition to these disincentives there was the fact that after 1979 grain became increasingly profitable relative to ground-nuts.

The problem of cost and supply of inputs to ground-nut producers is largely the story of credit. Because of the high cost of seed and relatively high cost of labour for ground-nuts, they are the crop which absorbs most of the credit dispensed to farmers in Darfur. One part of the story of credit is the Agricultural Bank of Sudan, which was set up in 1976 in order to provide cheap loans to small farmers. In the years to 1985 it failed: the challenge of setting up a structure that could both reach smallholders and ensure repayment was too great (de Waal 1987*a*, pp. 58–9).

The rural credit system known as *sheil* worked only slightly better. This is tied closely to ground-nuts, sesame, *tombac*, and other cash crops. It works entirely through private merchants. The merchant often relies on family links or friendship with the village sheikh to guarantee the loan. The merchant makes an initial loan of money or seed, and in doing so buys the forthcoming harvest at a price based on a proportion of the price of the previous year's crop, a price which is extortionately low. The creditor makes two further visits to the farmer to extend the other parts of the loan (if all is going to his satisfaction), once during the weeding season and once just before harvesting. Merchants complained of widespread and increasing default in the late 1970s and early 1980s. Many started to accept repayment in grain for the first time. Consequently *sheil* credit contracted sharply during these years, and in many areas it disappeared altogether. The area planted to ground-nuts stagnated, and fell sharply in 1984 (Fig. 4.10). In Angabo it almost halved between 1980 and 1984.

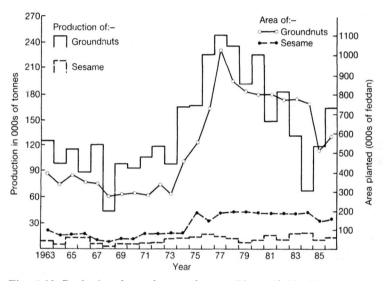

Fig. 4.10 *Production of ground-nuts and sesame (Note*: a 'feddan' is a Sudanese unit of land measurement equivalent to 0.45 hectare approx.)

Aftei the mid 1970s the price of ground-nuts in Darfur was unstable, but generally falling, both absolutely and relative to grain and livestock. This problem was compounded by marketing and transport problems. The best illustration is by a comparison between the price of ground-nuts in El Obeid (Sudan's main ground-nut market) and in Nyala. During 1982/3 the price in Nyala was only 7 per cent less than the price in El Obeid, a reflection of the transport cost between the two towns. During 1983–5 the difference in price increased so that in Nyala ground-nuts fetched only 56 per cent of the price they fetched in El Obeid. Fig. 4.11 shows the number of commercial trucks in Darfur over these years: at this time the numbers were declining. There was then a national fuel shortage, and the railway union was locked in a long and bruising battle with

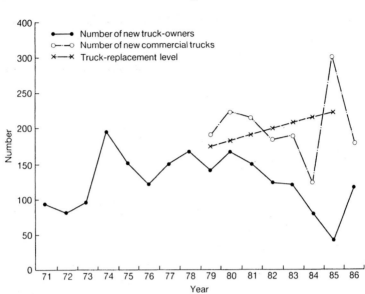

Fig. 4.11. *Trucks in Darfur*

the Nimeiri Government which practically closed down Sudan Railways. Darfur was becoming isolated, and farmers who grew for export were suffering as a result (Fig. 4.12).

Gum arabic has a similar history of decline in this period, due to a combination of ecological decline and its failure to provide an economic return. In 1982 production had fallen to 60 per cent of what it had been in 1970. During 1983 and 1984 the official markets received on average only 13 per cent of the 1970 figure. Production was not as low as that, because the government extracted no fewer than seven taxes from gum arabic, and hence producers preferred to sell outside official markets.

These are sad tales of the decline of rural incomes in Darfur. Nevertheless, the lowered income to cash-crop farmers was not critical in causing the famine of 1984/5. Cash crops are grown almost exclusively in the richer areas of Darfur, in areas where large amounts of grain are grown too. The contraction of commercial activity and the decline of *sheil* led to larger smallholders losing their dependence on merchants and gaining more autonomy in making

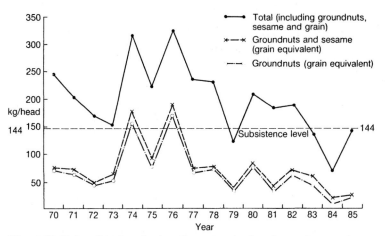

Fig. 4.12 *Value of total production of crops (production of ground-nuts and sesame, in grain equivalent per head, plus grain production per head)*

their production decisions. Farmers in villages such as Angabo were able to change their production priorities. As cash crops became less profitable, and grain became more so, they grew fewer ground-nuts for the national market, and planted more grain for the local market. Not a single one of the farmers in the sample who grew a significant area of cash crops was or became destitute during 1984/5.

Potentially, the most important effect of the decline in ground-nuts was the subsequent decline in the demand for agricultural labour in southern Darfur. In large part this was offset by the switch to growing grain instead. Hence, in Legediba the amount of labour hired was the same in 1984 as in 1980, and in Angabo it fell by only 25 per cent. At the same time the number of local villagers in both places who were seeking wage-labour doubled. However, wage-rates did not fall as much as would be expected. This was due to two factors. One was the escalation of the war in southern Sudan after 1982, which caused a drop in the number of migrant labourers from south Sudan to south-east Darfur, just as impoverished Darfurians were joining the market. The other was the drought, leading to a decline in southward resettlement to areas such as Legediba, so that there were in these areas fewer new settlers who would have been largely or wholly dependent on the labour market. In Nankose, there was even a growth in labour opportunities. Farmers expanded dry-season irrigated cultivation, almost doubling the demand for dry-season labour, and raising the annual amount of labour hired by 20 per cent.

Darfur had become partially integrated into the national economy since the 1940s, and then partially withdrew in the years after 1978. The impact of the advance and retreat of the national capitalist economy was mixed. In some ways the sequence was disastrous. For instance, the earlier integration created a demand for consumer goods such as sugar and tea in rural areas. During the years of retreat from integration this demand was only met through black-market supplies at appalling prices. These later years also saw the fragmentation of livestock, cash-crop, and labour markets in Darfur. In some cases, this fragmentation selectively penalized poorer households. The operation of the market in cattle was a case in point (see Chapter 6). The heightening of oligopoly in remote rural markets such as Legediba is another example, and other markets were excluded from traders' networks altogether. The performance of the national economy over this period caused stagnation in many sectors of Darfur's economy, and it would be wrong to deny that it was relevant to the causation of the famine. However, imperfections in the labour market served to keep labour rates relatively high, and the regional grain market became better integrated over this period.

The particular nature of the social economy of Darfur at the time when the famine struck was a creation in part of the processes of the advance and retreat of the national economy. The commercial economy was uneven in Darfur, both geographically and from year to year. However, it does not follow that this uneven integration brought Darfur to the brink of famine. Much of the resilience of the Darfur economy in the face of drought must be attributed to this very unevenness. It allowed producers in Darfur to change their production priorities so as to supply local markets with food, thereby blunting the impact of the national economic crisis. It made possible dramatic adaptations to ecological stress, such as the case of the Zaghawa. It created economic niches in wage-labour and low-status trades that poor people were able to exploit during the famine. These changes, which were critical in enabling people to withstand the effects of the drought, are largely invisible in aggregate national economic statistics. Hence such figures overstate the adverse impact of Sudan's national economic crisis on the living standards of the rural poor in Darfur.

Most poor rural people in Darfur (a category which excludes cash-crop farmers and traders) resist the notion that either the advance of the national economy or its retreat brought them to the brink of famine. The implication is that without such capitalism as there is, the famine would have arrived earlier and struck harder. This may be overstating the case. In some ways the poor in Darfur were more vulnerable than they had been one, two, or three decades earlier. In many ways, however, they were more secure. Hence, in both the short and the medium term, it seems likely that rural people were right in laying most of the blame for the famine on 'the drought' and its corollaries.

5

Hunger

Fifteen Months of Hunger

'Hunger: tie your stomach tightly and wait, it will leave you'. Ishag Mohammedin, from Furawiya, was stoical about the pains of hunger. There is little to say about hunger *per se*. Hunger was something that people had just to put up with. Families rationed the food they ate. Following the harvest failure that became apparent in August 1984, people began to eat fewer, smaller, and less pleasant meals. They ate less millet and sorghum (known as *'esh*) and more wild foods. Some had already been doing this for some time, after the failure of the harvest of 1983 in north Darfur. The meagre harvest of 1984 was gathered in during October and November. People ate some, and stored some. They anticipated being hungry until the first post-famine harvest was gathered in: this, they hoped, would be during October 1985, unless the rains failed again.

The idiom of hunger as poverty, suffering, loss, infertility, and many other unpleasant things need not be elaborated here. The whole period of hunger, in the other extended sense of a dearth or famine, consisted of just these things. The idiom of hunger was often used to describe destitution, which includes these negative attributes, and which is the concern of the following chapter.

'Last year [1984/5] we had money but no *'esh*, this year [1985/6] we have *'esh* but no money, and it is worse.' Ibrahim Abdala of Nankose was one of many farmers who valued his livelihood above satisfying his hunger. He was a richer farmer, and expressed an unusually extreme view, but others shared the sentiment. The analysis in this chapter will show that we cannot understand the famine simply in terms of the entitlement to staple foods. This is because the people who suffered the famine chose to make it otherwise: access to *'esh* was only one priority among several others, and in many cases it was a lesser priority.

This and the following two chapters discuss the trinity of hunger, destitution, and death. Throughout 1984/5 Darfur saw hunger and destitution. Excess deaths occurred during the second half of the

year (see Table 5.1, the 'famine calendar'). Nevertheless, analysis at
the level of households will show that these should not be seen as a
succession of stages through which famine victims pass, but rather
three co-present aspects of famine, with complex interrelations.

Table 5.1. *Famine calendar 1984–1985*

August 1984	It became apparent that the harvest would fail.
	People in the north gathered wild grains.
September and	The first trickle of would-be labourers came south for
October	the harvest. Some work was to be had in the south,
	particularly the south-west.
	Richer herders sold animals, anticipating a price drop.
November and	Most of the harvesting occurred. Larger numbers of
December	northerners who had gathered in their crops came
	south
	Pastoralists moved their herds southwards.
	Grain prices were at their least high.
January and	Threshing in the south, some work to be had, but many
February	wandered vainly looking for work in rural areas.
(1985)	Many came to the towns, selling firewood, fodder, etc..
	Wells were dry in many northern villages.
	Grain prices rose to reach new highs.
	Livestock prices fell to reach new lows.
March and	Children were dying from measles, diarrhoea, and other
April	diseases.
	Some work was available on irrigated farms in south-west Darfur.
	Most of the population concentrated in larger villages and towns, up to 750,000 people earned an income from selling firewood and charcoal alone.
	Pastoralists were desperate for grazing.
	First berries of 1985 *mukheit* crop became available.
May and June	As the nadir of the famine occurred, the rains began.
	Deaths reached their peak.
	North Darfurians began to return to prepare their fields.
	Many still relied on low-status trades.
	Grain prices at their peak, animal prices at their lowest.
July	Rains were looking excellent.
	Most farmers were active weeding their farms; southern farmers found few willing to work for money.
	Squatter camps around large villages and towns were now small.

Table 5.1. (*cont.*):

	Relief aid began to have an impact.
	Still many deaths, largely from malaria and diarrhoeas.
	Grain prices began to fall, livestock prices rose.
	Grazing in abundance; animals began producing milk; pastoralists returned northwards.
August and September	Dry spells affected crops in the north-east.
	Relief aid arrived in large amounts.
	Wild grains were harvested in the north, short-season sorghums in the south.
	Grain and animal prices had almost returned to normal.
	Death rate still high.
October and November	Main harvest came in, it was excellent.
	Mortality returned towards normal.

Maa fi 'Esh: 'There is no Food'

'Esh—millet and sorghum—is the normal staple food of all rural people in Darfur. It is normally eaten as *'asida*, which resembles a firm porridge, with a *mulaah*, a sauce made with peppers, vegetables, or meat. Richer people in urban centres tend to eat wheat, but this is marginal. Farmers, whenever possible, grow their own grain. Pastoralists, artisans, farmers with failed crops, and others obtain their grain mainly from the market.

In 1984/5 there was a huge deficit of grain in Darfur. This section looks first at grain production by smallholders, documenting the disastrous collapse of production, and with it 'direct entitlement' to *'esh*, particularly in northern Darfur. Then it turns to other sources of *'esh*, and shows that the amounts they could provide were also very low.

Production of Grain by Smallholders

The great majority of the *'esh* in Darfur is grown by smallholders. The amount of grain grown by small farmers, their direct entitlement to food, is therefore roughly indicated by the aggregate statistics for grain production in the region.

The long-term trends in grain production can be seen in Fig. 5.1. There was a general increase in the area planted to grain, but no corresponding increase in production. This was due to falling yields. In 1984, not only did yields fall dramatically, but the planted area

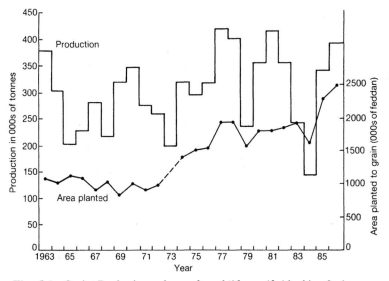

Fig. 5.1. *Grain: Production and area planted (Note*: a 'feddan' is a Sudanese unit of land measurement equivalent to 0.45 hectare approx.)

contracted as well. This can be explained by two facts. One is that many areas received too little rainfall to be worth cultivating. The second is that the crops on some planted areas failed to sprout altogether and were not included in the statistics.

Fig. 5.2 shows grain production separately for north and south Darfur. While south Darfur produced surpluses during the 1970s and only went into deficit in 1983, the north suffered a chronic deficit from the early 1970s. Furthermore, production in north Darfur varied greatly between districts. El Geneina and El Fasher districts are the main grain-producing areas in north Darfur. Much of the production in the vicinity of El Fasher goes to feed the town. El Geneina has a history of exporting grain to south Darfur and Chad. Hence the most northerly parts, the north-east, and the central mountains suffered an even more severe long-term shortfall in production of staple foods.

The years 1983 and 1984 were disastrous. In north Darfur only 18 per cent of the population's grain needs were produced in these years, a quarter of the per-head production of the 1970s. Production was best on the alluvial soils in the west and worst on the *goz* in the north and east. In 1983 south Darfur produced grain equivalent to

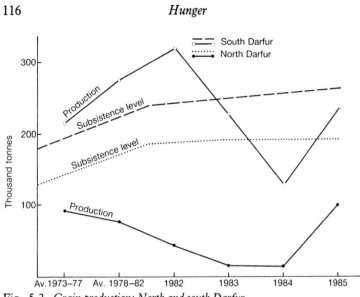

Fig. 5.2. *Grain production: North and south Darfur*

90 per cent of its needs, but in 1984 less than 60 per cent. These are official Ministry of Agriculture figures, and so should be treated with caution. However, one of the questions in the survey of 1986 asked farmers to recall the harvests of these years. The results closely replicated the official per-head production figures. The survey also found that only 5 per cent of farmers in southern Darfur and less than 1 per cent in northern Darfur had surplus grain production in 1984. Fig. 5.3 shows grain production per head for north and south Darfur together. 1983 and 1984 were the only two successive years in which production was well below the region's needs. 1973 and 1979 were the two other recent years when there was a significant shortfall. 1973 has been discussed. 1979 was a single bad year in which many of the reasons for a famine being avoided in 1973 also held good.

One of the most important reasons for the failure of household supplies of grain in 1984/5 was that there were two bad years rather than one. Farmers prefer to store a year's supply of grain or even more. Already in 1983 this was not possible for most farmers. In

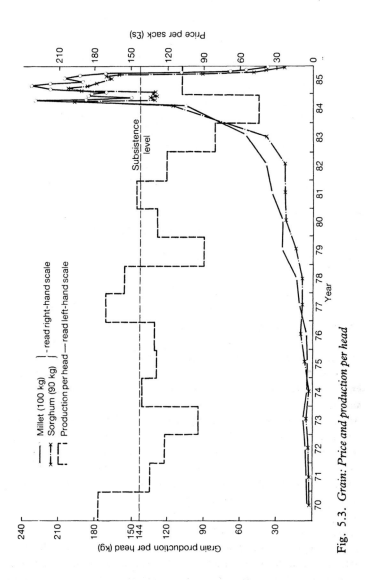

Fig. 5.3. *Grain: Price and production per head*

south-west Darfur, one of the main grain-producing areas, a survey of farmers' assessments of the grain they had in store was undertaken in February 1984 (JMRDP 1984). This found that 55 per cent of farmers had stocks below what they considered average for the time of year, and only 20 per cent had above-average stocks. Nankose lies in the centre of this area, and here only 20 per cent had stores above normal. Angabo and Legediba were equally badly off, with only one sixth of farmers having above-normal amounts of grain. In north Darfur, grain stocks were already exhausted by this time; only 2.5 per cent of farmers had what they considered a surplus of grain stored after the harvest of 1983. Therefore when the harvest failed in 1984, farmers had no stored grain in reserve.

In summary, two aspects of the failure of subsistence grain production can be identified. One was the long-term decline in north Darfur, leading more and more farmers to become dependent on the market for their 'esh. The second was the region-wide part-failure of production in 1983 and the nearly complete failure in 1984.

Other Supplies of 'Esh

There is no mechanized grain farming in Darfur of any note. Mechanized farms cultivated only 450 hectares during 1980–5, and average production was a meagre 1000 tonnes per year.

In 1984 there was a national failure of grain production in Sudan. Much of the national production is grown by smallholders and never reaches the market. The overall supply of grain on the national market is affected much more by commercial production, which is mostly mechanized. The fall in mechanized production in 1984 was truly precipitous. This meant that there was a huge fall in the amount of grain on the national market during 1984/5 (see Table 5.2).

Purchases of Grain

During the years 1983–5 there was simultaneously a local production failure in Darfur, a fall in the amount of grain available on the market in Sudan as a whole, and a rise in the number of people without a harvest of their own. This was not only a huge 'food availability decline', but a tremendous shock to the established food

Table 5.2. *National grain production in Sudan*

Year	Grain Production		
	1,000 tonnes	% (1960–79)	% (1979–83)
National			
1969–79 average	1,881	100	
1979–83 average	2,153		100
1984	1,155	61	46
Mechanized			
1979–83 average	1,420	—	100
1984	389	—	27

system. This section looks at how rural people responded to this, by buying and not buying grain.

The first subsection deals with an apparent paradox. People were not buying as much grain as they could afford to, apparently by choice. This observation is very unexpected and is worth repeating: people were not buying food they could afford at the height of the famine. Therefore it needs firmly to be established. It needs to be reinforced by data for sales, and objections to the 'choice' aspect need to be dealt with. This requires an analysis of how the economic and institutional structures of markets operated during the famine, which is the concern of the second subsection. This returns us to a central problem in the understanding of famine: if the markets worked so as to reduce peoples' entitlement to staple food, and people did not utilize what entitlement they had, and they had no significant subsistence production, then why did most of the people not starve to death? First, however, a few words on the price of grain in the markets.

A Note on Grain Prices

High grain prices are characteristic of famine. Fig. 5.3 shows the price of a sack of grain in El Fasher between 1970 and 1985. The fivefold rise from the end of 1983 and the high prices that persisted until 1985 are striking. The famine is clearly identifiable in this graph alone.

It should be noted that sharp but transient rises in the price of grain in 1973/4 and 1979/80 are masked in this graph, by the use of annual averages for those years, and because they appear dwarfed by the unprecedented rises of 1983/4.

Not Buying Grain

Amounts of grain bought

It is not possible to get a precise figure for how many people bought grain and how much. Nevertheless, the data available from the survey of 1986 can be used to show who was not buying grain, who had an income and so could buy grain, and whether that income was being spent on grain. The distortions in the data tend to underestimate income and underestimate non-grain expenditure: consequently the data are biased against the thesis being argued.

For the rural sites studied, two calculations were made. They were done for the dry-season (*seif*) months of 1985, when the famine was at its worst and grain prices were highest, and when rural incomes were at their lowest. One method involved taking all the households sampled, and taking out those who had no need to buy grain and those whose behaviour suggested they were not buying grain. This meant taking the sampled households, subtracting those with a grain surplus from the 1984 harvest, those receiving constant support from relatives or neighbours, and those collecting or buying wild foods at that time. The second method involved taking all those with a cash income in those months and calculating how much grain the stated income would have bought, at the prices which were current then. Both methods have the shortcoming that they ignore the possibility of stored cash being used to buy grain. The first also has the shortcoming that people who were eating wild foods were often mixing small amounts of millet or sorghum with them, and this may have come from the market. They also ignore the earlier buying of grain when the price was lower; there is evidence that poor farmers in south-west Darfur, where most grain was available, did this (JMRDP 1986, p. 21).

The first ('residual') method suggested that 31 per cent of the rural population, at most, bought grain during these months. The second ('income') method showed that 64 per cent of households had an income during these months (28 per cent from animal sales, crop sales, loans, etc., and a further 36 per cent from low-status trades and labouring only). In total, 18 per cent of grain needs could have been met by buying from the market, and probably more given the underreporting of income.

These aggregate figures do not converge neatly. Many people who had an income which could have bought food were behaving in a way that non-food-buyers typically did. In the extreme case, 5 per cent of the pastoral community of Furawiya were in the 'residual' category, but 68 per cent had a 'non-casual' income, mostly from selling animals. These 104 households had an income between them during these months that was over £s55,000. This could have bought 25 tonnes of grain at current prices, over 80 per cent of their normal grain needs, and 51 per cent of the needs for the entire community of Furawiya. Yet all but 14 households (9 per cent) were collecting or buying an average of 2.3 types of wild food in these months.

This paradox is further substantiated by evidence from household budgets. These budgets were obtained retrospectively many months after the *seif* of 1985, and only show the approximate proportions of income that were spent on different items. On average only about one tenth of the money was spent on grain, and a further fraction on other foods.

This is striking, especially in view of the many famine deaths during these months. We need to discover if this finding is general for Darfur. The answer is that it is, albeit in less extreme form.

The farming villages studied were all fairly similar to one another, with the exception of Arara in Dar Masalit (see Chapter 9). Income during the *seif* had no obvious relationship with 'need', assessed as the inverse of the size of the 1984 harvest. Table 5.3 shows the harvest of 1984 and income during *seif* 1985 (stated in terms of potential grain needs bought at current prices).

People in all of the north and south Darfur farming villages continued to eat wild foods when their income would have covered a small but significant part of their grain needs. The money was spent on water, fodder, labour, animals, and seed. Many households bought some grain, but this met only a fraction of their needs. Nankose was a partial exception to this: only a minority of people were eating wild foods, and people had bought in grain during the harvest season when prices were lower. A survey by the Jebel Marra Project in the nearby village of Ginniyho confirmed this, showing that villagers bought and sold grain when it was £s129 per sack, i.e. earlier in the season (JMRDP 1986, p. 22). Overall, a rough

Table 5.3. *Command over grain*

| Site | Location | 1984 harvest | | *seif* 1985 income (% of needs potent. met) |
		(kg/hh)	(% of need)	
Farming villages				
Saiyah	North	15	1.9	8.9
Jebel Si	North	40	7.4	11.8
Legediba	South	270	30.7	10.6
Nankose	South	400	49.9	10.6
Angabo	South	500	58.8	12.4
Other sites[a]				
Furawiya	North pastoral	25	2.7	51.5
Arara	West	155	24.5	4.3
El Fasher	Displaced	55	6.3	18.0
Nyala	Urban	NA	NA	134.0

[a] See above, below, and Chapters 6 and 9.
NA means not applicable.

calculation suggests that about 50 per cent of the income was spent on grain, which would have met on average a total 5 per cent of needs. Poorer households spent a higher proportion of their income on grain and other foods, but it was rare to find a household which had spent all its income on food, and many very poor households spent only a small proportion on food. These findings are confirmed for south-west Darfur by a detailed survey of household budgets undertaken by the Jebel Marra Project during these months (JMRDP 1986).

For the famine camp of Mawashei and the peri-urban settlement of El Nasr on the edges of El Fasher town we were unable to obtain estimates for how much income had been spent on staple food. In these communities, the income over these months would have met 18 per cent of needs. Estimates for the effective demand of the urban population can be calculated using data from a survey of Nyala town conducted in late 1986. The survey sampled 300 households, selected at random. The households were divided into high-, middle-, and low-income categories. The survey investigated current income and expenditure. Income was estimated to have risen 150 per cent since *seif* 1985. Table 5.4 shows the proportion of households in each category, their estimated mean weekly income during *seif* 1985, what percentage of grain needs that would have met at current prices

Table 5.4. *Command over grain in Nyala town*

Income group	No.	Weekly income 85	% of grain needs met[a]	
			Maximum	Actual
High	57	131	396	100
Medium	96	41	124	87
Low	147	13	39	27
Mean	—	—	134	60

[a] For the purpose of these calculations, the sale of subsidized relief food by the government in the towns during these months has been ignored.

if all the income had been spent on grain, and how much of their grain needs were actually met from the market (arbitrarily assuming that a maximum of 70 per cent of income was spent on staple food).

The total long-term urban population in the four main towns of Darfur in 1985 consisted of 320,000 people. This represented just over 10 per cent of the population. This analysis suggests that at the worst of the famine they met 60 per cent of their grain needs from the market, which implies that 6 per cent of the grain needs for Darfur were marketed in the towns. Casual observations of the grain markets during this period were, that more than half the marketed grain was sold in the towns. This confirms that the rural and displaced population of Darfur could be meeting only about 4 or 5 per cent of their needs from the market.

Therefore there was a situation in which although the rural population could have afforded to buy between 7 per cent and 51 per cent of their grain needs (and more if they had liquidated more assets or worked for longer) they in fact bought only 5 per cent or less.

There is one further way of substantiating this claim, which is by looking at data for the sales of grain.

Amounts of grain reaching the market
Quantities of millet reaching Nyala market are a good indicator of sales of locally-grown grain, as millet (as opposed to sorghum) is the major grain crop in Darfur. The amount of millet entering Nyala market fell during the early 1980s, rose sharply in 1983/4 (as grain prices rose) and fell sharply in 1984/5 (while grain prices rose even higher). After the famine, in 1985/6, they climbed back to pre-famine levels. This is one indicator that much less grain than normal was sold during 1984/5.

Did this pattern of lowered amounts of grain hold good in the rest of Darfur, and how much grain did this consist of? Grain sales, especially during famine, are a delicate subject. Answers to this question on the pilot survey of 1985 were evasive and unsatisfactory, so it was not asked in the survey of 1986: all we have are rough estimates. We have noted that only 3.5 per cent of farmers in Darfur had a surplus in 1984. Those surplus farmers had, on average, production equal to twice their needs, which suggests that 3.5 per cent of the region's needs was met by their sales. Many farmers without a surplus sold small quantities of grain too: perhaps as much again. However, many grain transactions occurred outside the market-place. These included paying farm labourers in grain, and loaning grain against future repayment in cash or kind. The gross total reaching the market must therefore be reduced. One third of the first consignment of USAID relief sorghum was also sold, in the towns. This amounted to 9,000 tonnes over six months, or 4.5 per cent of the region's needs. Small amounts of relief grain reached the market by other means. These calculations imply, very roughly, that a total of about 10 per cent of Darfur's grain needs were met through the market.

No significant imports of grain

There were no significant commercial imports of grain. This is an important point.

All sources of data confirm the lack of commercially imported grain from central Sudan to Darfur during 1984/5. One is Nyala market data for (imported) sorghum. Another is data for the commercial trucks (see Fig. 4.11), which show declining numbers at this point, and no evidence for grain haulage. A third is data from the railway: it was scarcely running a commercial service at all during 1984/5, and Sudan Railways also lost some trains on the Nyala route that year. A fourth is price data, which show dry-season grain prices lower in the west (furthest from central Sudan) and highest in the east (nearest to central Sudan). Nearness to the dry-season and wet-season roads in the dry and wet seasons respectively was not linked to a lower grain price. The grain price in eastern Sudan was similar to that in Darfur, so there was no commercial incentive to move grain. (During 1973/4 prices in Nyala were double those in Gedaref, but no significant amounts of grain were transported to Darfur because of the transport costs).

Conclusion

Consequently, the grain sold in the markets of Darfur during 1984/5 consisted of locally grown *'esh* and relief sorghum. This met no more than 10 per cent of the region's grain needs. Most of this was sold in the large towns. This figure closely matches that derived for grain purchases above.

The discrepancy between purchasing power and purchases is real and needs an explanation. Most accounts of the micro-economics of famine have assumed or argued that people suffering from famine spend what income they have on staple foods, until they fall below a minimum level of food intake, whereupon they starve to death, or are at least increasingly likely to do so.

There are two possibilities why this discrepancy occurred. One is that the grain could not reach the people, or the people reach the grain. In other words, people had money but no food to spend it on. The other alternative is that people were not chiefly concerned to maintain a diet of staple grain that nutritionists would consider adequate. In other words, they chose to go hungry. The second explanation is the correct one. The positive reasons why this is so will be examined in more detail later on. In the meantime we must examine the negative reasons. This involves showing that people could obtain physical access to marketed grain.

Access to Grain

The puzzle of people not spending their money on grain is real only if people had actual physical access to that grain: people might have had money, but no grain to spend it on. Ibrahim Abdala's 'money but no *'esh*' comment appears to back this up. But the point is that he did not consider this his main problem. Had he wanted to, he could have bought *'esh*. This section starts with an introduction to the operation of grain marketing in Darfur. Then I shall show how it might be argued that grain could not reach rural people, and finally show that this argument does not work.

Grain marketing in Darfur

Darfur has three tiers of markets. The upper tier consists of the major urban markets in the region, whose characteristics are that they meet daily, that they have a substantial resident commercial population, large numbers of trucks, and commercial banks, and that they are subject to close government supervision. There are six markets in this category: Nyala, El Fasher, Ed Da'ien, El Geneina, Mellit, and Zalingei (see Fig. 5.4). Large quantities of grain are bought, sold, and stored in the commercial sections of these markets.

The middle tier of markets consists of the large rural markets. These are weekly or twice-weekly markets. Dileij is a good example. These markets are normally controlled by market committees consisting of local people headed by a sheikh or a descendent of the owner of the original market franchise. These markets also see grain sold by the sack in large quantities, to go to the upper tier markets. Farmers also sell small quantities of grain, some of it 'vertically' to middlemen acting for large traders, and some 'horizontally' to other rural people for consumption.

The large rural markets are the most important in Darfur. Activity is intense, but the vertical trading of goods between these and the central markets is typically oligopolistic. Darfur is a huge region with scattered population, and the middle-tier markets require truck-owners to invest between one and three days' time and large quantities of fuel to attend them. There can be great variations in amounts of produce reaching the market from week to week. Consequently, marketing uses strong and inflexible merchant-middleman-retailer links, to eliminate as much uncertainty as possible, so the traders will be assured of selling all their goods and filling their trucks profitably on the return trip. The major trading on market-day is a foregone conclusion before the villagers even arrive. The frenetic bargaining occurs in the areas where small pedlars and market women trade vegetables, spices, and consumer durables with the villagers. Approximations to free markets may exist, but the idea and the ideology of a 'free market' do not. Markets are seen as regulated and controlled, and the notion of a 'right' or 'just' price is strong. This regulation and control should not be seen as a hindrance to commerce, but rather a precondition of it; only with the market stability created by control can traders operate at all.

·Finally there are village markets, where commercial interest is entirely seasonal and depends on the production of local cash crops. They are also periodic, and the markets in different villages in an area will fall on different days of the week so that small traders can circulate to them all. In these markets, grain is sold by farmers in small units of a few kilograms to middlemen who buy enough to fill several sacks, which they can then sell to traders in the middle-tier markets. Prices for small units of measurement such as the *rotel* (450 grams) are normally about 20 per cent lower per kilogram than for large units such as the sack. In northern Darfur many of these markets cease to function during the dry season as the population moves away to find work elsewhere.

Commercial interest in grain in Darfur has been extremely limited. There are few mechanized grain-producing commercial farms. Until the 1980s, merchants who made loans to farmers would do so only for the cultivation of cash crops, mainly ground-nuts. If the cash crop failed, repayment in grain was not acceptable. Above all there has been a lack of interest in selling grain to villagers. This lack of interest may seem paradoxical because there has always been exchange of grain between farmers and pastoralists and town dwellers, using cash as a medium since the 1920s. However there are good reasons behind it. The demand for grain from pastoralists has little impact on the traders because the pastoralists are mobile and have pack animals with them, so they can visit the grain-producing areas themselves and carry away what they need. The exception to this is northern Dar Zaghawa, where herders' migrations do not take them near farming areas. In this case the herders rely heavily on wild grains, but the marketing infrastructure there is also unusually well developed.

The townspeople do rely on traders to bring in grain, but a look at what this involves for traders will explain their reluctance to go any deeper into the rural grain market. The trader has a guaranteed market for grain in the towns, and can sell in bulk to retailers with whom he has long-standing relationships. Prices are predictable, and the time, money, and risk spent on negotiating a sale are low. Selling grain in rural markets is very different. Prices are lower, bulk sale impossible, demand is small and extremely variable, and may well be met by local farmers selling surpluses or stored grain horizontally, or by camel-and donkey-traders bringing grain from neighbouring villages. Selling grain in rural markets involves high risks. Hence a marketing infrastructure of retailers has not developed for selling bulk grain to rural areas.

Moving grain to people
Could the grain have been moved to the people in Darfur? It could

be argued that the actual demand for grain was so low because rural markets were entirely empty of grain. It could be that it was either physically impossible to move enough grain, or too expensive to do so, or that the marketing infrastructure effectively prevented it.

The point that it was physically or logistically impossible for grain to reach people can be made very forcefully. Roads in Darfur are awful. Fig. 5.4 shows how accessible or inaccessible places in Darfur are to commercial trucks in the months after the rains, using the year 1985 as an indicator. During the rains most commercial trucks do not even attempt to operate, but instead undergo repairs or simply sit under tarpaulins waiting for the roads to open. But this objection fails on a simple point. People are well aware of impending famine and plan accordingly. All important rural markets can be reached by road in the dry season; and if people in areas which are inaccessible in the wet season had the desire and means to obtain grain, they would make sure they obtained what they wanted before the rains came.

More significant than the state of the roads is the availability of transport itself: there might have been a shortage of trucks. Numbers of trucks in Darfur were dropping during 1983/4. Moreover, commercial interest in grain was less than in ground-nuts. But the surge in truck numbers during 1985, when Arkel-Talab began subcontracting to private operators to transport USAID relief grain, shows that trucks can arrive in Darfur if there is money to be made. The 1984 ground-nut harvest was also small, and fewer trucks than normal were required to transport it. If we assume average commercial truck turn-around to be four days, with one third of the time spent undergoing repairs or off the road for other reasons, the fleet available in Darfur in 1984/5 could have shipped about 500,000 tonnes in 200 days (the effective dry season). The transport was there.

A more real problem than the physical availability of transport was its price. It was expensive to move grain: the price to transport a single sack from Nyala to El Geneina averaged between £s15 and £s20 during the dry season of 1986. In the wet season of 1985, prices over £s80 per sack were quoted. Throughout 1984 and until April 1985 prices were higher because of a chronic fuel shortage, caused among other things by a diversion of fuel to Nimeiri's security services. Also, the prices just quoted do not include a premium to cover the higher risks of operating in a market that is not well

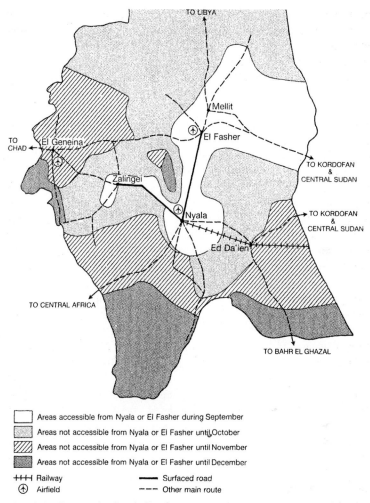

Fig. 5.4. *Communications in Darfur*

established. But if the price of transport were the determinant, the price of grain in the rural areas would simply have risen even higher.

Was the problem instead that merchants were simply not interested in selling grain in rural areas, however profitable it might have been, because of the lack of marketing infrastructure? The answer to this is also no, and this can be seen through a consideration of the special place that grain holds in rural market institutions.

The control of rural markets by market committees has already been mentioned. This control is mainly manifest in the collection of dues and the regulation of physical aspects of the market, such as who occupies which stalls (Civsec 64/6/42). Control over the commodities bought and sold is limited, with the exception of grain. This control, and the ideology underlying it, are probably more important in the lack of commercial interest in grain than the problems of transaction costs and risks outlined above.

The ideal of the autonomous, belonging farmer militates against grain being a marketable commodity: access to grain is seen as a right. People also have neither the concept nor the experience of a free market in grain. During the Sultanate, in Fur areas, grain was measured in *midds*. The *midd* was not a fixed unit of measurement, rather it was a standard of value. (The other two common standards of value in rural areas were the salt bar and the *takaki* length of cloth). The size of the *midd* varied with the size of the harvest and also according to the season. Each season the size was locally determined, and enforced (Darfur 6/6/17, p.XII-1). Vestiges of this system still remain in rural areas, to the despair of those who try to collect standardized market prices, and reflect the persisting ideology that grain is not a commodity like others. During the Condominium period the government frequently intervened to prevent hoarding and speculating in the grain market, and to restrict the amounts purchased by individuals. Local market committees also imposed restrictions. An example was the ban on exporting grain from the western district (Zalingei) during 1949, which was illegal under Condominium law, though not according to customary law (Darfur 6/5/12, 1949, p. 19).

Today, market committees still frequently restrict the buying and selling of grain in their markets without reference to higher authority. During 1983 and 1984 most of the middle-tier rural markets imposed restrictions on the amount of grain a single person could buy, usually about 100 kg. maximum in a week. This was intended to ensure that grain was bought only for the buyer's domestic consumption, not for trading or profiteering. The fate of these restrictions varied. Most had the desired effect of limiting the outflow of grain and lowering prices (by about 15–25 per cent), at least in the short term. Some were in place for many years, e.g. in Saiyah, but the market committees and village sheikhs were unable to maintain enough vigilance to prevent smuggling. Many were imposed during 1983, for instance in districts south and south-west of Nyala, but were forcibly lifted in 1984 when the people of Nyala town complained that they relied on buying *'esh* from these areas. The most successful restrictions appear to have been at Adila, near Ed Da'ien, where strict controls were combined with a provision which allowed larger farmers to sell a certain proportion of their crop in Ed Da'ien town.

Just as market committees could restrict the sale of grain outside the community, they could arrange for it to be brought in. Communally organized mass grain purchase has a history in Darfur: famines such as *Saafar Mellit* are so named because villages organized camel caravans to bring millet from Mellit. Market committees and merchants work closely together; the operation of each requires the co-operation of the other. If some of the members of the market committees are not the merchants themselves then they are at least their brothers, uncles, or cousins. To take the example of Furawiya again. Furawiya is a very long way from any urban centres. But it has a good trading infrastructure, and there are truck-owning merchants with family links there. The actual cash income to the community during the *seif* of 1985, when it was easiest to reach, would have bought five truckloads of grain. Other villages studied may not have had such a high cash income, but four of them had resident truck-owners, and all of them were more accessible. If moving grain to villages had been a priority of villagers, it would have happened.

People moving to grain

The previous section showed that grain could have been moved to people, at considerable cost, but was not. Part of the reason for this was that people were moving to places where there was grain. People were not moving solely to buy grain, but also because their destinations were the richer and wetter parts of Darfur, where work and water were available. These movements were evident in differences between the prices of grain in different parts of Darfur. Prices rose in southern Darfur in early 1985 as northern migrants came down south, and then fell again in July as the migrants left to return north. There are no reliable estimates for the total numbers of people from northern Darfur who came south, but they included most of the people from Furawiya and Jebel Si. For the duration of the dry season this created an integrated regional grain market.

Thus, grain may not be mobile in Darfur, but people are. High grain prices spread from northern to southern Darfur not because of merchants buying grain in the south and trucking it north, but because of migrants from the north coming to the south. People did not move because grain could not reach them in their home villages: on the contrary, one reason why grain did not move to the villages was because people were themselves moving southwards.

During the famine there were physical constraints on access to marketed grain. But these constraints were effectively overcome by migration, and could have been overcome still more. The puzzle remains: why did the rural population spend only a fraction of their cash income on grain?

Wild Foods

Hunger and Wild Foods

During 1984/5, people in Darfur chose not to eat *'esh* because they knew they could survive without it. They could go hungry. People were prepared to go very, very hungry for very, very long periods of time. They ate once a day, or once in two days. This was particularly so at the time when it was necessary to plant the fields and weed them. When people were asked what was their major problem with cultivating in 1985, many answered 'hunger' or 'weakness'; nevertheless they managed to cultivate.

People cannot live on prayer alone, though sometimes it seemed that they were doing so. Even more important than people's capacity to endure hunger was the availability of wild foods and the readiness of the people to eat them. Wild foods were far and away the most important factor in the survival of people in northern Darfur during 1984/5, and were critically important in the south.

During the rains of 1985, when the consumption of wild foods peaked, households were eating on average one and a half varieties of wild food regularly, with many eating four or five types. Throughout the year 1984/5, in only one site (Nankose) did people eat less wild foods than grain. Elsewhere in south Darfur most ate wild foods, and in rural north Darfur 96 per cent collected wild foods, and half of the remainder bought them in the market-place.

People bought only small amounts of millet or sorghum and used it to make meals of wild foods more palatable. The ordinary diet took a step downwards: wild foods had become the staple, and millet and sorghum the *mulaah*, the sauce or flavouring. The minority who ate only millet and sorghum did not do so out of necessity. They did so partly for reasons of taste, but largely for social reasons. Eating wild foods is something that is done by the destitute in normal times. Wild foods cannot be shared, exchanged, or given to guests in the way that millet or sorghum can.

Types of Wild Foods

There are many wild foods (Buckley 1987), and nutritional information is available for some (Berry 1985). They can be divided into various categories. The first includes those that constitute a normal part of the diet for some or all of the population (Table 5.5). The most important of these are the wild grains which are collected by the pastoralists in the far north (Tubiana and Tubiana 1977).

Table 5.5. *Wild Foods*

Local Name	Scientific Name	Description	KCal/100 g
Difra	*Echinochloa colonum*	Wild grass	n/a
Koreb	*Echinochloa crus galli*	Wild rice	377
Abu Asabe	*Dactyloctenium aegyptium*	Wild finger millet	n/a
Lalob	*Balanites aegyptiaca*	Fruit of *hajlij*	n/a

By comparison, millet has 326 kilocalories per 100 grams. One of the things that makes these foods important is their availability during the rainy season, when stocks of harvested *'esh* are lowest. However, they are not found in areas of widespread cultivation or intensive grazing. In Dar Zaghawa there are long-standing institutional controls to protect and regulate their harvesting.

Secondly there are distress foods, which are eaten in normal times only by the very poor. These are shown in Table 5.6. There is also the gathering of foods by unconventional means, such as digging up ants' nests or rat holes to recover the grains stored in them.

Table 5.6. *Distress foods*

Local Name	Scientific Name	Description		KCal/100g
Direisa	*Tribulus terrestris*	Thorny grass seed		n/a
Nabak	*Ziziphus spina-christa*	Fruit		314
Hajlij	*Balanites aegyptiaca*	Leaves		n/a
Hab	—	Watermelon seeds		n/a
Umbass	—	Groundnut meal residue		387
Mukheit	*Boscia senegaliensis*	Berry	(Dry)	341
			(Cooked)	92

Mukheit, the last food in Table 5.6, was the most important of these. During 1984/5 it was eaten by 94 per cent of those in northern Darfur who had access to it, and constituted the single most important factor in the diet. There are reports of pastoral groups planning their migrations specially so as to be able to take advantage of areas particularly rich in wild foods. For sedentary people, supplies in their localities often ran low or even ran out. *Mukheit* does not grow at all in some areas, and where there is extensive cultivation such as near El Fasher and Mellit, all the bushes have been cut down. In some areas people had to walk for a whole day to find *mukheit*. In other places the supply ran out, and for many villages the supply was enough only because many people had left. Raw *mukheit* is also toxic and needs to be soaked in water for several days to be edible; one migrant family arriving in El Fasher lost three children to poisoning. Early unseasonal showers in March also meant that *mukheit* berries fell to the ground; on clay soils they then rotted, on sandy soils they dried out and remained edible.

Knowledge about the edibility and properties of wild foods varies from area to area and group to group. In some areas certain wild foods are not found, and so migrants from these areas did not know how to make use of the wild resources in the areas they went to. On the whole, pastoralists know more about wild foods than farmers, and women know more than men. Some sections of society, such as itinerant blacksmiths and potters, who also specialize in gathering, tend to know most. Hunters are the most knowledgeable group in southern Darfur. Older people, who lived through *Julu* and the 1940s' famines, tend to know more than younger people. There are also examples of surprising ignorance. A Zaghawa visiting Dar Meidob in 1985 remarked on the number of edible wild grasses that the local Meidob were not making use of, not knowing they were edible or how to prepare them.

Finally there are the famine foods *per se*, those things that are not considered food except by people on the brink of starvation: refuse, fleas, ground up skins, some roots and leaves, the bark of trees.

The collection of distress foods is stigmatized, but this did not prevent people from gathering them. Because they are such low-status foods, few if any rights to them are held by individuals. There were no instances of people 'owning' *mukheit* or other distress foods, or of disputing others' rights to collect them. The problems of having to travel long distances and work hard to collect them were much more pressing.

Mukheit *and Millet*

It is worthwhile looking in more detail at *mukheit*, as it is the most important wild food. It looks somewhat like a green pea, but is more nutritious. It is highly toxic when raw and must be first soaked and then cooked. One hundred grams of *mukheit* when cooked contain about 70 per cent of the energy in cooked millet or sorghum. In this state it contains 5.4 grams of protein (millet: 7.2 grams). It is unappetizing.

In most parts of Darfur, notably in Dar Masalit, a market in *mukheit* opened up. This is interesting because analysis of the price data shows that parallel staple food markets existed, for *'esh* and for *mukheit*. This confirms the changed roles of the two foods during the famine: *mukheit* effectively became the staple food, and *'esh* became a luxury food.

The *mukheit* market is difficult to document. Prices are not properly known; no records were kept, it was often sold in small and irregular units (e.g. by volume rather than weight), the markets were highly localized, and different qualities of berry commanded different prices. The market was most developed in south Dar Masalit. Some spot prices were collected there. During late 1985 *mukheit* sold at the equivalent of £s12 per 100 kg. sack, and had reached £s50 per sack during the rains. These prices represented about a quarter of the price of *'esh*. This meant that the price of *mukheit* calories was approximately 35 per cent of the price of grain calories.

In other parts of Darfur, notably in the east, *mukheit* was also often sold, though markets as well-established as those in Dar Masalit did not develop. In some areas *mukheit* was used for paying farm labourers. Market data are even more scanty, but *mukheit* seems to have fetched lower and more variable prices than in Dar Masalit. In all areas there were two parallel staple-food markets, one for 'luxury' millet and sorghum, and one for the 'staple' *mukheit*.

Conclusion

Collecting, storing, and eating wild foods was usually people's first reponse to the impending famine. Already in the rains of 1984, when the famine became inevitable, over half of the population were collecting or consuming wild foods. This figure includes 'normal' wild foods, such as *difra* for the camel-herders; but if the pastoral community of Furawiya is excluded, the figure is still 45 per cent. The economic advantages of eating wild foods are clear: they are free. The social disadvantages are equally clear: they are stigmatized and shameful. Most taste unpleasant, but this was not considered important by those who ate them. Most people chose to eat wild foods in preference to grain

Other Foods

During the famine there were other sources of food, but they were of limited importance.

Meat

One of the ironies of the famine was that while people ate much less millet and sorghum than usual, many ate more meat. This was due to the large numbers of animals that were slaughtered because they were going to die, and because the fall in animal prices made meat very cheap. Livestock markets during the famine will be looked at in more detail in the following chapter. Here I shall examine two aspects of meat consumption. One is the consumption of meat from slaughtered animals, and the other a curious convergence in the prices per calorie for meat and grain at the nadir of the famine.

Livestock owners prefer to kill animals only on ceremonial

occasions or when the animal is clearly going to die anyway. Animals are slaughtered for the big feasts such as *id el kabir*, at weddings, or to entertain important guests. These obligations, though they provide meat for a short while, in fact mean a loss of food entitlement because the nutritional value of a carcass is less than that of the grain which could have been bought if the animal had been sold. This is recognized by livestock owners.

During the famine it was often impossible to sell animals which were likely to die. This was because they would not have survived the journey to market, or because the owner was too busy to be able to make the journey. Consequently the animals were often slaughtered and eaten in the villages or the herders' camp. Informants described how the meat was then distributed free among the people present, as people in small villages were not able or ready to pay for it. The resulting meals can hardly have been joyful occasions, nevertheless the maintenance of the principle of sharing food was important. In contrast, eating the carcass of an animal that has already died, without being slaughtered in the correct Islamic fashion, breaks an important social taboo. There are no confirmed reports of people eating carcasses.

During the famine the prices of animals dropped markedly. The resulting deterioration in the 'terms of trade' between livestock and grain is common during famines. It is striking how the terms of exchange of animals with millet reached lowest levels where the sale of one animal bought grain of almost exactly the same energy content. During the 1970s, the cost of a calorie from meat was between six and ten times as expensive as the cost of a calorie from grain: in June 1985 the differences fell to a tiny 3–14 per cent.

Elsewhere I have discussed this phenomenon in more detail (de Waal 1987*a*, pp. 48–9), concluding that it shows that at the nadir of the famine, the value of these animals to the people who were selling them lay only in the food they could provide immediately. But this is puzzling: there is no plausible explanation for how people could understand that the prices per calorie for meat and millet were approaching parity. Moreover, the effect is not robust: the price statistics and estimates for carcass weights are of unknown accuracy. Also, the staple food market was not in millet or sorghum but in *mukheit*, so that the per-calorie prices for meat were approximating to those for 'luxury' foods, not staple foods. This striking convergence of calorie prices is too scanty a base on which to build a theory, and there is no plausible explanation for it. Provisionally, it should be regarded merely as coincidence.

Milk

There is no category of people in Darfur for whom milk is a staple food, but it does provide an important item in the diet of many during the wet season. At this time grain is usually scarcest and animals, grazing on new pasture, produce most milk. In the case of the camel pastoralists who take their herds up to the *jizu* pastures of the Libyan desert, milk is essential; the camels graze for a month or more on the succulent grasses without needing water, and the herders drink camels' milk. Milk can be an important part of the diet of sedentary livestock owners too. In a drought year the quantity and quality of the milk each animal produces is depleted, through poor pasture and low fertility, and herders have fewer milking animals because of deaths and sales.

Access to milk (or lack of it) proved to be a significant factor in mortality differentials during the famine. Households which owned a milking animal were less likely to suffer a death in the family. This relationship probably holds during normal years too. Animal milk is an important weaning food. The analysis of mortality in Chapter 7 shows how weanlings were the group most likely to die during the famine. With other weaning foods in short supply, milk came to be of even greater importance in weaning children.

Additional Foods

In Darfur the most common additional foods are ground-nuts, sesame, hibiscus, and vegetables. These foods are potentially valuable to a hungry population, but normally they are grown as cash crops, not for home consumption. They are of limited importance in the normal diet. Moreover, most are wet-season crops which were hit by the drought. Ground-nuts are the prime example. They are highly nutritious, but the nature of ground-nut growing in Darfur means that a few people have a large number of ground-nuts, many more than they can eat, and a large number of people have none, but will buy only small quantities. Ground-nut production in 1984 was the lowest for fifteen years. The dry-season crops, such as tomatoes, onions, and okra, are grown only by richer farmers and have limited nutritive potential anyway.

Tree crops such as oranges, dates, and mangoes form a limited part of the normal diet. In south Dar Masalit mangoes are so plentiful they are practically free, because they are too perishable to be transported out. Even during the famine, however, people sold a bagful for a few piastres when they could.

These crops were therefore marginal to the hunger of most people. They were more critical for that special vulnerable group, weanlings. Weaning practices during food crises is an area urgently needing research: very little is known about them. Ground-nuts and sesame, made into a thin paste, form one weaning food in Darfur. It is not known whether mothers made a special effort to obtain this and other weaning foods during the famine.

Water

People need water as much as food. Here I shall consider drinking water for people. Water for animals will be discussed in Chapter 6. People can only live where potable water is available in sufficient quantities. Water availability is a problem principally in eastern Darfur and in the far north. Water quality is poor in almost all parts of Darfur. People in Darfur see water as a major problem they face, perhaps *the* major problem. During the 1960s, the government saw the provision of water to rural villages as a way of ensuring rural votes. When asked why the famine occurred, a frequent answer was *maa fi moya* ('no water'). This meant mainly 'no rain', but lack of ground-water was implied too. In their belief that Darfur was undersupplied with water, the rural people disagreed with the 'experts'. 'Experts' have agreed with one another that Darfur is overprovided with water points, which has encouraged 'over-farming' and 'overgrazing'.

During the drought many hand-dug wells ran dry, often for the first time ever. In the past people had methods of storing water in baobab trees or growing it in water-melons. The introduction of pumped water from bore-holes led to a neglect of the former and the drought itself caused a failure of the water-melon crop. Many diesel engines proved as unreliable as the weather. The drought came during an economic recession, and spare parts and diesel were not available for many bore-holes. Many people had to travel to neighbouring villages for water. This could involve up to twelve hours' walk on foot. Even with a donkey this was time-consuming and cut into the time available for other necessary activities such as cultivation or working for money. The alternative was buying water, which could be very expensive: a forty-four-gallon drumful of water cost up to £s15 in parts of eastern Darfur, and a price of £s5 per drum was common. Lack of water led to the abandonment of whole villages in north-east Darfur during the dry season of 1984/5. The wells took a while to refill after the rains returned, which meant that planting after the first rains was difficult in some areas.

People had to go 'thirsty' as well as hungry. 'Thirsty' in practice meant washing less or not at all, paying money for water, spending large amounts of time travelling to fetch water, or storing it in unsatisfactory containers. If there was not enough water even to drink, people were forced to move elsewhere. In contrast to past droughts, in 1984/5 there were no reports of deaths from thirst. Nevertheless, the consequences for health and income from 'thirst' in this extended sense were considerable.

The quality of water deteriorated too. In northern Darfur wells had less water, and throughout Darfur large villages had more people and animals taking water from their wells. In Chapter 6, water supply is identified as a main problem facing farmers and herders in their response to the famine. In Chapter 7 the quality of drinking water is identified as probably the main determinant of famine mortality. This section on 'thirst' is short and comes at the end of a chapter entitled 'hunger', but water was actually a central issue in famine destitution and mortality.

Conclusion

This chapter has shown that the pattern of the famine in Darfur during 1984/5 cannot be understood by reference to people's entitlements to staple grain. It has shown that people were not simply motivated to avoid hunger. On the contrary, people appear to have chosen to forgo eating grain. Why they did so is the concern of the next chapter. Two other issues have been introduced which will recur. One is water. The other is the question of what is happening to children due to be weaned.

6

Destitution

A Way of Life under Threat

The previous chapter presented a paradox which strikes right to the centre of how we think of famines. Famine victims had exchange entitlements to *'esh* which they did not fully utilize. This paradox is partly resolved by looking at the consumption of wild foods, and partly by the observation that people simply went very hungry. Two questions remain. One is: if people were not spending their money on grain, what were they spending it on, and why? That is the concern of this chapter. The concept of famine held in Darfur has a focus on destitution. People see famine primarily not as a threat to their lives but as a threat to their way of life. Their central aim during the famine was to preserve the base of their livelihood, so that they could return to a normal or acceptable way of life after the famine. This leads to the second question: were people struggling to preserve their way of life at a risk to their lives, were they really choosing to starve? That is the concern of the next chapter.

The analysis of how famine victims struggled to prevent themselves becoming destitute falls into three sections. The first concerns farmers, the second herders, and the third those who were destitute already.

The Farmers of Jebel Si: A 'Worst Case Scenario'

Jebel Si is an example of an area in northern Darfur which has been hard hit by chronic ecological decline, which has forced major changes in the pattern of livelihood. By 1984 it was poorer than any of the other rural communities studied, with half of the households already below normative subsistence level. It was impoverished still further during the famine year; more so than the other sites. Thus Jebel Si represents the 'worst case scenario' in Darfur. Nevertheless, despite greater difficulties than anywhere else studied, most people managed to avoid complete destitution. This is shown by the fact that most farmers were able to plant their land in 1985.

A Fur Heartland

Jebel Si is actually a mountain, a spire of bare rock standing 6,000 feet high in the northern reaches of the Jebel Marra range. Close to the mountain lie a number of small villages, of which two, Ora Jebel Si and Jutei, were studied. The people of this area are Fur. It is a mountainous area, where cultivation is possible only by building terraces. The rich volcanic soil, the high altitude, and the rainfall attracted by the mountain range make Jebel Si more fertile than other areas at the same latitude. Nevertheless, it is an area where yields have been declining steadily. This is partly due to the declining rainfall. For a long time the 400 millimetre rainfall isohyet passed through Jebel Si; now the area is bounded by the 200 and 300 millimetre isohyets. The decline in yields is also partly due to a drying up of perennial springs that used to water the area until three decades ago, and partly due to exhaustion of the soil. The mountains used to be forested and infested with wild animals, now they are bare and empty.

Jebel Si used to be famous for its farming. Millet, cotton, and vegetables were among its crops, which were sold in a large rural market to merchants from Kebkabiya town and El Fasher. The money earned was invested in animals and in expanding the terracing on the mountainsides. This fertility and the cash income it provided remained until after the Second World War. Since the 1950s there has been little cash flowing into Jebel Si on account of its agricultural production. The ecological and climatic changes there have forced farmers to abandon growing cash crops and turn almost exclusively to millet. Since the late 1960s the area has been generally in net grain deficit. One result of this is a massive inexorable loss of capital in the form of sales of animals. Even numbers of goats were declining during the pre-famine years. Another is that the people have looked for paid work elsewhere. Jebel Si saw two types of out-migration; movement of men to central Sudan for long periods, and seasonal labour migration of families within Darfur.

Massive male out-migration has become a dominant feature of Jebel Si. Almost half the households are headed by women. The average household size was 3.7 people, compared to 5.5 for Darfur as a whole. There were 80 males per 100 females overall; in the age group 20–39 there were 49. Moreover, this is long-term out-migration. Most emigrants had gone to central Sudan. This was the highest rate of migration to central Sudan we found in Darfur. It is a relatively recent phenomenon: while most parts of Darfur were sending large numbers of young men to Gezira to earn money from the 1920s onwards, this did not occur in Jebel Si until the 1960s and 1970s. The men who leave remit money only occasionally: less than 60 per cent of the Darfurian households interviewed in central Sudan had sent money home in the previous two years. These remittances, though small, are important in sustaining the wealth of the area. Out-migrants to central Sudan also tend to return home when they have earned enough money, and become farmers again, using their stored cash to subsidize grain-deficit farming.

The remaining households consist largely of women and children. They have tended to leave the area during the dry season to seek work elsewhere in Darfur. They mainly move south; to Jebel Marra to work in irrigated orchards, to southern Darfur to work harvesting and threshing, and to alluvial areas of western Darfur to work in irrigated vegetable cultivation. Jebel Si had the highest proportion of farm labourers found. More recently the people of Jebel Si have also started to earn dry-season incomes by selling firewood, fodder, and water, largely in towns such as Kebkabiya.

These strategies provided income to cover the grain deficit for most years since the 1960s. People were following famine strategies before the famine struck. Most of these activities illustrate that people were, in their own terms, destitute: they were poor, a dependent or client community, and reliant on a seasonal dispersal and a long-term separation of spouses. They refer to the whole period since the late 1960s as one of *maja'a*: hunger or dearth, and chronic threat to the traditional way of life. Famine, understood in these terms, with its focus on destitution, is itself becoming a way of life.

Fall-Back Strategies: Farm Labour

In 1983 only five households in Jebel Si harvested surplus *'esh*. In

1984 the harvest averaged 41 kg. per household: enough for four weeks' food. In the hills of Jebel Si there were wild foods to be had, but not enough to feed the whole population throughout the year. There was no paid work to be found locally, and scarcely any in other parts of northern Darfur. People could have eaten their seed or sold their animals, but their priority was precisely to avoid having to do these things.

Instead, to find alternative sources of food and income, the people of Jebel Si moved southwards, in larger numbers than ever before. During the 1970s many of them had worked in the irrigated gardens of Jebel Marra. The labour market there was strongly segmented along ethnic lines, and the Fur of Jebel Si received preferential treatment. Employers acted in a similar manner to patrons, and supported the labourers when times were hard. But by the early 1980s this market had collapsed under the pressure of drought. The people of Jebel Si had to look further west, to villages such as Nankose. During 1984 this was the best area for finding work: the grain harvests were least bad, and richer farmers were starting irrigated gardens. Seasonal aspects to farm work are shown in Fig. 6.1. However, the labour market here was more open and competitive. By 1984/5 the number of would-be labourers was double the number of 1980. Many failed to find work.

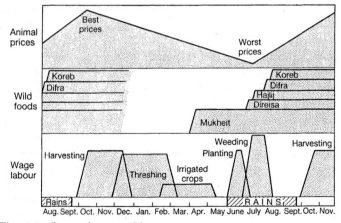

Fig. 6.1. *Seasonal opportunities*

Most of the labourers from Jebel Si are women. Women are at a disadvantage compared with men only for two types of agricultural labour: clearing land and digging wells. For planting, weeding, harvesting, and tending irrigated gardens both men and women are employed. For threshing it is only women. Men are almost always paid in cash, at current market rates. Women are paid to harvest and thresh with a fixed payment in grain, usually one tenth of the crop. In normal times this works to the advantage of men, as the real value of the cash wage is higher.

During the dry season of 1984/5, cash wages were extremely low. The daily rate fell to £s1.00, even to 75 piastres per day. Labourers were also given a meal. This wage could just buy another meal for two adults at current grain prices. However, the pattern of paying female workers with food persisted. They mostly received grain, though sometimes it was *mukheit*. As grain prices were so high, this meant that in real terms the women were receiving a higher wage than the men (and also more than they had received in non-famine times). The relative scarcity of men in Jebel Si thus became an advantage.

As the dry season wore on, work became scarcer and rates lower. Migrants moved from village to village, looking for work with increasing desperation, or congregated in towns. The villages of Jebel Si re-formed in the south, as groups of labourers and beggars, living in squatter camps on the margins of villages such as Nankose. The consequences of these movements for health and mortality will be discussed in Chapter 7. People became thinner and more visibly desperate.

But in June, as the rains began, the situation changed abruptly. These apparently destitute and dependent people left to return north. This was just as more farm work became available. Richer farmers in Nankose complained of a shortage of labourers to hire. The daily wage doubled to £s2 or £s3. Throughout south-west Darfur, farmers were increasing their cultivated area and needed more labour than normal. They hired an average of seven hours' work planting and twenty-five hours' work weeding during June and July (JMRDP 1986). In Nankose, only 65 per cent of this work was done by local labourers. The remainder was done mostly by Chadian refugees: the migrant northerners had gone. In Angabo the migrants supplied 36 per cent of the hired planting labour and a mere 1 per cent of the weeding labour. After the rains they trickled back, doing 28 per cent of the harvesting, and 62 per cent of the threshing.

With no prospect of a harvest for five months, the migrants from Jebel Si had turned their backs on the only food and money available and returned north to cultivate their own farms. In economic terms, they relinquished the chance of a current income in order to preserve their farming assets. Working for wages on another's farm means very different things during the wet season compared with the dry season. From October to May, people from Jebel Si could work without endangering their future livelihood. But during June or July, a labourer who planted or weeded another's fields was doing this at the expense of jeopardizing her own harvest. In their own terms, the migrants were leaving the shame, dependence, and exclusion of working for others, for the dignity, autonomy, and community of working on their own farms, despite the huge hardship and hunger it involved.

Low-Status Trades

After the failed harvest of 1984, many more people than normal fell back upon the activities normally followed only by the poorest. One of these was paid farm work, others were a variety of low-status trades. During 1984/5, and especially during the late dry season when farm work became scarce, these trades became vitally important, as Tables 6.1 and 6.2 show.

Perhaps three-quarters of a million people were partly relying on money earned by selling wood during the first months of 1985. Almost two-thirds of the population followed (temporarily) the

Table 6.1. *% of sampled households following low-status trade (1984/1985)*

Category	%
Agricultural wage-labour	53
Crafts (pottery, mat-making, rope-making)	7.5
Casual paid labour (e.g. brick-making, portering, building houses, roads, fences)	11
Gathering/selling (firewood, fodder, wild foods, also charcoal burning)	34
Charcoal and firewood alone	23
Other, requiring capital (blacksmith, water-carrier)	10

Table 6.2. *Numbers doing low-status trades and wage-labour in each site*

Site	Area	Low-status trades		Agric. wage-labour (%)	Total doing one/both (%)	Wealth order
		%	Mean LSTs			
Legediba	S	53	2.1	83	85	3
Saiyah	N	75	2.2	63	79	5
Angabo	S	45	2.1	58	71	2
Jebel Si	N	46	2.3	54	69	6
Furawiya	N	24	2.0	26	41	4
Nankose	S	23	1.5	33	41	1
TOTAL		45	2.1	53	65	

activities of those who are normally counted as destitute and non-belonging.

Jebel Si lies fourth in Table 6.2, but here agricultural labour and low-status trades provided a greater proportion of the income than elsewhere. Their importance in Jebel Si was reflected in their treatment of donkeys. Donkeys are critical to low-status trades. People with donkeys can carry water, and earn far more money from collecting firewood and fodder than people without. Donkey numbers in Darfur declined by 27 per cent during the famine year. Deaths outnumbered sales by four to one. In Jebel Si, where the losses of all other animals were the greatest among the sites studied, the total number of donkeys declined by only 9 per cent. Only two respondents admitted to selling a donkey, whereas four actually bought donkeys. 70 per cent of households had a donkey after the famine, a higher proportion than in the other sites studied. As a result of this, households from Jebel Si were able to follow relatively profitable trades, such as selling water, twice as often as households in the other rural sites, and gain a higher income from selling firewood and fodder. Jebel Si was becoming a permanent provider of low-status services to Kebkabiya town and south-west Darfur.

As in the case of farm labour, the low-status trades are followed in a markedly seasonal manner (Fig. 6.2). In Jebel Si the number of households following them fell from sixty-two during the dry season to four during the rains. They have to be seen as only part of a response to the famine, the complementary part being the return to farming during the wet season.

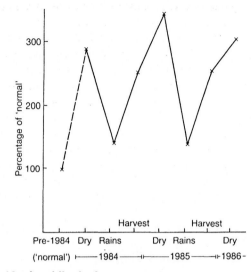

Fig. 6.2. *Numbers following low-status trades*

Cultivation during 1985

In late 1985 the farmers of Darfur reaped a record grain harvest of millet and sorghum that had been planted and weeded during the months of the greatest hunger. This harvest was a remarkable achievement. Its origins lay in the fact that farmers planned their responses to the famine precisely in order to be able to return to farming afterwards.

In order to cultivate, it is necessary to have labour, land, and seed. The management of labour has been described. People hired out their labour in the dry season and tried to conserve it for their own farms in the wet season. In Jebel Si they were least successful. Thirty-three families were compelled to work for money during July and August. There was no work to be had nearby, so they had to move south to Kebkabiya. Six fell into normative destitution as a result.

Land is the second factor. In most places in Darfur land cannot be sold, so distress sales were impossible. The few areas where it is possible are richer areas close to towns, where most of the land had passed to rich farmers already. In south Darfur, farmers mostly tried to expand landholdings by renting or clearing new ground allocated by the village sheikh. The pattern of land acquisition in villages such as Nankose shows that preference was given to established villagers, and recent arrivals could not expand. In northern Darfur, land rights affected the farmers' abilities to follow other strategies, notably out-migration. Jebel Si is a prime example. Here land is held on a customary system that approximates to freehold. Women own separate fields from men, in their own right. Thus a man can leave for a long stretch and know that his own fields will remain for him to reclaim on his return, and that his absence will not jeopardize his wife's access to land. Women can also leave for a season, and know their rights will persist. The one difficulty is that male labour during the dry season is needed for building terraces. This problem has been overcome by changing the terracing system from broad and high terraces to narrow and shallow ones, which require only a little unskilled labour to maintain.

This contrasts with Saiyah, the paradigm case for the disaster tourist. The land-rights system in Saiyah militated against any responses to famine that involved out-migration. Only usufructuary rights exist to *goz*. With falling yields, a household's prosperity depends on being able to expand cultivation. A man dare not leave for fear that his family's fields will be reallocated by the sheikh, or simply expropriated by an individual farmer, who will continue to plant it while the litigation drags on. At the same time the first farmer is looking for the opportunity to acquire someone else's land. Unplanted land in Saiyah is not evidence for deliberate fallowing, but simply for lack of labour or seed.

Seed is the third factor in cultivation. Farmers went to great lengths to preserve and acquire seed for planting. In Furawiya, one woman described how she had harvested just enough millet to provide seed for the next year. She had buried it, mixed with sand and gravel to prevent her children digging it up and eating it, and then gone south for the dry season. In June she returned, dug it up and planted it, together with some seed she had been given by the Red Crescent. In Nankose the richer farmers chose to plant short-season sorghums, in order to have an early harvest in August, and

drought-resistant millets, in case the rains were poor. Some had only
the seeds of long-season sorghum, and travelled to Nyala to search
for the ones they wanted. For northern farmers the situation was
critical. In Saiyah the harvest of 1984 was an average of 16 kg. per
household. This could not even provide seed for the 1985 season,
and relief distributions were important in averting disaster. In Jebel
Si the situation was worse. The harvest was only slightly better, less
seed was given by relief agencies, and people were poorer and many
could not buy it. A third of the householders admitted to eating seed
that they had intended to plant. This was the only rural community
in which the figure was over 5 per cent. Through combinations of
weakness, working for others, and lack of seed, twenty-one
households (one seventh) failed to plant. Table 6.3 shows the
acquisition of seed for 1985, by site.

The management of labour and seed showed not only tenacity, but
a large amount of forward planning too. When the harvest failure
became apparent in August 1984, people knew that they would have
to wait another fourteen or fifteen months before they could harvest
their own crops again. In the meantime they had to budget what
resources they had. People knew that farm work could be had until
about January, that the markets in water and fodder were strongest
from February until June, that *mukheit* would ripen in about April.
The sequence of strategies reflected these opportunities.

As people followed their strategies, they became more visibly
desperate, until May. This was as much a function of their visibility

Table 6.3. *Origin of seed for cultivation in 1985*

Site	% who had				
	Stored all	Stored maj.	Bought maj.	Donated[a] maj.	Failed to plant
Nankose	40	29	17	8	6
Angabo	15	51	17	8	9
Legediba	15	50	17	11	10
Furawiya	4	37	11	40	8
Saiyah	0	46	15	36	3
Jebel Si	4	23	40	18	15
TOTAL (weighted)	16	40	20	16	8

[a] This category includes people who received seed from the relief distribution, and
people who were given seed by a relative, neighbour, or patron.

as of their desperation. From February to May most of the countryside was empty of people. The famine came to town. After that came the *mukheit* crop and then the rains. People dispersed: hungrier but less visible. The crisis was visibly waning.

Labour in Dar Sabah

The sufferings of the Darfurian people in central and eastern Sudan— known in Darfur as *Dar Sabah*—are not our concern here. Two issues are important, however, and should be mentioned. One is the extent to which the Darfurian people in *Dar Sabah* were joined by more people from Darfur during the famine.

In 1985 World Vision estimated that there were 60,000 destitute Darfurian migrants in central Sudan. The real figure was certainly lower. Many of those claiming to be from Darfur were in reality Chadians, and others were destitute Darfurians already living in central Sudan. The Darfur survey of 1986 found that 2.3 per cent of the sampled population had left for central and eastern Sudan during the previous two years, implying a total of 76,000 migrants. The survey also interviewed a further 187 households in Omdurman, Gezira, and Gedaref. This included a question on when the household had arrived from Darfur. The numbers need some

Table 6.4. *Migration to* Dar Sabah

	Mean of 1979–82	1983	1984	1985
No. of Households	17	15	18	18

attention. First, some of the people who arrived in earlier years had left again, so the earlier figures should in fact be higher. Second, the 1985 arrivals came mainly at the end of the year, when the Gedaref labour market improved, and when the famine was over in Darfur. Third, though 1984/5 migrants represented 19 per cent of the households, they had fewer people per household and represented only 14 per cent of the people. Lastly, most migrants were young men; fewer had brought their families over: adult men outnumbered women by three to two.

A common estimate for the total number of Darfurians in central and eastern Sudan was 500,000 people. If the survey was representative, 14 per cent of that total or 70,000 people arrived in *Dar Sabah* during 1984 and 1985. This figure is close to the estimate of 76,000 derived from the Darfur survey.

These data show that in fact, no more Darfurians than normal came to *Dar Sabah* during the famine. It made little sense to come: grain prices were as high as in Darfur, and work was as hard to get. Because of the expense of travelling it was not something the very poor could do. Nevertheless some did come, mainly from western Darfur.

The second way in which Darfurians living outside Darfur are relevant to those who remain behind is the extent to which they send them money. Because of the distance involved, remittances to Darfur have never been regular in the way they have been to areas such as Kordofan. During the famine years the labour market in Gedaref and Gezira slumped severely. As a consequence there was less money to remit. It also became more difficult to send it; fewer people could afford to travel and it was more likely to be stolen or pocketed by the carrier. Only 16 per cent of the sampled households received remittances. Even during 1985/6 when the economy in central Sudan was recovering and communications with Darfur had improved, a JMRDP survey found only 2 per cent of households receiving any sort of remittances at any one time, whether from towns in Darfur or *Dar Sabah* (JMRDP 1986).

Livestock

Deaths of Animals

The farmers of Jebel Si struggled to preserve the base of their future livelihood. More people there failed than did in any other site: during 1985/6 many continued to live from wage-labour and low-status trades. However, even these people retained their land, and during 1986/7 began to return to farming. A pastoralist, such as a herder from Furawiya, faced greater dangers. A herd of thin and thirsty animals, weary from a long trek through strange country, may be decimated by unfamiliar diseases in a matter of days. One herder from Furawiya recounted how he awoke to find that 'half my sheep had died that same night'. The numbers of animals lost during droughts tend to be exaggerated both by herders and by those who make surveys of them. But it is true that some herders see their herds annihilated, and the threat of mass death hangs heavy over all of them.

In Chapter 5 it was shown that the pastoral community of Furawiya had an income during the worst months of the famine which could have bought most of the staple food the people needed. Instead, the herders chose to eat wild foods, go hungry, and spend only a fraction of this income on grain. The money was spent on their animals.

During the drought many animals died through one or more of hunger, thirst, and disease (Fig. 6.3). The figures for deaths given here are lower than most other estimates. They are probably still too high. This is because of the propensity to exaggerate losses and understate existing herds, and because transhumant herds, which suffered less, were underrepresented in the sample. For instance the migratory herds of Furawiya were depleted by 39 per cent by the famine, whereas the sedentary herds of Saiyah and Jebel Si were depleted by 74 and 75 per cent respectively. No southern trans-humant herds were sampled, so the figures for losses in the south, especially for cattle, are exaggerated. Livestock losses were much greater in the north than in the south. Cows suffered most, sheep suffered least. Animal deaths peaked during the dry *seif* months of 1985 and the first month of the rains (*rushash*). Deaths during the dry season were caused by lack of water and grazing, and the stresses of long migrations. Mortality during the rains was due to the sudden change in climatic conditions and abundance of pasture, which provided a shock that many weakened animals could not withstand (see Topps 1977, p. 103). Deaths among livestock amounted to 53–54 per cent, and 32–33 per cent remained after the famine. The difference is accounted for by births (of which there were few during the drought), and sales.

Keeping Animals Alive

It takes great skill to care for a large herd in a semi-arid climate. Some of the knowledge of plant ecology which is necessary for a pastoralist was described by Tubiana and Tubiana (1977). The Tubianas worked in Dar Zaghawa during the 1950s and 1960s. Since then there have been huge changes in herding patterns, and Zaghawa herders have had to acquire knowledge about the ecology

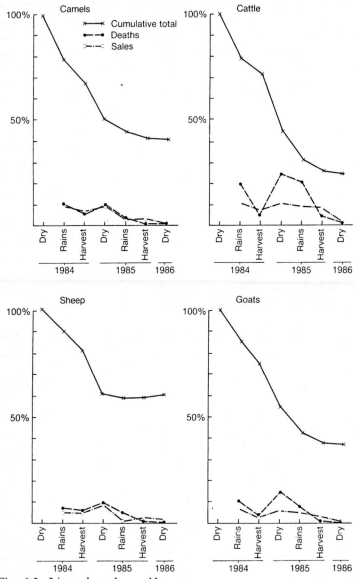

Fig. 6.3. *Livestock numbers and losses*

of southern Darfur as well. In times of drought, herders rely on an extensive system of intelligence as to where grazing and browse is available.

Grazing and browse, when available, may not be useful or may not be free. They may be too far away from a source of water. In this case herders have to plan their movements to pass the area soon after the rains, when there are surface pools, or pay people to collect fodder at that time and store it for later. It may be too close to planted fields or enclosed grass-fields that are being kept for villagers' donkeys. In this case grazing will have to be paid for, either by formal purchase or in the form of a fine. It may be in areas infested with tsetse flies or livestock diseases. It may be available but be so thin and sparse that a large herd has to be moved on every day because of exhaustion of the grazing, and under these conditions an animal may not be able to spend enough hours in the day eating to be able to avoid starvation. In this case a large herd has to be divided into small herds, and more herders hired.

A further problem is the absolute lack of water in some areas. Water is difficult to transport. Consequently fodder is brought to water, and not vice versa. In other areas it is available but costly. Herders in their home areas, if there are shallow wells, usually pay only a nominal price or none at all. In unfamiliar areas the herders will be charged larger amounts for each animal that drinks from a well.

The right to move a herd through a certain area can be a problem with an expensive solution. Farms do not actually block herders' transhumance routes, because farmers who do cultivate too close to established routes are not entitled to compensation when a herd of animals eats and tramples its way through the farmers' millet. But problems arise when a herder wants to use a non-established route, or to use an established route normally used only by another ethnic group. This is especially the case when grazing is short. The owners of the route typically demand a compensation payment. If this is not agreed, the situation can become violent. One of many examples that arose during 1984/5 concerned the movement of Fellata cattle herds to the Bahr el Arab down the stock route that passes through Legediba, which the Habbaniya (also cattle-herders) have rights over. Fellata herders were accused of numerous small infringements of the 'code of practice', including non-payment of compensation to local farmers whose crops were damaged. The situation was largely contained during the famine, but soon afterwards blood was shed and the Fellata were unilaterally banned from using the stock route. In Nankose, relations between farmers and herders deteriorated during the drought. More northern herders came south. There were accusations of theft and trespassing against the Arabs, and some local farmers deliberately burned grazing so that the herders would be unable to stay in the vicinity. This situation has also worsened since the famine.

Thefts of animals were invariably blamed on pastoral groups, notably the Bedeyat, the traditional scapegoats for any lawlessness. During the famine, and especially at the end of 1985 when livestock prices went up, camel thieving became epidemic, and thefts of other types of livestock also increased. There were much-reported instances of 'Bedeyat' going further than livestock theft. In El Sereif, close to Kebkabiya, they raided a village and took off all its *'esh*. A local sheikh who organized local resistance and police protection was assassinated shortly afterwards. After another incident in which a village was stripped of its grain and a policeman killed, the villagers took the law into their own hands, and the Bedeyat raiders were met with a barrage of rifle fire. Subsequently the Bedeyat have armed themselves with automatic weapons.

The point of these stories is not so much their truthfulness, but that they were widely held to be true. One farmer in Nankose sold his camel, fearing that it would be stolen, and that he might lose his life in the process. Any groups of strange northern pastoralists were extremely unwelcome in settled communities. The people of Furawiya suffered from the ethnic association between Zaghawa and Bedeyat.

The financial costs of maintaining a herd during the drought therefore escalated enormously. Herders had to pay for water, fodder, hired herders, and the rights to move through certain areas. They also had to pay to keep the peace. These costs are what absorbed the income of the people of Furawiya.

Sedentary farmers with large herds faced an acute dilemma. Grazing and water were in short supply near villages. The animals could be entrusted to a herder who would take them south. But this required considerable trust: the herder could sell the animals and credibly claim that they had died.

Fifteen per cent of all the sampled households (both farmers and herders) that became normatively destitute during the famine year did so mainly because of animal deaths. This was most significant in Furawiya. Though Furawiya lost fewer animals than other sites, they were of much greater importance than elsewhere, so that just over 10 per cent of the whole community (sixteen households) became normatively destitute because of animal deaths during the famine.

The Livestock Market

Livestock marketing in Darfur is much older than grain marketing. Darfur was exporting camels to Egypt certainly during the eighteenth century and probably before. There is less evidence concerning the marketing of animals within Darfur before this century. During the 1920s, herders exchanged animals directly for grain in villages: we do not know whether this was a longstanding tradition or a forced retrenchment following the upheavals of the previous decades. In the later part of Condominium rule the direct exchange of livestock for grain died out and was replaced by cash transactions. There are no formal or customary hindrances to the marketing of livestock other than inspection by the veterinary department of those destined for export from the region. However the way in which animals are bought and sold is just as complex as the market in grain.

Small stock, sheep and goats, can be sold in any market. Much of the small stock seen in markets is bought early in the day by middlemen who stay in the animal enclosure all day, selling the animals they bought earlier on.

Large stock, cows and camels, tend to be sold in middle- and upper-tier markets, especially in specialized livestock markets. The butchers in a lower-tier market may buy and slaughter one or two cows every week, but this is a minor affair. Cattle marketing in major centres such as Abu Matarig, Ed Da'ien, and Nyala involves large merchants with considerable amounts of capital buying whole herds, most of which will be transported by rail to central Sudan. Big camel markets such as Foro Baranga and Mellit also involve powerful merchant interests. These markets are highly seasonal because large stock are generally owned by transhumant pastoralists who are only in the vicinity of the markets at certain times of year. The cow and camel owners are more economically powerful than people who sell only small stock and the buyers and middlemen are likewise more powerful than the traders in small stock.

Patterns of Sale during the Famine

The famine saw a sharp increase in sales of animals and corresponding drops in price and quality. Approximately 20 per cent of all animals were sold during the famine. This represented a huge increase—more than a doubling—on normal years. Coming on top of the 50 per cent depletion of numbers due to deaths, the sales represented a huge loss to livestock owners. The impact of sales on gross animal numbers was less than the impact of deaths, but in terms of creating destitution it was greater. Fifteen per cent of the households becoming destitute during 1984/5 did so because of deaths, and a further 25 per cent became so because of sales. The sales hurt more. Why this was so will become clear later.

Why were households selling their animals? The obvious reason was to buy grain. Though grain purchases were limited, they were important outlays of cash at critical times. Many poor farmers bought grain or wild foods in order to work on their own fields during the planting season. Many northern farmers needed money to migrate south, migrate back north, or to buy seed. Many of these sales occurred late in the famine, at the onset of the rains, when prices were lowest. They were true distress sales.

People also sold through fear. In the north, many people sold animals because there was no grazing or water, and they feared that their animals would not survive. This was especially the case for farmers selling cows, the most vulnerable animals. In Saiyah and Jebel Si, most of the villagers' cows were sold right at the start of the famine year. In wetter southern villages where cows were more likely to survive, this did not occur, and the peak of cattle sales was towards the end of the famine. In the towns, fodder became prohibitively expensive and people sold animals they could not afford to feed.

The main fear, however, was that the price of animals would fall. In normal years, prices are high at harvest time and then drop to a low point as the rains approach. Every herder knows this, and also knows that during a drought the seasonal differences in price are exaggerated. So, richer owners sold animals they could safely spare during the 1984 harvest season, when the prices were relatively good. In the richer villages of Furawiya, Angabo, and Nankose there was a surge of sales during these months. Because these people had many more animals than the poorer people who sold later, the aggregate number of animals in this surge overshadows those in the later surge. These early sales could prove dangerous; the herder could miscalculate and sell too much. One farmer-herder in Nankose sold a 'surplus' cow early in the famine, only to see his other animals die later and leave him destitute.

Richer herders, particularly transhumant herders, sold a steady trickle of animals to buy water, fodder, and the rights to move their herds to pasture, and to pay fines.

The data from rural areas therefore show a two-peak pattern of sales. The early (harvest 1984) peak represented mainly 'pre-emptive' and 'fear' sales, and the later (dry season/rains 1985) peak represented mainly 'distress' sales.

Ability to Use the Market

During the famine the market structures became distorted. The price of small stock dropped too low for small middlemen in rural markets to be able to obtain an adequate percentage, and the number of animals rose so that they were unable to exercise the same degree of control over the buying and selling. In some rural markets powerful middlemen came to buy cheap animals in order to sell them in the towns or even export them to central Sudan.

The structure of camel and cattle markets worked to the disadvantage of poorer livestock owners trying to sell their animals. These large animals are 'lumpy'; they have to be sold as a whole unit, even when the owner needs only a proportion of the money the sale will bring in. Even when prices were at their lowest, one cow cost between £s45 and £s175, and one came over £s200. These prices were too high for almost all rural people to afford. Therefore, the buyers consisted of rich middlemen and long-distance traders. In a small market during the famine there were often only one or two middlemen buying cattle: they could effectively fix the prices. The seller could obtain a better price from a larger market, but it would not be worth travelling that distance to sell only one or two animals. The sellers' relative powerlessness shows up in the comparative minimum prices for cows in different markets. Where the position of the herders was strongest (Ed Da'ien), cattle prices fell least, and where the sellers were weaker *vis à vis* the buyers (Zalingei, El Fasher), the prices fell most. Spot prices for rural markets show prices lower still. This gradient in prices ran roughly west–east or 'periphery–centre' and can be seen in the relative prices of one cow in different markets (Table 6.5).

Table 6.5. *The price of one cow in June 1985*

Market	Nankose[a]	Zalingei[b]	Nyala[c]	Ed Da'ien[a]	El Obeid[c]	Omdurman[c]
Price (£s)	45	58	128	175	261	700

[a] Data from spot.   [b] Data from JMRDP.
[c] Data from LMMC.

The timing of sales combined with the place of sale to work against poorer livestock owners. The first peak of sales consisted of richer herders selling, at a time when the prices were relatively good. They sold whenever possible in large markets. Middlemen who bought in small markets resold as quickly as possible, anticipating the price drop. The sales peaks for central markets occurred during November–December 1984, only shortly after the peak in sales by individual owners (September–October).

The second peak occurred when poorer people sold in rural markets, when the prices were low. The number of rural people selling animals peaked during April–July. This was most noticeable for sales of goats, the poor person's most common animal. This peak in sales affected the central markets in north Darfur only marginally, and those in south Darfur not at all. These animals were bought by middlemen who had no desire to sell them when prices were so low. Normally such animals would appear in central markets during the rains. In 1985 the surge in goat sales did not affect Nyala at all: they were being bought in middle-tier markets by richer herders and farmers (for instance in Angabo and Furawiya). More sheep arrived in Nyala market during August and September, and a surge of cattle did not appear until October and November. Many of these cows were resold to central Sudan only at the beginning of 1986. Many merchants made a great deal of money by exploiting the west–east gradient of cattle prices shown above, and the enormous (tenfold) increase in prices in the six months after June 1985.

This second peak of sales does not appear in statistics for central markets except in a delayed and distorted form. This is an illustration of the dangers of using such data, especially for cattle, to try to understand animal marketing during the famine.

Between these two peaks the prices of animals had fallen dramatically. Fig. 6.4 shows livestock prices in Darfur, using official data. There are many problems with the data. In normal times herders sell mostly male calves and bulls, and fewer female animals, which fetch a lower price, and which they need for maintaining the structure of their herds. In the famine, herders sold more female animals, and this factor alone contributed to a price drop. The quality of animals also varied. With the changes and breakdown in the structure of livestock marketing, the difference in prices between the seller–middleman and middleman–buyer transactions fluctuated. More animals were also sold outside regular markets. Nevertheless the trends were clear, especially when the prices are translated

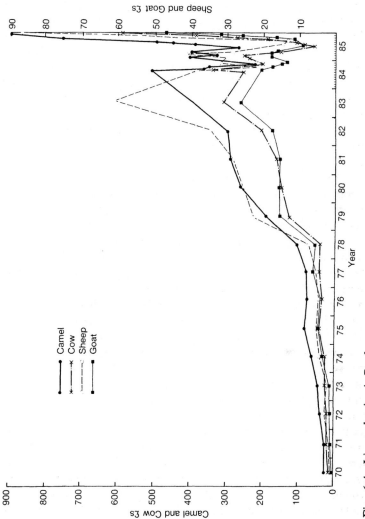

Fig. 6.4. *Livestock prices in Darfur*

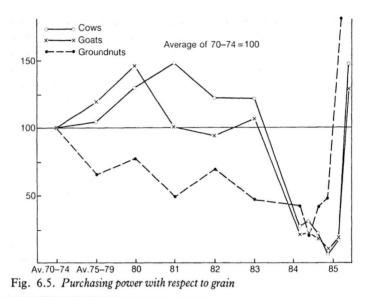

Fig. 6.5. *Purchasing power with respect to grain*

into grain equivalents (Fig. 6.5). In the middle of 1984 prices began to fall. They reached a low in September and then rose slightly, remaining at about the same levels until February–March 1985, when they began to drop precipitately. This second drop was caused not only by poor farmers' and herders' desperate need for money, but the weaker position of the sellers *vis à vis* the buyers, and the need to sell in rural rather than central markets. Prices reached all-time real lows during June and July, when animals were worth a tenth or less of their pre-famine values in terms of grain, before starting to rise again to reach all-time real highs during 1986.

Every livestock owner knew in August 1984 that this was going to happen. They might not have foreseen the actual extent to which prices would fall (and subsequently rise), but the general pattern was known. Rich herders were able to obtain the best prices and still retain a herd large enough for subsistence. Poor herders chose to retain their animals as long as possible, going hungry and clinging to the chance of retaining a few after the famine. The rich could use their knowledge of the market to their advantage, but the poor could not. This shows how the uncertainty of the famine worked against poorer livestock owners, who could not sell surplus animals early, but had to wait until the last moment to see if they would be forced to sell. By waiting until that moment, the nadir of the famine in May–June 1985, the whole structure of animal marketing in Darfur was operating against them. Consequently animal sales selectively penalized the poor, unlike animal deaths, which were more equitable. This was why a smaller number of sales than deaths led to a greater amount of destitution.

Buying Animals

In southern Darfur, the right to grazing and the price of fodder were the main constraints on animal survival. It follows that richer people who bought animals could bank on probably keeping them alive and then profiting when their price increased after the famine.

The fifteen years previous to the famine had seen an important restructuring of herds, away from cattle and towards sheep and goats. During the famine there was a further shift in herding strategies away from cattle and towards small stock. Most of this consisted in the preferential selling of cattle. But some cattle-owners sold cows and bought sheep. A good example of this was Angabo in southern Darfur.

The sample in Angabo contained six households that had owned sheep in mid-1984. This number was the same as in 1980. Two lost their sheep in the famine year. Others started to buy, selectively. At the nadir of prices in June 1985 the sale of one cow could buy four to six sheep or goats. By the end of 1985 there were eight new sheep-owners. The number of sheep had doubled during the year, and was still rising. In 1986, the five richest sheep-owners (four of them new to owning sheep) owned an average of eighty-five sheep each. Over 75 per cent of these sheep had been bought in the market during the famine and in its immediate aftermath. Of the eight new sheep-owners, four had sold cows in order to buy sheep, and two had previously owned cows which had died. Only one also bought cows, and then only three. In mid-1984 cows outnumbered sheep in Angabo by 2:1, by 1986 sheep outnumbered cows 3:1.

A Case Study of Mawashei Famine Camp

Most of the rural population followed, temporarily, a variety of low-status trades in order to live through the famine. They lived for a short while in the interstices of society. This was unfortunate for the people who were already occupying these niches and relied on an income from low-status trades before the famine occurred. These people were hit hardest by the famine. Not only were their markets diminished by the impoverishment of the people who bought their goods and services, but they found themselves competing with huge numbers of extra people trying to follow the same activities. It would be tempting to see these people as the ultimate victims; already destitute and 'non-belonging', deluged with competitors just as the economic niches of their existence were disappearing. Yet, even among the very poorest people, at the very nadir of the famine, it was possible to discern what peoples' long-term priorities were, and that they were struggling to achieve them in a coherent way.

Mawashei camp was situated on the western side of El Fasher city. The name *mawashei* is used to designate an animal market, and the camp was called this because it was situated next to the old camel market of El Fasher. In the middle of 1985 Mawashei was one of the most dreadful places in Darfur. People were iller and thinner than almost anywhere else; every day people were dying. It was a place where people were competing for the most unpleasant, unprofitable, and lowest-status trades. Everyone was poor and getting poorer. Among these trades there was a definite hierarchy, and certain groups of people were gradually forced down this hierarchy, and in some cases out of it altogether. There were two groups in the camp. One consisted of the people who were there to stay, who had been permanently forced out of the rural economy. The other consisted of short-term famine migrants, who would for the most part return to their villages to plant. The hundred households who remained in the camp in 1986 were studied.

The dynamics of the low-status trades can best be examined by breaking the population into groups according to when they arrived in the city: the 'core' group who came before 1983, and the arrivals of 1983 and 1984 respectively. The activities can also be divided, according to a hierarchy. Petty trading and craft activities were 'higher-status' activities. The more profitable trades (charcoal, water, fodder, etc.) were 'middle-status' and the remainder (labouring) were 'lowest-status'.

Table 6.6 shows how the core, 1983, and 1984 groups fared at the beginning and end of the famine year with respect to the 'higher-status', 'middle-status', and 'lowest-status' trades and activities. The

Table 6.6. *Differences in destitution in Mawashei camp*

Group	July 1984			July 1985		
	Core	1983	1984	Core	1983	1984
No. of households	14	13	57	14	13	57
Trades and activities[a]						
Higher-status	0.8	0.2	0.4	0.8	0.2	0.4
Middle-status	1.1	1.1	1.0	1.7	0.7	1.1
Lowest-status	0.1	0.4	0.3	0.1	3.0	1.4
Resources[b]	1.0	1.1	1.4	0.8	0.3	0.6
% of animals remaining July 1985[c]				19	17	25
% of farmland planted 1985				85	26	73

  [a] Figures refer to the mean number of activities per household to the nearest tenth.
  [b] Figures show mean resources relative to normative subsistence level, with 1.0 representing subsistence.
  [c] Numbers calculated in economic livestock units.

table shows the relative downward trajectories of the three groups. The 'core' group started off the poorest, but ended the least poor. The 1983 group started off in the middle, but ended up very much the poorest. The 1984 group started off at the top, but slipped so as to end in the middle.

The core group came to El Fasher between 1970 and 1982. Some of them had lived in El Fasher for years on the margins of the economy. Their economic profile prior to the famine resembled that of the poorer townspeople: they owned or rented small plots of land and found niches in petty trade and craft work (see de Waal 1987a, pp. 111–13 for a description of the urban poor in the Hai el Nasr quarter of El Fasher). They owned very few animals, because of the expense and difficulty of maintaining them in the town (in normal times the number of animals owned tends to decline with length of time in the town). All were Tunjur or Zaghawa, the ethnic groups that dominated the low-status activities in the town before the famine. Like the urban poor, they also relied upon activities such as selling water, charcoal, and firewood, often collected and carried by hand. To a lesser extent they also did some labouring, on farms and building sites, and portering and brickmaking.

During the famine year this 'core' group maintained their dominance of the 'higher-status' activities, and expanded their 'middle-status' activities. They managed to avoid complete impoverishment through their intimate knowledge of the workings of the town, and their established connections. For instance, over half of them were able to use their links in the market-place to obtain credit, compared to less than 10 per cent for the later arrivals. Eight of these fourteen households were above normative subsistence in 1984, and only two fell below by mid-1985.

The group of people that came to Mawashei during 1983 were devastated by the famine year. Their net economic resources in mid-1984 were higher than the core group; by 1985 all but one were normatively destitute.

During the famine, the new immigrants with donkeys displaced the 1983 group from selling charcoal and firewood into labouring and selling wild foods, trades with even lower status and less profit, and into planting fields for money. Planting was the lowest-paid work of all in 1985, and because planting near El Fasher occurs straight after the first useful rain, interfered with their own chances of cultivating. Many moved ultimately into begging and searching for scraps. It might appear strange that the newer immigrants pushed them downwards, rather than vice versa. This was because they were squeezed between the core group and the newer arrivals. They had not had time to become well-established, and acquire the skills, knowledge, and connections of the core group, and they were gradually losing their burden animals, and so losing their competitive edge in the 'middle-status' trades to later arrivals.

Only one of the households in this group had any animals left after the famine. These people planted very little of their own land in 1985. They had lost most of their staple 'middle-status' activities. They finished the famine year not only poorer than the other people in the camp, but also getting poorer faster. They were the people who collected around the warehouses of relief food in the rains of 1985, picking up each fallen grain of sorghum from the ground; they also claimed to have eaten half the population of camel fleas that still infested the site of the camp. The case of these people demonstrates how the sections of the urban poor without any regular income were pushed downwards into utter destitution by the coming of large numbers of famine migrants.

The 1984 group was much larger (fifty-seven households). These people were the rural poor of northern Darfur who had already suffered a succession of harvest failures even before the failure of the 1984 rains. Twenty-four of them were above subsistence in mid-1984, eleven a year later. Most of them planned to come only for the dry season and return home when it rained; but the rains failed and they went home for a month or two at most, long enough to see the millet seedlings wither.

The 1984 immigrants had one advantage over previous arrivals: more donkeys. Hence they followed a set of activities that was complementary to the core group, bringing firewood, fodder, and charcoal from outside the city. They were not a homogeneous group, and many also followed other, 'lower-status' activities too.

The people of Mawashei sold half of the animals they owned during 1984/5. Poor townspeople complained that the Mawashei immigrants were selling their animals for money so that they could subsidize working for wages that were below the minimum needed to sustain life. With no animals to sell, the urban poor could not compete. This implied that the immigrants' major concern was to maintain an income in the camp. An alternative explanation for the sale of so many animals was put forward by the immigrants themselves. This was the opposite: they strove to preserve their animals, and sold them only when they could not afford to feed them, or had no work at all and were truly desperate. This can be seen as a direct test of whether famine victims were motivated by entitlement to food, or by the longer-term goal of preserving the basis of their preferred way of life.

In the former 'subsidy' case we would expect the animal sellers to hold their position among the 'higher-' and 'middle-status' trades, with non-sellers and others being pushed downwards. In the latter 'desperation' case we would expect to find that people in the 'higher-' and 'middle-status' trades could afford to keep their animals, but those in the 'lowest-status' would be forced to sell them.

The core group sold some of their few animals to subsidize their continued dominance of the 'higher-status' trades. However, this group was exceptional. For years their way of life had depended on crafts and petty trading, both 'acceptable' activities, and they did not intend to return to rural life. Among the immigrants the story was different. There were 41 (non-burden) animal-owners in Mawashei in mid-1984. Twenty-nine of them sold animals. The 29 were on a downward path through the hierarchy of activities: in mid-1984 they

mainly followed 'middle-status' trades, but by mid-1985 they
mainly followed 'lowest-status'. Excluding one exceptional household with 35 camels, there were 11 households that did not sell:
these were also on a downward path, but not such a steep one. In
mid-1985 their 'middle-status' trades still outnumbered their
'lowest-status' activities. This suggests that people sold animals only
when forced to do so. It is an example of how even the poorest
people in Darfur were planning their activities around maintaining
the base of an acceptable future livelihood, not simply gaining access
to food.

Many people came to Mawashei during 1985; the total number of
immigrants during that year outnumbered those from all the
previous years by five to one. In mid-1985 the camp held 5,000
migrants, and El Fasher as a whole perhaps 25,000. It was their
coming that swamped the market in the low-status trades for a few
devastating months.

Out of the hundreds of households that came during 1985, only 15
remained a year later. One of these households was headed by a
woman who had 35 camels (we found no satisfactory explanation for
why she was there). There was also a group of Zaghawa potters, all
women, who set up just outside the main camp: even in a famine
camp the rules segregating the potters were kept. They were
something of a special case. Ten of them came in 1985 to join 6
already working in the camp. They had a marketable skill, and they
came in the 1985 wet season, when the camp was decreasing in size
and the market in low-status trades was improving as a result. The
potters were also all Zaghawa, and belonged to the special itinerant
potter-blacksmith caste; so their migration to Mawashei was distinct
from the distress migration of the other 1985 arrivals. Leaving aside
these cases, only 4 households that came in 1985 stayed. This is too
few for a socio-economic profile. But the very absence of the 1985
arrivals in 1986 is significant. Unlike the earlier arrivals, migration to
the town worked for them as a short-term safety-net. They came to
the town for a single dry season, when no farming was possible, and
were able to return to the villages to cultivate when the rains came.
What had seemed to outside observers like last-ditch migration on
the brink of death by starvation was in fact one part of a year-round
strategy for avoiding destitution. As these people left and the camp
became smaller, economic conditions improved for those who stayed
behind.

Mawashei received little attention from outside. The Red Crescent fed children and provided some medical care. But the city turned its back. The El Fasher Charitable Committee, led by worthy citizens such as sheikhs and merchants, organized distributions to the poor of the city. These included old and disabled people and widows, but that emphatically did not include the famine migrants (*nazihiin*). The term *nazihiin* was newly adopted during the famine years, and was used with strong derogatory connotations. A prominent member of the Charitable Committee described the Mawashei people as being 'thieves', 'beggars', 'lazy', and 'rich', not to mention 'Chadians'. He said 'If you were to go there at night, you would find the camp deserted as the inhabitants will be out stealing and hiding their loot.' The epithets served to exclude the people of Mawashei from the 'deserving' poor. The term 'Chadian' was significant, because 'Chadians' are by definition not citizens, and so it legitimated their exclusion. The term 'rich' excluded them from the category 'poor' altogether. The descriptions of the famine migrants by the citizens of the town provided a thesaurus of words which illustrate the social dimensions of normative destitution, and at the same time a huge and contradictory set of reasons for denying relief to them. The famine migrants did dispense charity among themselves, however. A notable instance was when they collected money to buy a donkey for a man whose wife had died, so that he could earn money by selling water.

This case-study shows that a famine camp is not a place where people sit and passively await relief or death. It is not a place where purposive behaviour gives way to irrationality, and neither is it a place where social structures and values dissolve. Even when people are eating spilled grains and camel fleas picked from the ground, they still plan ahead and keep their long-term priorities clear. Within the category of the destitute, the non-belonging, there are hierarchies and subdivisions and excluded castes: subsistent society re-creates itself among the destitute.

Women During the Famine

In Mawashei, women were doing significantly better than men. The 37 households headed by women were not only less poor, but getting poorer more slowly, than the 63 households headed by men. This holds even when the potters and the woman with 35 camels are excluded, and holds for all groups classified by year of arrival.

If all the sites are taken together, an interesting relationship emerges. The poorer the site, the better female-headed households were doing relative to male-headed. Table 6.7 shows this. The

Table 6.7. *Female : male advantage index*

Site[a]	F:M Advantage Index	Wealth of FHHs (ordinal)
Mawashei	174	6=
Jebel Si	118	6=
Saiyah	83	5
Hai el Nasr	76	4
Angabo	67	1
Legediba	52	2
Furawiya	51	3

[a] Nankose has been omitted because of the small number of female-headed households which it was possible to interview.

'female:male advantage index' was derived by taking the ratio of wealth (normative, adjusted for household size) in female- versus male-headed households, and multiplying it by the ratio between the rates of impoverishment of female- and male-headed households during the famine. This is expressed as a percentage. Thus a score over 100 represents an advantage to female-headed households, and under 100 an advantage to male-headed households.

Why were female-headed households faring better in some places? The most likely reason is to do with female advantages at the lower end of the hierarchy of occupations. In farm labour, women do the threshing: a thankless job in normal times, but a rewarding one during famine, because it has a fixed payment in grain. Women are also more likely to be paid in grain for harvesting: in normal times the man's cash wage is worth more in real terms, in famine it is the other way round. Women know more about wild foods. Many low-status trades are preferentially or exclusively open to women: gathering firewood, making pots, building. Those that are reserved for men, such as blacksmithing or selling water, may be more profitable, but require some capital. Hence the sexual division of agricultural labour and low-status trades favours men when times are good, but it favoured women when times were hard.

There was also a difference between poorer and more conservative north Darfur and richer and more 'progressive' south Darfur. In the conservative land-rights systems and family divisions of labour found in north Darfur, women have greater control over growing, storing, and disposing of grain than in the south, where 'joint' households are more common. In these joint households the woman does not own land or grow grain crops in her own right, and female-headed households have difficulty in acquiring enough land. (Pastoral communities such as Furawiya follow a different pattern altogether.)

A partial explanation is also that there had been selective out-migration from northern Darfur by richer male-headed households, thus leaving poor male-headed and female-headed households only. The 'advantage index' controls for such pre-famine distortions by including relative rate of impoverishment during the famine. The mean wealth ratio was 86, the mean rate of impoverishment ratio was 101. That is, households headed by women were generally poorer than those headed by men in 1984, but during the famine they did not get poorer faster.

7

Death

'Allah Takes from the Rich, and from the Poor'

Kuwebe lies in Dar Zaghawa, a hamlet of no more than a dozen households. In one desperately poor compound lived two co-wives, abandoned by their husband, and the brother of one of them, with his wife. In October 1985 these three women had five living children between them. A few months earlier, in the space of three weeks, these children had seen seven of their siblings die, of 'swollen heads'. We did not want to press the mothers any further with our questions. Instead we spoke to the sheikh, who merely commented 'Allah takes whomever he wishes.'

This response was universal. People were aware that children were most likely to die; otherwise the answers were consistent: 'It is God's will.' This type of answer is not incompatible with a deeper, or at least more complicated, model of why people might be dying. (By comparison, most people said drought was God's punishment, but then went on to elaborate on why and how this was occurring.) But when pressed as to whether the poor were dying more than the rich, there was no secondary explanation: 'Allah takes from the rich, and from the poor'; 'It is God's will'. The most specific answers were along the lines of 'We have no medicines.' This was frustrating. These otherwise articulate people were refusing to acknowledge the 'well-known fact' (demonstrated by Professor Sen, among others) that it is the poor who starve in famines, and not the rich.

Their attitude could be put down to simple fatalism, a stoical resignation in the face of the inevitable. The prevalent moral idiom of thinking about deaths might have made people unwilling or unable to consider patterns in mortality. Alternatively, people could have been influenced by hearing of deaths in richer families. One expatriate in Libya was remitting money back to his family near Furawiya; unbeknown to him they had all died. A government clerk just south of Kuwebe, with a good salary and many animals, lost all three of his children. These cases are a salient influence on thinking, whatever their statistical insignificance. I questioned people who registered the population, such as sheikhs, who would be more likely to see patterns in mortality. But all remained insistent, even in the face of blatantly leading questions. I dropped this line of questioning after a few dozen interviews.

For whatever reason, people in rural Darfur believed that wealth and poverty did not affect differences in mortality during the famine. This relates directly to the issue of 'choosing to starve'. The previous chapters have shown that people were not using all their resources to buy grain, but were choosing to go hungry and eat wild foods, in order to preserve the base of a future livelihood. Their comments suggest that they did not believe that going hungry would involve an increased risk of death. Either rural people were wrong, albeit for understandable reasons, or they were right, and we are faced with a very unexpected finding: rich and poor died indiscriminately. In this chapter I present the evidence to show that when rural people rejected the view that the poor were more likely to die than the rich, they were right.

Methods

Collecting and analysing demographic data involves many complex and technical issues. I have described the methods used in drawing the sample, analysing the data, and deriving a 'normal' mortality rate for comparison elsewhere (de Waal 1989). Here it suffices to make a few points. One, the sample consisted of 1,182 households in eight villages and two peri-urban areas (see Fig. 7.1). Two, famine causes disruptions to the rates of mortality, fertility, and migration found in a population, with the result that the population is, in demographic terms, not 'stable'. Most of the procedures used for checking the reliability of demographic data obtained from surveys or censuses can only be applied to a stable population. Hence the data are presented in a relatively raw form, without corrections for bias. However, this is a serious problem only for infant mortality rates: the data for other age groups are more reliable. Three, the 'normal' death rates are based on the Census of 1973. This implies a normal life expectancy at birth of about 49 years, an infant mortality rate

Fig. 7.1. *Darfur, showing sites of case-studies*

(under 1 year of age) of 124.6 per thousand and a child death rate (ages 1 to 4) of 63 per thousand.

During the years immediately before the famine there were many fewer births than normal, and during the famine the number of births dropped sharply, to about half what would be normal. There were thus fewer young children in the population than would be expected during normal times. This can be seen clearly in Fig. 7.2; the small cohort of children under 5 is due not only to higher

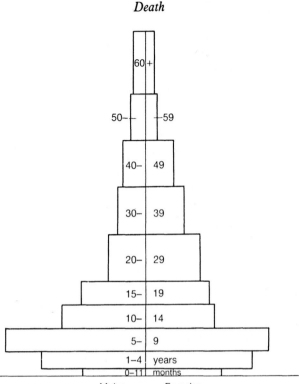

Fig. 7.2. *Age and sex structure of the population during 1986*

mortality, but also to the lower fertility. Lower fertility has been often recorded during famines (Watkins and Menken 1985; Ladurie 1979). Possible causes include amenorrhoea, anovulation, sexual abstinence, and separation of spouses. It is likely that the post-famine period has seen a 'rebound', with a high birth rate for a short period.

Children are more likely to die than adults, both during normal times and during famines. Consequently the 'normal' or 'expected' death rate, for all age categories for a population like that of Darfur in 1984 would have been comparatively low. We can calculate this 'expected' crude death rate to be between 13.0 and 13.3 per thousand per year.

The age–sex pyramid (Fig. 7.2) also reveals a marked lack of young adult men in rural areas. Overall, the sex ratio was 93.5 males per hundred females. For the age group 20–39 the ratio was 66.9. The missing men were to be found in urban areas and *Dar Sabah*. In Nyala town in a survey of 300 households the sex ratios were 96.3 males per hundred females overall and 117.0 for ages 20–39. In a survey of 187 households from Darfur in Omdurman, Gezira, and Gedaref the overall sex ratio was 117.7, rising to 149.6 for the ages 20–39.

Mortality Data

Excess Deaths

The crude death rate was 56.2 per thousand for the two years June 1984–June 1986, or an average of 28.2 for the two years taken separately. For the year from January 1985 the rate was 40.15.

If we assume the population of Darfur to have been constant at 3,149,000 throughout the years 1984–6, and the expected crude death rate to be 13.0, we can calculate figures for excess deaths. These are shown in Table 7.1.

Table 7.1. *Estimated gross deaths*

	Deaths		
	Expected	Actual	Excess
1984 (Jun.–Dec.)	27,300	36,800	9,500
1985	40,900	126,400	85,500
1986 (Jan.–May)	13,600	13,600	0
TOTAL	81,800	176,800	95,000

It is possible that these figures conceal an under-reporting of infant deaths amounting to up to 30 per cent. If we revise these figures on the basis of this possible underreporting, the average crude death rate rises to 30.2, the 1985 crude death rate to 42.6 and the total 1984–6 excess mortality rises to 107,800. On either assumption, death rates for 1985 were something over three times the normal.

If the conditions of 1984–6 had persisted indefinitely, life expectancy at birth would have been 32.5 years for males and 35.2 years for females. This compares with life expectancies at birth in 1973 of 47.7 and 54.3 years for men and women respectively. If the conditions of the calendar year 1985 alone had persisted, life expectancy for both sexes would have dropped to around 22 years.

Mortality Differentials

Season

Most of the excess deaths occurred during the dry season and the rains of 1985 (Fig. 7.3). In fact, only in these two seasons was the overall death rate significantly higher than normal (this and following significance figures are based on the Chi-squared test). The normal seasonal pattern of mortality was grossly exaggerated and slightly distorted during the famine year.

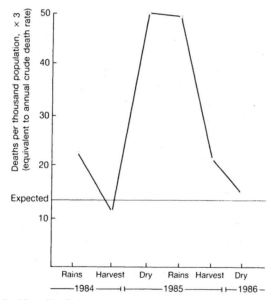

Fig. 7.3. *Mortality during each season*

Sex

Mortality was higher for men (30.8 per thousand per year) than women (26.7). This difference is not significant at the 5 per cent level, except for children aged between 5 and 9, who will be discussed later. Mortality was higher for men in most age groups, but among children aged 1 to 4 years, more girls died than boys. Higher mortality of men has often been noted in famines (Watkins and Menken 1985, p. 656; Dessalegn 1987).

Infants

Excess mortality was closely related to age (Fig. 7.4 and 7.5). The normal infant mortality rate is 124.6 per thousand. If we assume complete enumeration of deaths, infant mortality was *not* higher than normal during 1984–6. Infants were not dying more frequently than they did during normal times.

Even during the rains of 1985, when infant mortality was highest, it was still not significantly above normal (see Fig. 7.6). However, if we assume an underenumeration of infant deaths by 30 per cent the infant mortality rate was significantly above normal.

At worst infant mortality rose considerably less than child mortality. A rise of 30 per cent closely corresponds to the 32 per cent rise in mortality between ages 10 and 59.

The main reason why infant mortality did not rise as much as child mortality, if indeed it rose at all, is probably related to the weaning practices followed in Darfur. Infants are weaned late, always after twelve months, frequently only after eighteen. There is no bottle-feeding in rural areas. The infants are, therefore, less vulnerable to many of the diseases associated with unclean water supplies, and have the protection against infection provided by their mothers' milk. Mortality among women of child-bearing age was also very low. It is possible that weaning of children was delayed during the famine.

Children

Most of the excess mortality—over half the excess deaths—occurred among children between the ages of 1 and 4 years (Figs. 7.4–7.6). Among children aged 1 to 4 years the annual age-specific death rate jumped five times from 15.7 to 79.5 per thousand. This implies a jump in the child mortality rate from 63 per thousand (already very high), to 282. Child mortality was higher than normal during the

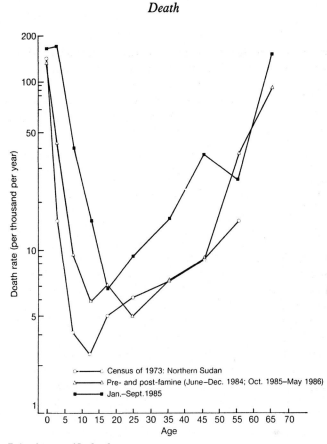

Fig. 7.4. *Age-specific death rates*

rains of 1984, when deaths among all other groups remained at normal levels for another six months. Mortality was exceptionally high during the dry season and rains of 1985. If the conditions of these months had persisted, 567 out of every thousand children would have died before their fifth birthday. The rate was slow to fall after this, remaining high during the 1985 harvest season, when the death rates for other age groups had returned to normal. Girls died more than boys, but the difference was not statistically significant. These children were the group at greatest risk by far during the

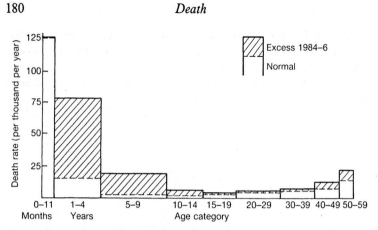

Fig. 7.5. *Excess deaths by age category (Source*: survey data; width of columns proportional to size of age cohort.)

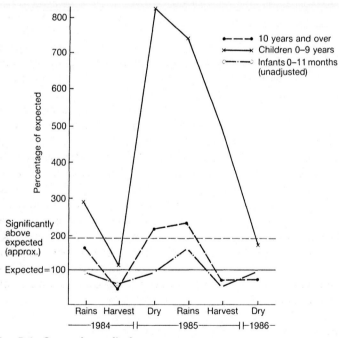

Fig. 7.6. *Seasonal mortality by age category*

famine. They had the lowest threshold of increased vulnerability, being the first to suffer increased mortality, and the last to return to normal mortality.

Children between the ages of 5 and 9 were less at risk than their younger brothers and sisters, with an annual death rate of 19.5 per thousand (compared to 3.2 normally). The increased mortality here was found only among boys. Mortality of girls of this age was never significantly above normal during the two years, whereas for boys it exceeded normal levels throughout 1985.

The 5–9 age group was the only one with a significant sex difference in mortality. This may be related to the difference between the domestic roles of boys and girls. Girls of this age are expected to help their mothers with the cooking. In Arab and African societies it is generally regarded as the norm for men to eat first, and women and children afterwards. Whatever may be true elsewhere, this does not apply to Darfur. It is true that women cook meals for their menfolk and then consume what is left over; but they also cook meals solely for themselves and their children. It is often said 'the cooking pot does not go hungry'. This would imply that a nutritional difference was the cause of the difference in mortality. Other aspects of the data suggest that this nutritional difference, if indeed it existed, was unlikely to have affected mortality. This factor, along with other factors mentioned in the discussion on female independence, is important, but not for mortality.

Looking more closely at the data shows that only in one site was there a significant difference between rates for boys and rates for girls among these children. This was the pastoral community of Furawiya, which alone accounted for 70 per cent of the excess deaths among boys of these ages. Here the boys are enormously more mobile than the girls, because they are responsible for herding animals. During the famine they covered huge distances southwards and thereby came into contact with many other communities, and also congregated with their animals around places where surface water was available. Surface water is notorious for its poor quality. It is likely that these migrations led to increased exposure to diseases. These exposure factors offer a more consistent explanation for this higher mortality.

Adults
Adolescents and adults below the age of 50 were marginally more at

risk than in normal times, but fewer than one in ten of the excess deaths occurred in these categories. Their death rates were significantly above normal during the dry season and rains of 1985. Older people were more at risk than before; the death rate for people in their 50s increased from 14.0 to 21.0 per thousand.

Interpretation of the data is once again more complex for those aged 60 and over. The raw age-specific death rate for people aged 60 and over exceeded 70 per thousand. This is certainly a substantial increase on normal levels, but the exact size is unknown.

The pattern of excess mortality attributable to famine was therefore highly specific with regard to season and age.

Other Factors Affecting Mortality

Destitution

What is most interesting about the socio-economic factors which would be expected to influence mortality is that they had little or no effect. The most obvious factor is poverty. Indicators of poverty had no evident relation to mortality, either for individual households or for communities. Mortality was actually slightly higher in house-holds that were subsistent in mid-1985 (30.1 thousand per year) than destitute ones (27.5) (difference not significant). For subsist-ence and destitution in mid-1984 the difference was in the expected direction, but also not significant. This result held for all the sites studied, except Angabo, where destitute people were more likely to die than the non-destitute ($p<0.05$). This will be discussed later. Related to this is the expected timing of mortality. Mortality would be expected to be highest when destitution was greatest and consumption least (during the *seif* of 1985), falling away as destitution lessened during the rains, and returning to normal by the harvest season as the rural economy recovered. This was not the case: there was a 'lag' in mortality, both its rise and its fall lagged behind indicators of destitution and food consumption (and child thinness).

It has been argued that during famines the relationship between destitution and mortality is concave, that is, the marginal effect of a unit of consumption increases with poverty (Ravallion 1987). It is certainly true that as nutritional status declines to the point at which it is classed as 'severe' deficiency, the risk of death accelerates

(Martorell and Ho 1984). If this relationship held in Darfur we might explain the absence of a difference between the mortality of subsistent and of destitute households as being due to the fact that only among the very poorest households did the risk of dying increase enough to show up in the statistics. However, mortality in the 125 very poorest households, all with a level of normative destitution of 0.1 or less, was not significantly higher than in the others.

Later I shall show a close relationship between location and mortality. Location is also correlated with wealth. It is possible that the influence of location masked the effect of wealth or poverty. To control for this, relative poverty in each site was looked at. Households were divided into ranked quartiles by normative subsistence for each site. Wealth in the year 1984 was considered, as this was closer to a significant relationship with mortality differences than that of 1985. Though death rates were highest in the poorest quartile, the differences were not significant. Fig. 7.7 shows the results of this exercise, summed for all the sites.

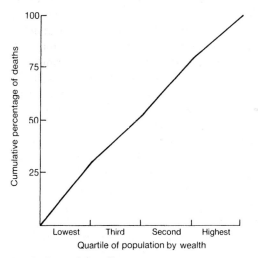

Fig. 7.7. *Destitution and mortality*

Occupation

There was a weak link between the kind of activities followed to prevent destitution during 1984/5 and the risk of dying. Risk of dying was not significantly higher for people who followed low-status trades during the dry season of 1985 than for those who did not.

This lack of a significant difference masks some interesting interactions which illustrate that what was important was not the fact of following a low-status activity, but the migration that was involved. It was not what people did that mattered, but where they did it. If we take the six cases where following a low-status trade during the dry season of 1985 involved leaving the village, the picture becomes more interesting. In five of these cases the mortality difference was in the expected direction: death rates for people who were following low-status activities were higher than for those who were not ($p<0.05$ for the five taken together, $p<0.05$ for Legediba and Sabola, the others approached significance). In one case, Furawiya, the difference was in the opposite direction, approaching significance.

Knowledge of local conditions makes these differences explicable. In Furawiya there was an outbreak of measles during the dry season, which out-migrants missed. Out-migrants went to towns such as Kebkabiya and Zalingei, where there were no large famine camps, and where sanitary facilities were generally good. In the villages where death rates among out-migrants were raised, but not significantly (Jebel Si, Saiyah, Angabo), the local towns where the out-migrants went (Kebkabiya again, Mellit, and Ed Da'ien respectively) were similarly not too bad. For the people of Sabola and especially Legediba, the local town was Buram, in which there was an appalling famine camp containing 20,000 people, with minimal sanitation and severe crowding. Hence the link that existed between dry-season occupation and mortality was created by the different locations where people were living.

Ownership of Livestock
Mortality was linked to ownership of animals. The mortality rate for people who owned animals was 24.2 per thousand per year, which is significantly lower ($p<0.05$) than that for those owning no animals. Animals are a form of wealth, so this finding would appear to contradict the earlier finding that poverty, as defined by normative destitution, did not affect mortality. However, the numbers of animals owned made no difference to the risk of dying. Instead there was a simple threshold, above which the risk of mortality was

reduced. This threshold was at a level slightly above one animal. The implication is that the important factor here was access to milk, which followed from ownership of one mature female animal.

Location

In three of the sites studied mortality was different from the overall rate. The sites were Sabola (high, $p<0.01$), Nankose (high, $p<0.05$) and Saiyah (low, $p<0.05$). In all the other sites mortality was not significantly different from the average for 1984–6.

The reasons for these differences are revealing. Sabola was the southernmost site studied. Ethnically and demographically it is closer to Bahr el Ghazal region, where very high mortality rates are normal. In Bahr el Ghazal life expectancy at birth was 34.2 years in 1973. The (adjusted) crude death rate of 'western southerners', an ethnic grouping that includes the people of Sabola, was between 32 and 36 per thousand in 1955/6 (Demeny 1968): a figure double that of Darfur at the same date. In Sabola there is no protected water source, no health service and a high prevalence of malaria. Seasonal variations in mortality were much smaller there than in the other sites studied.

Saiyah was the village with the lowest mortality, despite being in one of the poorest areas. Saiyah has protected wells and received supplementary foods from the Red Crescent Society throughout the famine. These included milk and oils. Much of the credit must also go to the medical assistant who was able to provide a continuously functioning health service. Almost all the excess mortality occurred here during the dry season of 1985. At this time the normal population of 1,600 people in Saiyah was swelled by an additional 6,000 migrants who encamped on the northern side of the village, and there was an outbreak of typhoid.

Nankose, with mortality significantly higher than average, demonstrates the reverse. It was the richest site studied. It has no health service to speak of (the health assistant is known as 'Malaria', after his only diagnosis), but plenty of milking animals, and the best food supply (grain and vegetables) of any of the sites studied. There is a 'protected' well in the village, but people stand on its rim to draw water, having stepped up from a marsh of animal excreta surrounding it, and the area is notorious for its poor water. It is low-lying and damp, and malaria was common.

The other sites all have one of the following: a health service (El

Fasher, Jebel Si), clean water (Legediba), and plentiful milk (Furawiya). Some of the mortality in Furawiya was due to an outbreak of measles. Angabo has a partially functioning health service and partially clean water: there is a deep bore-hole, but drinking water is scooped from the same trough that the animals drink from. In Arara, fertility was very low in the years preceding the famine, largely because of high out-migration of men. This served to depress the death rate during the famine. Still, with no health service, no protected water supply, few animals, and less food aid than any other site, but only average mortality, Arara remains something of a mystery. In a sense, however, geographical variations in excess mortality need no explanation, because the effects of a health crisis can be almost random. It cannot be predicted where a major killer such as measles will strike.

Causes of Death

Rural clinic records provided a guide to the major diseases that were killing people. These consisted of the normal pattern of diseases in rural Darfur, but amplified. The most frequently mentioned cause was diarrhoea. This fits well with the age-specific and seasonal pattern of mortality identified. Weaned children are most vulnerable to diarrhoeal diseases. In drought-stricken Darfur, diarrhoea was both a dry- and a wet-season disease. During the dry season many wells ran dry, and those that did not were often short of water. The drought itself was a major health crisis, irrespective of food availability. When water became this scarce, bacterial concentration increased. When the rains did come, they were very heavy at first, and it is likely that though the quantity of water increased, its quality did not, due to pollutants being washed into the wells. Even where water was no scarcer than in normal years, the population concentrations around large villages put a strain on the water and sanitation facilities.

The other most mentioned causes of death were, first, measles and, second, malaria. Measles is a dry-season disease, and was found in all parts of the region. Malaria is a wet-season disease, found largely in the southern part of Darfur. Other diseases mentioned included typhus, meningitis, and pneumonia. Tuberculosis seemed relatively rare. Some records were less than informative, including the frequent certified cause of death as 'fever', and on one occasion 'found dead'.

Social disruption itself caused death. Society became more violent during the famine. People were poisoned from eating improperly prepared wild foods. A man in Furawiya was buried when trying to deepen a well that collapsed on him.

Starvation itself was never cited as a cause of death. This omission is common during famines. It is usually attributed to the fact that health records allow for the mention of only one cause of death, so that the proximate cause (a disease) is normally recorded, rather than a supposed underlying cause such as starvation (Sen 1981, p. 203).

Models of Famine Mortality: The Starvation Model

Diseases were the proximate cause of death in famine-stricken Darfur. The most commonly adopted model of famine mortality is the 'starvation model'. This accepts that diseases may be the proximate cause of death in famine, but claims that undernutrition is the underlying cause (Sen 1981). Lack of food consumption is the engine of excess deaths, with epidemics of disease reduced to an 'error' factor (Ravallion 1987, p. 32).

The model is represented schematically below, with the arrows representing 'increases the risk of':

Model 1: 'Starvation Model'

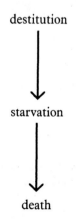

destitution

starvation

death

Mortality is driven by starvation, though manifest in disease. This appears to be so self-evident that it would seem foolhardy to deny it. Yet the evidence from Darfur suggests that it did not hold there in 1984/5. This model does not fit the data presented.

Models of Famine Mortality: The Health Crisis Model

The main evidence against the 'starvation model' is the fact that socio-economic indicators failed to predict differences in mortality, but public-health factors did. Evidence on the proximate causes of death is secondary.

It is possible that if the sample had been larger and more carefully selected, some of the variance in death rates could have been explained by measurements of poverty, implying undernutrition, without intervening variables of differences in access to health care. But even if this were so, the greater part of the variation could only be explained by community-health factors. Unfortunately, because quantification of these community-health factors is not possible with the data available, statistical testing of this hypothesis is not meaningful. Moreover, there are problems with using socio-economic status variables to stand proxy for nutritional status. If maintaining a nutritional state is not the priority of a household, the wealth and income of a household may not be related to the nutritional status of its members in a simple manner. Also, chances of dying may be related to factors such as physique, which are to a large extent genetically endowed.

The 'health crisis' explanation of famine mortality is therefore a residual explanation. It is also an explanation at a socio-economic level (like entitlement theory) and not at the level of clinical epidemiology. However, it is worth presenting and refining, because it is least at compatible with this and other data. In the 'health crisis' model, famine causes both destitution and death, but it causes death in parallel to destitution, not because of it. What was seen in Darfur was drought and social disruption leading to severe but localized health crises throughout the region. This model fits the facts on mortality and mobidity. The challenge is to make it fit the known ecology of nutrition and disease as applied to Darfur, and develop a simple explanation for how some 100,000 people could die of famine without starvation contributing to any deaths.

Model 2: 'Health Crisis Model'

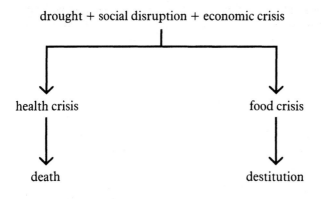

drought + social disruption + economic crisis

health crisis   food crisis

death   destitution

The increase in mortality could be due either to an increase in exposure to potentially fatal diseases, or to an increase in susceptibility to them, or to a combination of the two.

An increase in susceptibility to diseases is an obvious possibility when a population, or large sections of it, are suffering from a shortage of food. Yet, there is little evidence for this occurring. Three lines of argument are relevant here. One is a reiteration of the points already made concerning the lack of a link between destitution and mortality. If the shortfall in food consumption increased susceptibility, we would expect it to increase susceptibility most among those who had least to eat, and we would expect food consumption to reflect access to food and money to buy food. Yet, food and income indicators, with the sole exception of access to milk, completely failed to predict mortality. If undernutrition affected mortality, the effect was slight relative to other factors.

The second line of argument refers explicitly to evidence on undernutrition, specifically among the most vulnerable category, children under 5. In Darfur during the famine, child malnutrition rates were abnormally high. However, almost all of this malnutrition was classed as 'moderate' (by anthropometric classification). The debate on mild and moderate malnutrition and mortality has generated controversy but few hard data. What few studies there are suggest that mild or moderate malnutrition does not increase the likelihood of death at all, or at worst, only slightly, when other factors are controlled for (Chen *et al.* 1980; Kasongo Project Team 1983; Martorell and Ho 1984; Tomkins 1986*a*). Severe malnutrition does strongly affect mortality. But in Darfur severe malnutrition was relatively rare. The cases that did occur were almost always a consequence of disease rather than the result of lack of food consumption *per se*.

The third line of argument is based on access to health services. It could be argued that the famine caused a breakdown of health services, which reduced the capacity to treat illnesses that did occur. It is certainly true that rural (and urban) health services in Darfur had deteriorated by the time of the famine. In Dar Masalit in particular, most rural health centres ceased to function in the early 1980s; by 1985 many of them had even lost their roofs. But the decline was chronic rather than acute. Health services reached their lowest point when the famine started, before the sharp rise in mortality. The increase in mortality was not caused by the failures of the health service.

Nevertheless there is an interesting, though minor, interaction at work. This interaction consisted of differences in access to sanitation and health services, based on wealth, in a few places. Thus there was a destitution–mortality link, albeit an indirect one, and an effect of lower susceptibility to disease among certain groups.

In Darfur this type of differential access to health services based on social class or wealth is found mainly in towns. In villages everyone shares the same water supply, and there either is or is not a health service.

In Nyala town there were mortality differences that appeared to be based upon differences in access to sanitation and health care. The survey found marked differences in death rates between households in high-, middle-, and low-income areas of the town. In the areas defined as 'high-income' the annual crude death rate during 1984–6 was 8.4 per thousand, in the 'middle-income' areas it was 31.2, and in the 'low-income' areas it was 45.6. The difference between the medium and low groups was significant at the 1 per cent level, that between the high and medium groups was not significant. This was also the case in Angabo village, where a mortality difference linked to wealth existed. Angabo is close to Ed Da'ien town, so that members of richer households could take advantage of the medical facilities there.

Severe undernourishment and differential access to health services are the exceptions that prove the rule. There is little evidence for supposing that the people of Darfur became significantly more susceptible to disease during the famine. Why then, did up to 100,000 of them die? The answer lies in analysing increased exposure to disease.

One important factor in this was the decline in both the quantity and the quality of water. A second was the large-scale movement of people, which exposed both the migrants and their hosts to infections carried by the other group. Large concentrations of people accelerated the rates of transmission of infectious diseases. The new situation was equivalent to a sudden change from a dispersed or rural-type environment to a concentrated or urban-type environment. This also put pressure on water supplies and sanitation facilites in the host communities: the public health environment became degraded, for hosts and migrants alike. The increase in exposure to diseases meant that more of the most vulnerable group (weaned children) fell ill of one, or more seriously, two diseases. With simultaneously increased exposure to several diseases, as the chance of contracting a disease increases arithmetically the chance of complications increases geometrically. For diseases such as measles, it is the presence of complications such as pneumonia or diarrhoea that is the single most significant factor in raising the risk of mortality (Foster 1984).

This can be modelled in a simple manner (Fig. 7.8). Imagine a population of 400 people exposed to two diseases, M and D. Exposure and susceptibility are such that each disease has a prevalence of 40 cases, and the prevalence of the two diseases occurring together is 4. Assume that the diseases only threaten life if

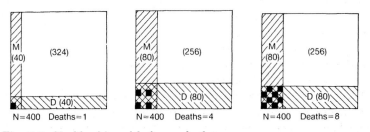

Fig. 7.8. *Health-crisis model of excess deaths*

they occur together, with a case–fatality ratio among these cases of complications of 1 in 4. Hence, the number of persons likely to die is 1. Now assume that exposure to both diseases doubles, and susceptibility remains constant. The number of cases of M or D or both will rise from 76 to 144; that is almost double. But the number of life-threatening cases of both M and D together will quadruple, from 4 to 16. With an unchanged case–fatality ratio (unchanged susceptibility) the number of deaths will also quadruple, to 4.

In addition, if diseases spread faster, children will catch them when they are younger and more vulnerable. Measles is the prime example. In dispersed rural communities, children are likely to catch measles at the age of perhaps 3 or 4 years, when the case–fatality rate is between 1 and 2 per cent. But in concentrated urban-type environments the faster rate of transmission means that children catch the disease at 1 year old. At this age, the case-fatality rate is 6 per cent (Foster and Pifer 1971).

Developing the M-and-D model, if the population is exposed to the diseases at a younger age, we may (conservatively) assume a doubling of the case–fatality ratio, in this case from 1 in 4 to 1 in 2. The number of deaths from the model population will thus rise to 8: which is 8 times the initial number.

It is well documented that disease is a major cause of under-nutrition. With a huge increase in the incidence of life-threatening disease among children, it follows that rates of undernutrition will rise. Children who are or have been ill will be thin, they will look as though they are dying of starvation. Disaster tourists, seeing these stick-thin children with their protuding bellies and visible ribs, will jump to their erroneous conclusions. At this stage, malnutrition will contribute to children being more susceptible to catching a further killer disease. But in Darfur it was disease itself that had brought them to this stage.

Therefore, famine mortality in Darfur can be explained simply by a changed disease environment. It was mostly or wholly disease-driven and not starvation-driven.

One proviso must be included, and one objection addressed. The proviso is that weanlings were the most vulnerable group. Access to milk was a factor in differences in mortality. In Saiyah, access to dried milk and oils may well have been important to the diet of weanlings. The status variables used to stand proxy for consumption are likely to have been better predictors of consumption of staple foods than of weaning-foods. Access to grain did not affect differences in mortality, but access to these other foods may have done so to a small extent.

The objection is that the migrations and consequent social and environmental disruptions which create health crises are themselves unleashed by a failure in people's access to food. Thus, while undernutrition may not directly contribute to increased mortality, through increased susceptibility to disease, it may indirectly contribute, because the hungry are forced to migrate. This has some truth. However, it is an explanatory schema that yields little. People migrate for many reasons. Lack of food is only one reason, albeit an important one. In addition, in some instances those who migrate find healthier conditions that those who do not. We have found a focus on hunger to be inadequate for explaining rural people's responses to famine. It follows that a focus on hunger is also inadequate for explaining the origins of health crises. Instead, in order to identify the underlying causes of famine mortality, the focus should be on the entirety of social disruption that constitutes famine. In order to identify the immediate causes, the focus should be on the nature of health crises themselves.

Conclusion

The central problem was to explain a threefold increase in mortality over a single year, including a sixfold increase in child mortality. That has now been done. The model in its simplest form assumes an increase in exposure to diseases such as diarrhoea and measles. Underconsumption of staple foods as an influence on mortality does not occur. This is contrary to commonsense, but seems to be true.

The account of the famine in Darfur in 1984/5 includes neither mass starvation unto death nor mortality manifest in disease but driven by starvation. This does not mean that starvation-driven mortality does not occur in famines. A more severe famine than that in Darfur could result in the appearance of a destitution–starvation–death sequence. This would supplement but not replace the health crisis model, by adding starvation and death as consequences of destitution at the bottom right: in effect appending the starvation model to the health crisis model. Most modern African famines appear to approximate to the experience in Darfur.

It is important to note that the theoretical claim that famines do not imply starvation is *not* based on the empirical finding that starvation and undernutrition were not the causes of excess deaths in Darfur during 1984/5. The two claims are theoretically distinct. If starvation had occurred in Darfur, the conceptual centre of the famine, for its victims, would still have remained destitution. If no excess deaths had occurred during 1984/5, the event would still have been a famine, and a *maja'a*. The striking empirical finding presented in this chapter is incidental to the main arguments of this book concerning the concept of 'famine'.

The people of Darfur refused to recognize any effects of poverty or destitution on mortality, insisting that it was merely 'God's will' that determined which children were going to die. Given that respondents were drawing their information from their locality, and could not be expected to compare places which were far apart, such a 'random' model is a better predictor of patterns of mortality than the starvation model.

People in Darfur believed that going hungry in the way that they were doing was acceptable: it did not increase their risk of dying. They were right. They were not 'choosing to starve', with its implications of choosing to risk death. Instead, under enormous stress, they were choosing to suffer hunger in order to try to preserve their way of life.

8

Relief

Perceptions of Outsiders

The famine in Darfur became most visible to outsiders during the first half of 1985. Journalists began to visit Darfur, and relief agencies began their operations (although there was to be no sign of major UN agencies such as UNICEF and World Food Programme for many months). Aid agency officials, journalists, politicians, and other sundry disaster tourists flocked to Darfur. Disaster tourism reached its peak shortly after the EEC relief programme launched an airlift of grain in May 1985, making it possible to visit Darfur with relative ease.

These disaster tourists saw the issues of famine and relief in simple terms. The harvest had failed, thin people were to be seen congregating around towns and relief camps; unless huge amounts of food aid were supplied, most or all of the population would starve to death. In *The Times* of 27 June, a journalist wrote with all sincerity that there would be 'half a million people [dead] in the next two months, maybe more'. Other journalists and relief workers made predictions that were similar or worse. In fact, based on the figures presented in Chapter 7, we can estimate that about 20,000 people died over the following two months. Even the most cautious estimates of imminent mortality turned out to be exaggerations. The lowest published predictions were made in an unsigned article in *Africa Confidential* in April: '500,000 to 2 million of Sudan's 24 million population will be dead before the harvest in November'. A breakdown of the numbers of 'affected' and 'severely affected' people puts one third of them in Darfur, implying that excess deaths in Darfur would number between 167,000 and 667,000—between two-and-a-half and ten times the actual number who died.

Outsiders' estimates of imminent famine mortality in Darfur in

1985 were fortunately wrong. The outsiders did not deliberately exaggerate the severity of the crisis in order to alarm the world. These were sincerely held sombre predictions. The outsiders who made these predictions were ill-informed, but no better-informed outsiders were available to correct them, and local opinions were too often not sought or were ignored.

Outsiders' complementary concern was with food aid. They reasoned that unless food aid arrived in huge quantities, mass death through starvation was unavoidable. The outsiders saw Darfur as a problem—an emergency—which only they could solve. Previous chapters have shown how the victims of this emergency were in fact very skilled and tenacious in the way in which they faced the crisis: to an extent the emergency dealt with itself, the problem solved itself. This chapter continues the story of how the people of Darfur faced the famine, by analysing indigenous modes of famine relief, and looking at the role of the international relief effort.

Non-poor people who give aid to poor people have a marked tendency to see their aid as central to the poor peoples' lives. Most outsiders who have contact with famines in Africa do so through the work of aid agencies. All too often famines are discussed as though the successes and failures of relief were the most important factor in the survival of people affected by the famine. This study shows that this is not the case. Food aid was not the most important element in surviving the famine. This does not mean that the aid programmes were not important, just that they were less important than the people who worked on them and publicized them often believed.

During the famine there were at least four different 'ideologies' of relief-giving, leading to different ideas of who was entitled to relief. The people holding each ideology rarely paused to consider the legitimacy (or even the existence) of the other ideologies. As a result the relief programmes were full of struggles and misunderstandings, over and above the problems caused by greed, mismanagement, and what might euphemistically be called divided loyalties.

Indigenous Famine Relief

There wasn't much indigenous famine relief. But during most of the famine the meagre amounts of local assistance were more important to people's survival than the food aid donated by international agencies. The ideologies, understandings, and power relations that lay behind local relief can also be seen in the responses to the millions of sacks of relief sorghum that arrived later.

Two Relief Ideologies

In Darfur two indigenous ideologies of relief existed side by side. One ideology can be glossed as 'Sudanic', and the other as 'Islamic'. The two have contrasting claims concerning who is entitled to relief.

The 'Sudanic ideology' draws the boundaries of those who are entitled to relief at the boundaries of the community: at members of the same kinship group and those who have become 'fictive kin' by having assimilated to the community. Newly arrived people and those such as artisans who have no status in the community are excluded. Inside the community, the people who receive help are typically those who are physically unable to support themselves even in normal times. This includes old and disabled people, and young orphans, who form a group that might be described as the 'deserving' or 'belonging' poor. People who may in material terms be even poorer but who do not belong to the community are the 'undeserving' or 'non-belonging' poor, or are not regarded as poor at all.

The 'Islamic ideology' makes a set of claims that often conflict. All Moslems, including strangers, are entitled to relief. Islam makes a virtue of migration, and the *haj* pilgrimage to Mecca is one of the 'five pillars' of the religion. Mahdism in western Sudan has also been associated with migration: the *tahjir* forced migration during the nineteenth century to join Mahdist armies in Omdurman, and during the twentieth century to the neo-Mahdist centre at Abba Island on the Nile. More generally, all natural things are seen as created by God for the use of humankind. It follows that any Moslems can make use of any natural resources so long as they do not infringe the rights of others: 'a group of [West African] Fellata in the Sudan when asked why they left their country and came here replied "[we] came and found land without a master but Allah"' (al Bashir 1978, p. 38). The corollary of the encouragement to migration is the duty of hospitality, and the giving of sanctuary. The customary Arab greeting is 'Welcome! My house is your house.'

Strangers are to be welcomed and assisted in their further travels. One eighth of the Islamic tax *zaka* is to be given to travellers, including pilgrims.

Another aspect to Islam is that it contains a material notion of the poor, which has a wider constituency than those included under the 'Sudanic ideology'. According to the Koran, one eighth of the *zaka* is supposed to be given to the *fagiir* and one eighth to the *miskin*. Koranic law as interpreted by the Condominium authorities glossed the *fagiir* as 'the poor and indigent, being good Moslems, who are without means of subsistence' and the *miskin* as 'those who can support themselves throughout the year only with difficulty' (Civsec 56/3/26). This implies a material basis for judging who are the 'deserving' and 'undeserving' poor, irrespective of membership of the community.

The Arabic words for 'poor' mentioned above, along with other terms such as *mohtaj* ('needy'), are closely associated with the Islamic duties of giving assistance to the poor. This is the familiar issue of 'the poor' being defined by the non-poor, with respect to their right or need to receive assistance. These terms suggest a sophisticated tradition of charity. However, in rural areas, the subtle distinctions between the terms for 'poor' are often not understood, and in practice the 'Sudanic ideology' of giving is dominant. Insofar as the categories of *miskin* and *fagiir* are used in Darfur, they refer to people within the community who are disabled or old, and those threatened with slipping into destitution and non-belonging. The most common distinction drawn between the categories is that the *fagiir* do not have food enough for one day, and the *miskin* do not have enough for one year. Although strangers are usually given hospitality, systematic charity as enjoined by the Koran is rarely extended to them, and travellers are regarded as disreputable. Artisans are likewise regarded as untrustworthy.

Some local charitable institutions, such as the Red Crescent Societies, were notable exceptions to this. In the discussion of Mawashei camp it was noted how the Red Crescent supplied relief aid to the migrants there, on the grounds of their material poverty, while the Charitable Committee of El Fasher town refused to do so. In other parts of Darfur the story was similar. There was a notable spread of Red Crescent branches through northern Darfur during 1984/5. Much of the time they were concerned with precisely those people who were neglected by the traditional forms of charity, and demonstrated universalistic humanitarian principles (York 1985).

Forms of Relief

Most of the charity given during the famine consisted of gifts within extended families. The help took the form of money, food, or labour. The recipients were mostly old people, disabled people, widows, or orphans. 'Grass orphans' were commoner than 'real' orphans, because adults were more prone to leave than to die. These children mostly joined the families of relatives. Old or disabled people typically remained alone in households, unable to work to support themselves. These people were much less mobile than younger and fitter members of the community. Consequently in communities with net out-migration, the net flow of assistance was from outside inwards, and vice versa. Hence Saiyah and Jebel Si were net 'recipient' communities, whereas Angabo and Nankose were net 'donor' communities. Furawiya played host to many people from scattered satellite villages where wells had dried up, and was a net 'donor' community, while itself receiving assistance from southern Darfur. This was similar to the pattern of relief given in normal times, as households moved through the demographic cycle, and the population slowly moved southwards. These flows of aid diminished and sometimes dried up altogether during the famine.

There were some acts of relief peculiar to the famine, but most were either reluctant, idiosyncratic, or brief. Some people had abandoned children thrust upon them. In a publicized case a woman found herself a day's work in a town house, and brought her children along, only to disappear, leaving them to the care of the household. There were some spectacular individual gifts. One Jalul Rizeigi from Kutum sold 100 camels in El Fasher in 1984 and gave the money to his kinsmen. Some merchants provided meals for all the children in their home villages. There are also reports that during Ramadan 1985, which fell in June, more *sadaga* alms were given to the poor. Certainly the onset of the rains saw frenetic performances of the *istisgha* rain prayer, which involves the performance of religious duties, one of which is giving alms.

As normal links of assistance began to break, famine relief itself, based on action by the community or its leaders, became more important. The nature of this varied with the normal patterns of political life in communities. The discussion will contrast two patterns of indigenous famine relief. The first case is that of the Zaghawa, who tended to dispense patronage, with a corollary of control. The second is that of the Berti, who relied on the distribution of material relief by institutions, whether village committees, Red Crescent societies, or local government.

The 'Zaghawa Pattern' of Relief

Among the Zaghawa, most help was given in the form of repayable loans of cash or grain. These were not akin to commercial credit for productive activities, the *sheil* system, which had anyway virtually ceased to function by 1984/5. They were loans from shopkeepers, middlemen, petty traders, herders, and farmers as well as professional merchants. They were most often known as *gorda* or *deen*. This system is found throughout Darfur, though it is most prominent among the Zaghawa.

The creditor advances money or food to the household, usually before the beginning of the rains when money and food are expensive, and accepts repayment after the harvest, when they are cheap. Interest is often as much as 100 per cent, doubling for the following year if the debtor reneges. The creditor can also confiscate collateral, such as animals, and sometimes even land. Although many loans appear to be interest-free, there is a hidden profit made by the creditor on the fall in the grain price between granting a loan of grain and its repayment in cash.

The commercial overtones of the *gorda* system conceal the fact that it is primarily operated as a means of extending power in community politics. To obtain a loan it is more important to have kin ties than material collateral. Specifically, a prominent member of the community needs to guarantee the repayment of the loan. This excludes sections of the community from obtaining loans, such as immigrants, and sometimes single women. On the other hand, poor people who are in good standing are considered creditworthy.

This could be seen clearly in Legediba. Eighty-five per cent of households tried to obtain *gorda*. The difference between those who succeeded and those who did not was not collateral or income, but ethnicity: three-quarters of the borrowers were Zaghawa. No Zaghawa men and only four Zaghawa women were refused a loan. Kinship ties, not collateral, were what counted. This was despite the fact that in Legediba, unlike other sites, the creditors were mostly professional merchants and commercial farmers. They were all Zaghawa. In Legediba these merchants wield the power that in the north is held by the Zaghawa aristocracy in their traditional role as senior sheikhs. Most are the brothers, sons, or *mandubs* of these sheikhs. They were perfectly aware that many of the loans they had made were irrecoverable. After the harvest of 1985 about two-thirds of the debts remained unrepaid: merchants estimated that half of these would have to be written off, and fully 20 per cent of those in debt admitted that they could not pay and would default. Debtors were concerned more with the social aspects of debt, the shame associated with dependence and clientship. The creditors gave loans not only as a commercial enterprise but also as a form of patronage, in place of the traditional loan of milking animals to poor relatives in return for political allegiance. This was related to the Zaghawa *mandubs'* need to consolidate power in the face of the dispute over land and authority with the Habbaniya.

In Dar Zaghawa itself the practice of loaning milking animals had virtually stopped by the time of the famine. Loans of animals to rebuild herds were also rare. *Gorda* was becoming commoner, along with assistance to an impoverished household to migrate south. There were also few gifts or sharings of grain among the Zaghawa, perhaps because having been previously herders, they had no tradition of distributing grain.

Community politics appears at the heart of charity among the Zaghawa. This was relief with many exploitative strings. Yet even in the depths of the famine, Zaghawa families could obtain loans of money or *'esh*, in a way that more equitable communities could not.

The 'Berti Pattern' of Relief

The Berti provide a contrast. They have a more egalitarian ethic, based on the village community and on the production and consumption of millet.

The Berti have a longer history of diaspora than the Zaghawa. From the eighteenth century Berti villages have been moving south. The largest movement occurred during *Julu* and its aftermath in 1913/14, when much of eastern Darfur was colonized. A steady trickle of settlers followed until today. These newly settled areas have a similar *goz* ecology to the Berti homeland, and settlers re-created similar farming and social systems to those found in their northern homelands. The Zaghawa diaspora has created economic and ecological diversity, the Berti diaspora only re-created extensive cultivation of millet on *goz*. Moreover, the northern and southern Berti are not politically linked. When eastern Darfur was settled, the four most prominent settlers petitioned Ali Dinar to become *shartais*. Sultan Ali obliged, and made them answerable only to El Fasher, and independent of their northern kin. Traditionally, a Berti sheikh has jurisdiction over a strictly limited geographical area. Despite the continuing southward migration, Berti political authority remains geographically fragmented. South–north assistance occurs only within extended families. Because donor and recipient both farm millet on *goz*, their periods of want are likely to coincide, and the northerners will need relief just when the southerners are least able to give it. 1984/5 was a case in point.

During the famine, Berti villages were thrown back on their own resources. *Zaka* grain-tithe payments were suspended, and in the few cases where a little grain remained in the *zaka* stores, some redistribution occurred. A traditional measure during famine is the *dara*, whereby rich and poor alike eat in public, sharing their food. A few instances of this occurred in small villages near Mellit, Saiyah, and Um Kedada, but only during the early days of the crisis. These measures lapsed because they centre on gifts of millet, and even richer Berti farmers did not have spare millet during 1984. Unlike the 'commercial' charity of Legediba, the 'pure' charity of the 'Berti pattern' broke down under the stress of the famine.

There is also a second strand to the Berti pattern of relief. This is a strand that the outsider is liable to miss, because he himself is a part of it. This is exemplified by the case of Saiyah. In Chapter 2, Saiyah was presented as a 'disaster tourist-spot', and as a misleading paradigm for Darfur. Partly this was because the institutions of Saiyah (the sheikhship, land tenure) have militated against change in a way that is unusual in Darfur, so that the visitor is given a false impression of rural stagnation and helplessness. The second reason is because the people of Saiyah do have an effective strategy of meeting the threat to their way of life: they obtain assistance from outside.

Saiyah is situated on the old 'Forty Days' Road' that linked Darfur and Egypt across the desert. It was the first water-point north of Mellit. The people made their living from travellers and long-distance traders in luxury goods. They still do. A road to the el

Atrun oasis and Libya runs through Saiyah. Of equal importance is disaster tourism. Saiyah has been outstandingly successful in obtaining relief from outside. In 1984 the Kuwaiti Red Crescent started a feeding programme in Saiyah, almost the very first in Darfur. Throughout Dar Berti, local Red Crescent committees have been very active, and relatively successful in attracting outside support. During 1984/5 the Mellit Area Council, which includes Saiyah, received the most USAID food relief per head of any part of Darfur.

The government also plays a part in this strategy. From early times, the Berti have been politically loyal. Their settlement in Korma in the eighteenth century was facilitated by a grant of land from the Sultan. In 1913/14 they were one of several groups trying to move south and east. They were loyal to Ali Dinar, and succeeded. By contrast the neighbouring Zayadiya and Ma'aliya were unable to resettle in Darfur because Sultan Ali did not trust their loyalties. The Anglo-Egyptian government restricted the movement of most groups outside the boundaries of their newly created 'tribal dars'. The Berti, uninvolved in neo-Mahdist uprisings, were able to continue their southward movement.

In most rural areas of Darfur, people expected the state to supply them with services such as schools and clinics, and in some cases bore-holes. The notion that the state might be obliged to feed villagers was considered curious. This was not the case in the towns, nor in parts of Dar Berti. The citizens of El Fasher rioted over food shortages in 1984. Rural areas remained quiet, with the single exception of Mellit. Government food aid in 1983/4 was highest in the towns, but second came Berti areas north of Mellit. In the survey of 1986, 36 per cent of the respondents in Saiyah said they considered help from the government and relief agencies to be the most important factor in their prospects for the coming year. In the rest of Darfur the figure was only 7.6 per cent. In 1987 the *shartai* of Saiyah met with the governor and suggested that the government facilitate resettlement for the people of the area. The governor agreed. During 1986, when Prime Minister Sadig el Mahdi needed a loyal and uncontroversial choice as governor of Darfur, he chose a Berti from Saiyah Village Council. Accusations of tribalism did not arise. *Shartai* Adam is an astute politician, and he waited a full nine months after the governor's appointment before first visiting him.

It would be unfair to accuse Saiyah and the surrounding areas of manifesting the 'dependency syndrome'. The government and international agencies are in important ways also dependent on Dar Berti. The result of this mutual dependence was that during the famine year, Saiyah did far better than its production alone would have predicted. The harvest was poorer than in Jebel Si, fodder and water were scarcer, and 6,000 displaced people congregated around the village. Yet relatively few became destitute, death rates were low, and the channels for change remained open.

'Who is this Reagan?'

Rural people in Darfur are used to relying on themselves: their own production and the forms of charity found in their local communities. Before 1985, Darfur had never known a major food aid programme. The arrival of food aid from outside, known as *Reagan* after the man who had supposedly donated it, was greeted with bafflement and surprise—and delight. The idea of the government (which, to the people of Darfur, embraces the 'international community' as well) having an obligation to supply villagers with food was a novel idea. 'Who is this Reagan?' said one farmer, 'He ought to be promoted!' Food aid was a bonus. Nobody expected it to continue. Outside Saiyah, only a minority said that assistance from government or aid agencies would be important in helping them through the coming year, the first one after the famine. Only 32 out of 622 said that it was more important than other factors such as their own farming skills or hard work. If the questioner had not come from an aid agency, the numbers would probably have been even lower. One farmer was asked why he was repaying his debts when he could renege on them, safe in the knowledge of food aid, and replied that he trusted the merchant to be around to lend to him in the next famine, but not the aid agencies.

Two More Relief Ideologies

People in the towns felt strongly that the government was obliged to supply them with cheap grain. When such grain was not available, riots followed. Government employees such as clerks and policemen also felt that the government had an obligation to provide them with staple food at a price they could afford on the salaries the government was paying them. The government responded to these demands. Their relief ideology was based on their 'special obligation' to certain groups. Whenever possible, they provided food relief in the towns by means of sales of grain at subsidized prices. Villagers received a smaller share. Herders were lucky if they received anything.

Distributions of grain organized by the regional government started in late 1983 in northern Darfur. Sorghum was sold at a subsidized rate of £s39 per sack, about one third of the prevailing market price. Tobert (1985) commented that in Kebkabiya, where 4,000 sacks were sold at this price, it was still out of the reach of poor people. A second distribution was made in early 1984. For this, sheikhs drew up lists of people in their villages who had 'no possessions and no animals', who received a free ration, and grain was sold cheaply in the towns. In September 1984 the regional government drew up a more ambitious distribution plan. The 'poor' were divided into three categories. The poorest were to receive 36 kg. of sorghum a month, about half a full ration. Those who were slightly less poor were to receive a third of that. Those who were merely 'poor' were to be sold up to a quarter of their needs at a subsidized rate. Townspeople and government employees could also buy grain at 'cost price'. This scheme reveals how regional government would have liked to have managed a major relief operation, meeting both their 'special obligations', and fulfilling humanitarian needs in a manner similar to the demands of the *zaka* distribution.

In practice these distributions were small and urban-centred, hampered by lack of grain, money, and transport. The main reason for this was the refusal by the central government to recognize the existence of the famine, and co-operate with attempts to relieve it. The 1983 distribution was made without any support from Khartoum. It consisted in a meagre 3,650 tonnes. In December 1983 the governor, Ahmad Diraige, went into exile after making a public stand on the issue of the famine. In early 1984 a team from FAO estimated Darfur's immediate grain needs at 39,000 tonnes. Under pressure from Khartoum, this was revised down to 7,000 tonnes. This grain was to be released through the Agricultural Bank of Sudan. Central government released only 5,400 tonnes, late. The ambitious September 1984 plan for relief needed far more food. Khartoum promised only 13,500 tonnes, which also arrived late.

Only in December 1984 did Nimeiri recognize the crisis. Fortunately by then USAID had already unilaterally committed emergency food aid to western Sudan.

A second reason for the inadequacy of relief attempts was that, because of the famine, the Darfur regional government had practically no revenue (Doornbos 1986). It could not transport the food, and any source of income was urgently needed. Consequently most of the relief food in 1983 and 1984 went no further than the main towns, and most of it was sold. The government struggled to meet even its minimum special obligations.

USAID and the international agencies had a relief ideology based on contrasting principles. According to USAID guidelines, government employees and people earning salaries of £s100 per month or more were not entitled to receive relief food. Neither could relief aid be sold. The priority was to reach the people in 'greatest need', seen to be the farmers and herders. They also believed that if grain were distributed in towns, this would draw rural people there. They would abandon their farms, and live in famine camps. The agencies were anxious to avoid camps, because of the very high death rates that occur in them.

The conflict of ideologies was compounded by the foreign relief workers distrust of the government's motives, and resulted in a damaging clash of policies. At first, the government's 'special obligation' ideology prevailed. One third of the first batch of USAID sorghum was sold in the towns. This was seen by the agencies as evidence for urban bias and corruption. There is some truth in this. However, the government was not unitary. The Sudan Socialist Union (SSU) had the prime task of protecting the stability of the regime, and thus had a strong urban bias. The civil service had stronger concerns for local government and rural needs. After the abolition of the SSU in the April 1985 uprising, and with more grain and transport available, it is likely that the relief distributions would have reverted more to the September 1984 plan. The agencies, however, pressed for an end to all urban distributions and sales. They were now strong, regional government was now weak, and they prevailed. Local government, however, never fully understood nor appreciated the 'greatest need' ideology. In order to implement it fully, as they did in 1986, the agencies ultimately had to take all aspects of distribution into their own hands, and bypass local government altogether.

Delivery of Relief

The delivery of food aid to the west of Sudan in 1984/5 was one of the world's largest relief operations since the end of the Second World War. USAID consigned two batches of sorghum to Darfur. Grain from 'Project West Sorghum I' arrived in Darfur between December 1984 and May 1985. 'Sorghum II' started in May, and grain was still arriving at the end of the year. The overall target was to distribute 125,000 tonnes of relief grain before the harvest in October 1985. Table 8.1 shows how much grain was received in the

Table 8.1. *Receipts of relief sorghum by month (September 1984–December 1985)*

Month	Tonnes received	Cumulative total
September–November 1984 (Government Relief)	13,500	
December (USAID Relief)	6,790	6,790
January 1985	3,181	9,971
February	801	10,772
March	5,901	16,673
April	8,383	25,056
May	2,835	27,891
June	9,742	37,633
July	10,527	48,160
August	10,527	58,687
September ('target month')	25,413	84,100
October	9,651	93,751
November	3,300	97,051
December	100	97,151

district headquarters each month. The figures are optimistic, in that onward transport to villages took further time, sometimes weeks or months. Delays were particularly bad at the start of the rains. It is clear that during the main crisis period, the dry season, the distributions were small. USAID's initial plan was for all the grain to go to rural areas in the north. This was amended, so that much went to the south, and one third of 'Sorghum I' was sold in the towns. Table 8.2 shows how much relief sorghum was distributed in rural areas in north and south Darfur. Again the figures are optimistic. Partly this is because of delays in forwarding relief sorghum from district headquarters. Partly it is because, particularly in the early

Table 8.2. *Distribution of USAID sorghum to rural areas (December 1984–December 1985)*

	Rural Population	Target Distribution	Actual Distribution			Kg. per Head
			Dec.–May	Jun.–Dec.	Total	
North	1,241,000	73,350	10,287	43,517	53,804	43.4
South	1,798,000	51,560	7,947	27,003	34,950	19.4
Total	3,039,000	125,000	18,234	70,520	88,754	29.2

months, small towns and large villages not included in the urban quotas took large shares of the grain.

During the dry season of 1985 the relief programme was disappointing. It failed to deliver as much grain as it promised, and failed to distribute that effectively to the population 'in greatest need'. However, the amounts distributed should be compared with the harvest of 1984, which was 14,000 tonnes in northern Darfur. In mid-1985, most of the grain available in northern Darfur consisted in relief supplies. During the rains, the amounts distributed were higher, and more reached rural areas because of greater control by SCF and USAID. However, many districts received little or none because roads were cut. Fortunately, most of the areas of greatest food scarcity were the relatively accessible areas of the north-east. Dar Masalit was the principal area of great need which was inaccessible for relief supplies during this time.

Food Relief and Mortality

USAID and other donors gave food to Darfur in order to save lives. Yet there is surprisingly little evidence that the food relief had any impact on mortality. During the dry season, the only site studied which received significant amounts of aid was Saiyah, which was given not only sorghum but supplementary foods as well. The death rate in Saiyah over these months was equivalent to an annual rate of 56 per thousand, higher than the average for the other sites. This was due to a huge congregation of migrants around the village, and the resulting health crisis. During the rains, Saiyah, Jebel Si, and Furawiya all received significant amounts of food relief. The death rate in these three sites over the rains was equivalent to 36 per thousand, less than in the other sites, but not significantly so. The difference is probably due more to the ecology of these areas than to the consumption of relief sorghum. During the rains, malaria was a major killer. These three sites are all relatively dry, and so malaria is less prevalent. In Saiyah there was a dramatic fivefold drop in the death rate from the dry season to the rains. This was related to the dispersal of the squatter camp which surrounded the village, as people returned home to cultivate.

The evidence presented in Chapter 7 suggested that consumption of staple foods had little or no influence on the risk of dying during the famine. If this is true, it follows that consuming relief sorghum likewise did not improve people's chances of surviving.

It is possible that food relief could have had a more subtle and indirect influence on mortality, by drawing people to where it was available. Relief distributions might have attracted people to towns and large villages, where they formed camps, and were exposed to health crises. In this way, it would have contributed to higher mortality. Although Darfur saw no huge relief shelters like those in highland Ethiopia, there were many smaller camps. Outside Nyala there was Damaya, which contained 17,000 refugees and local people in early 1985. In El Fasher there was Mawashei camp. Around El Geneina there were a number of migrant camps, and most of the refugee camps there also contained some local people. Small towns such as Mellit and Malha also had camps, and all towns and large villages had migrant populations. Some of these appear to have come into existence as the result of food distributions. For instance, the camp at Hujerat in Buram grew from nobody to 20,000 people in a few weeks between March and May when the council started to distribute food there. Saiyah is another example. However, in each case, people had already come to the town for another reason: relief food was an incidental bonus. The reasons included lack of water in home villages, finding work, and obtaining help from relatives. People went only to relief camps when these did not interfere with their other economic activities. It is an open question as to whether mortality was higher in relief camps than in the informal squatter settlements the migrants occupied otherwise.

Later in the year, relief was distributed to the villages partly with the intention of drawing farmers back to their fields, thereby dispersing migrant camps. There is no evidence that the village distributions had this effect. People did return, but not because of food relief. This can be illustrated by the inhabitants of Mawashei.

These people came to the city to try to earn an income. Most came from villages in El Fasher district, an area where people had been receiving more relief per head than anywhere else in Darfur. They did not leave in March or April, when relatively large amounts of food (compared to the previous and succeeding months) were distributed. They left towards the end of May, a month in which only a third of the food distributed in April was given out. They said they were leaving to plant their fields, not to obtain relief. We have every reason to believe them.

Consequently it is unlikely that food relief reduced mortality, either directly or indirectly, or that it inadvertently served to increase mortality.

Food Relief and Destitution

The discussion on food relief and the formation of peri-urban camps has shown that rural people did not plan their strategies during 1984/5 around the possibility of receiving relief food. When people received it they were thankful, but they regarded it as a free bonus rather than a reliable source of food around which they could plan.

The weeding season is the time of peak labour demand and a critical moment in the agricultural year. For farmers, the famine represented a subsistence crisis up until the point when the fields had been planted and weeded. If food relief was of assistance to rural people, one of its immediate effects would have been to allow more people to work on their own land, thereby creating labour shortages. In the weeding season of 1985, labour shortages occurred in *all* parts of Darfur, irrespective of whether relief aid was received or not. These included areas as diverse as Zalingei and Dar Meidob. In the latter place people had perhaps fewest resources of anyone, and were also not receiving relief food in significant amounts: an indication of the lengths to which people were ready to go in order to plant their fields. The labour shortages obscure the fact that in 1985 more hired weeding labour was done than ever before. This was the case even in Saiyah. There is no evidence that labour shortages were greater in areas reached by food during the weeding season than in others.

Until July, the amounts of food relief given out were small. With the exception of Saiyah, the receipt of relief had made no difference to people's choice of strategies during the famine, and had only marginally affected their success at avoiding destitution.

Food relief had a much greater impact during the second half of the rains. By this time farmers had planted and weeded their crops. The strategies to avert destitution had for the most part succeeded or failed by this point. In all of the villages studied except Arara (see Chapter 9), the subsistence crisis was over. However, there followed a period of two months before the first crops could be harvested. The exception to this was Nankose, where farmers had planted some quick-maturing varieties which could be harvested at the end of August. Wild grains also became available at this time, and were important in Furawiya. For most places the end of the rains presented a potential second crisis. These months—August and September—are normally ones of great physical hardship and hunger, comparable to the end of the dry season. Sales of animals and rates of indebtedness usually peak at this time. These were also the months when most grain was distributed.

The relief distributions had a dramatic effect on grain prices. There was a slight decline in August, a bigger fall in September, and by October they were back to normal levels. These price changes rippled throughout the region, affecting areas where no relief was able to reach. This alone served to lessen impoverishment.

The impact of relief upon destitution can be assessed by comparing the sites where food aid was not received in significant amounts with the sites where it was. Table 8.3 shows how the rates of indebtedness, the sale of goats, and the consumption of wild foods

Table 8.3. *The impact of food aid on destitution: Comparison of post-July 1985 with pre-July 1985*

Site	No. of New debts	No. of goats sold	Wild food consumption
Receiving relief aid			
Saiyah	−81	−64	−17
Furawiya	−67	−56	−10
Jebel Si	−52	−56	+23
Receiving little or no relief aid			
Arara	+160	−62	+23
Nankose	+150	+26	+10
Legediba	+ 30	−33	+19
Angabo	+310	−28	+21

for the sites studied, changed over this period compared to previous twelve months. All the sites were getting poorer, but for some the downward trajectory was steepening, while for others it was bottoming out.

Indebtedness increased everywhere, as it always does during the pre-harvest months. In the cases of little or no food aid, the number of new debts taken out rose sharply. Where food aid was being received, levels of new debts show a contrasting pattern, with many fewer new debts. This suggests that food aid had the effect of helping people to see the wet season through without going into debt.

The sale of animals is much less clear cut. Animal sales certainly declined everywhere in Darfur. This is due to a combination of factors: improved terms of trade between animals and grain as grain prices began to fall and animal prices began to rise, less livestock to sell among the poor; and less need to sell among the rich. Sales of cows, camels, and sheep, the animals of the rich, do not tell a consistent story. Sales of goats tell us most about those at risk of destitution, and although the rate of sales declined everywhere except Nankose, in general it declined most in places receiving aid. There is evidence, therefore, that receipt of food aid prevented distress sales of livestock during these months.

Food aid had an effect on other strategies too. In August and September, wild foods become an important part of peoples' strategies. Collecting wild foods does not interfere with subsistence prospects, and so it is a strategy which is preferable to borrowing or selling animals. As things improved we would therefore expect it to have continued for longer than these other less preferable strategies. This was the case. Consumption of wild foods during the rains fell only in two sites, which were two of the three receiving relief aid. This was particularly striking because in these two sites wet-season wild grains are important, so an increase in consumption would have been expected.

By the end of October the population of Darfur had received over 90,000 tonnes of relief grain, most of it free. This was only three-quarters of the target. It was enough for 22 per cent of a year's consumption, 33 per cent in the north and 15 per cent in the south. More food aid delivered earlier would have been desirable, and would have certainly prevented much impoverishment. When it did arrive, it blunted the impact of the second period of annual stress, the pre-harvest months. Food relief was one factor among many which enabled people to pull through the famine year.

In October 1985 there was an almost tangible feeling of exhaustion and relief among rural people in Darfur.

How Could it Have Been Done Better?

The famine relief programme in Darfur during 1984/5 was not very successful. It is subject to two lines of criticism. The first is that food aid itself was not the most appropriate form of assistance to famine-stricken Darfur. Food aid did not address properly the causes of excess deaths, and so was marginal to saving lives, and it did relatively little to prevent destitution. The second line of criticism is that the food aid programme failed in its own terms. The food was committed late, delivered late, and failed to reach the right people.

These are severe charges to bring against a relief programme, and by implication, against the agencies that planned and implemented it. However, the purpose of this section is not to put the relief agencies in the dock for what they did and failed to do in Darfur during 1984/5. The principal organizations involved were USAID and the Save the Children Fund. Both have been subjected to much criticism for the mistakes they made. For instance USAID has been harshly criticized for its decision to hire a commercial haulage company, Arkel-Talab, to transport the grain within Sudan. Foremost among the critics were organizations who had shown themselves incapable of making any response at all to the crisis of 1984/5 (though some of these started relief operations in 1986, when the famine was over). Nimeiri's government had made it impossible for international organizations to respond to the famine until it was almost too late to do anything. In the circumstances, both USAID and SCF deserve credit for risking institutional humiliation in an attempt at least to do something to relieve the famine. The proposals for better responses to famine which are outlined below would have been possible only if the government and the UN organizations had been more willing to recognize the existence of an impending famine and act to relieve it.

Many of the problems of logistics and targeting were subsequently overcome during the continued relief operation of 1986 (Buckley 1988; Eldridge 1988). Some of the problems of providing timely relief have been addressed by the setting-up of a 'famine early-warning system' for Sudan.

This section will not provide an audit of the relief operation, or follow up the second line of criticism. Instead it will outline radically different proposals for relief, under three headings: saving lives, preventing destitution, and early warning. These should be considered only tentative suggestions, rather than definitive answers to the problem of famine in Darfur. More research and more consultation are needed before properly effective relief programmes can be designed.

Saving Lives

Most if not all of the excess deaths in Darfur during the famine could have been prevented if the health crises that caused them could have been prevented.

One way to prevent the occurrence of health crises would have been to make it unnecessary for people in small villages to leave home and migrate to large villages and towns. In northern Darfur, many people abandoned their villages because of the drying of wells. Providing deep bore-holes to small villages would overcome this problem, but this would be an expensive solution. Moreover, it would not address a second and more important reason for people leaving their villages: to earn an income during the dry season. This income was needed to buy grain and other food items, provide for animals, buy seeds and tools, meet social obligations, etc. Some out-migration during the harvest and the dry season could be prevented by supplying relief grain to the villages. People whose chief need is to obtain food would be less likely to move. This would help to reduce health crises. However, many people would still need to migrate. They would have needs for cash, fodder, and water. In addition, they might not trust the relief agencies to continue the food distributions. In this case people would migrate during the harvest season to find work, so as to have some stored cash in case the relief supplies dried up. Such food distributions would be more effective in helping farmers return to their villages before the start of the rains. At this point, food relief would be supporting people's strategies, not restraining them. This would serve to reduce the health crises that occur in squatter camps after the first rains, when low-lying areas are flooded, wells become polluted, and malaria becomes epidemic.

Preventing migration during the harvest and dry season would also have undesirable side effects, because richer farmers in south Darfur depend for a labour supply on seasonal migrants from the north.

The second and more effective way of preventing health crises would be to prevent the adverse effects of population movements. This means improving the public health environment of the large villages and towns to which villagers are likely to migrate. This has several advantages over the policy of discouraging migration: first, discouraging migration is likely to be only partially successful; secondly, the interventions can be started well in advance of a famine occurring; thirdly, they will benefit the inhabitants in normal times also.

There are five main issues in the prevention of health crises in large villages and towns. The first is supplying clean drinking water. Shallow wells must be protected. Facilities for taking water from wateryards should be improved and made more sanitary. In cases where an inflow of people will lead to excessive crowding around wells, more wells should be provided. Some wells should be allocated for use by livestock and others by people.

The second issue is sanitation. Most towns in Darfur have grown larger than their services can cope with. Poor areas are frequently not served at all by waste-disposal services. Provisions are never made in advance for squatter camps. Contingency plans can be made for siting such camps and extending services to them. Funds, directives, and organizational support are needed. The same principles apply, on a modest scale, to villages.

The third issue is measles. Measles immunization must be a priority. Worldwide immunization campaigns are currently targeting five main childhood diseases. These are tuberculosis, polio, whooping cough, diphtheria, and measles. Of these only measles was a major killer during the famine in Darfur. Unfortunately, of the five vaccines, the measles vaccine is the most vulnerable to breaks in the cold chain (the vaccine deteriorates rapidly if it is not constantly refrigerated) and hence measles vaccination requires the greatest logistical support. On occasions this has become a reason for dropping measles vaccination, and concentrating on the other four. However, if the prevention of famine mortality is a priority, a good case can be made for doing the opposite: overlooking the other four diseases and concentrating on measles alone, as it kills more than all the others combined.

The fourth issue concerns diseases which are not normally prevalent in Darfur, but might break out in certain places during or immediately after a famine. Such diseases include meningitis, cholera, relapsing fever, and typhus. Widespread preventive measures against these diseases would be prohibitively costly and for the most part unnecessary. However, it is necessary to be vigilant and to be prepared for the contingency of an epidemic of one of these diseases. This involves security stocks of vaccines and contingency logistical planning.

The fifth issue is malaria. In Darfur, malaria becomes an acute problem where irrigated agriculture is practised, and where the water-use and waste disposal of aggregations of people leads to standing water near houses and shelters. This can best be dealt with by careful siting and maintenance of migrant camps, in a manner similar to planning for sanitation. As mentioned, there is also a role for food relief (or cash relief) in helping to disperse migrant camps before the rains start.

Underlying all these public health interventions is the need to strengthen the infrastructure and morale of the health service in rural areas.

A final issue in saving lives during famine is a nutritional issue. The category of the population most at risk during the famine was children due to be weaned. The provision of weaning foods would probably help to save these children from diseases and severe malnutrition.

If these proposals had been followed in Darfur during the years immediately before the famine, and during the famine itself, it is likely that very many fewer excess deaths would have occurred, or even none at all.

Preventing Destitution

Faced with famine, the people of Darfur were tenacious and skilled at survival. When they failed to secure their livelihood it was most often because, faced with the huge uncertainties of famine, they made decisions that in retrospect were wrong. An effective relief policy should make use of this great resource, and aim at enabling rural people to use their skills to greater effect. The most effective interventions will be those that make rural people's planning more reliable, and reduce the uncertainties of famine. These should include assisting the survival of their livestock, guaranteeing the prices they will receive for selling livestock, giving a guaranteed income for a certain period, and giving resources such as grain in bulk, which they can use as they see fit.

Animals

The largest single factor in people becoming destitute during the famine was loss of animals, through death or sale. It follows that if preventing destitution is to be a priority, the most effective assistance involves helping people retain their animals, by providing fodder to keep animals alive, preventing distress sales due to exceptional cash needs, and assuring that those who do sell obtain a fair price.

For animal owners, fodder aid can be more important than food aid. This is particularly the case for people who cannot move their animals to where grazing is available, because they need to stay where they can earn an income. For many poor people dependent on low-status trades, feeding their donkeys is both a necessity and a major expense. Feeding their goats, sheep, and cows is a necessity if they are to have a livelihood after the famine. Providing free or cheap fodder would be an enormous boost to such people.

Providing fodder is only one way to help maintain livestock. There are others, such as facilitating the movement of herds (by hoof or by lorry) to areas where grazing is available, paying the costs of maintaining wateryards and wells so that animal owners need not pay for water, and providing veterinary services.

These proposals would not only serve to keep animals alive, but remove many of the expenses that animal owners face during drought, in turn making it possible for them to sell fewer animals. Livestock owners do face other needs for cash, however, so other means of making money available should be explored (see below). Food relief is an inefficient way of providing animal owners with an income. Buying grain is only one expense among many that they face during famine, particularly the owners of large transhumant herds.

During 1984/5, those who sold animals often received pitifully small amounts of money. After the famine, they saw the same animals fetching ten or more times the price, which was far more than they could afford. The rise and fall in animal prices was greater than the rise and fall in grain prices, and worked more selectively against poorer people. Poor people were hurt more by the inequity of the animal market than by the inequity of the grain market. If there has to be a choice between intervening to keep grain prices stable and intervening to keep animal prices stable, the animal prices should be the priority. Intervening in the livestock market would be an effective way, not only of maintaining rural people's livestock, but increasing their cash income during famine.

It is important that rural people are enabled both to receive a good price when they sell under pressure, and to buy animals after the famine at a comparable price. Setting legal controls on the prices of animals would be ineffective. Insofar as they could be enforced, buyers would simply not buy during the famine, and so sellers would receive nothing. The most effective intervention would be for an agency to buy up animals during the famine, in rural markets, at a price fixed at slightly below the normal yearly low. The animals could then be moved to where water and grazing were available, best done by employing nomadic herders to look after them. After the famine the animals would be resold, again in rural markets. The numbers sold would be smaller than the number bought, due to deaths and slaughterings. The price would also have to be higher, to cover the costs incurred in keeping the animals alive. Market controls, such as allowing individuals to buy only a few animals, would have to be invoked to avoid mass buying by speculators and merchants. Nevertheless this would be a huge improvement on the current inequity of the livestock market during famine.

Employment

Many poor farmers have no animals. Others have too few animals to risk selling some, even at a good price, and even with assurances of being able to buy them back later. These people are those most in need of assistance. They do require food, but, like other people, they also have cash needs. They engage in the low-status trades, such as cutting firewood and burning charcoal. During the famine, hundreds of thousands of people in Darfur were dependent on the destruction of trees for earning an income. Legal restrictions on the cutting of trees were ineffective. Providing alternative employment would have benefited both the tree-cutters and the environment.

Organized employment on famine-relief works was tried in Sudan during the Condominium period. It was one of the principles of the

Sudan Famine Regulations of 1920, which followed the model of famine relief laid down in the Indian famine codes. Organized employment had limited success in Sudan, for several reasons. One reason was that there was rarely an absolute shortage of work in Sudan. This was in contrast to India, where famines were 'rather famines of work than of food' (Baird-Smith quoted in Drèze 1988, p. 8). Instead, the areas where there were people needing employment, such as Darfur, were simply a long way from the areas of labour shortage, such as Gezira. It was therefore government policy to organize transport of labourers to the central labour-shortage provinces, in preference to starting relief works in the outlying provinces. Second, the demand for employment existed only during the dry season, and the work-force tended to disappear at the first sign of rain. Thirdly, the very mobility of the labour force made it hard to plan for the size of relief works. People might have gone elsewhere for work, so that very few would-be labourers would turn up. Alternatively, fully manned relief works could be surrounded by a crowd of people, attracted from great distances, looking for employment. Most importantly, administrators in rural areas were hard-pressed to find construction projects, and provide the support and supervision necessary to make them a success. However, on some occasions relief works were highly effective. In 1942, the aerodromes at El Fasher and El Geneina and a number of roads were constructed largely using famine labour.

Three recommendations follow from this: first, to facilitate travel to labour-shortage areas; second, to make employment available during the dry season, and close the projects during the rains; third, to be prepared for a difficult logistical and management exercise, perhaps with a disappointing outcome in terms of the number of roads or dams built or trees planted.

Seed

Supplying seed to famine-stricken farmers has both great advantages and great difficulties. Since shortage of seed is an acute problem to many farmers, providing cheap or free seed would greatly help poorer farmers secure a post-famine harvest. However the problem is that Darfur has a varied ecology and farmers use a variety of strains of millet and sorghum. Farmers in some villages use particular strains which are rarely found elsewhere. A uniform distribution of one or two types of seed throughout Darfur would do little good. An effective seed programme will need to build up stocks of local seed varieties for distribution.

Food Relief

The shortcomings of free food relief have been evident for some time. It is slow and cumbersome to transport and distribute. It is a blunt instrument, largely irrelevant for saving lives and inefficient for preserving livelihoods. Under some circumstances it creates disincentives for local farmers, thereby disrupting local food production, or displaces commercial grain traders from the market, creating further disruptions. It is easy to abuse.

Nevertheless, free distributions of food can be extremely effective in certain circumstances, and for particular categories of people. One such circumstance is during the wet season when farmers need to plant and weed their fields. This is a time of peak labour demand, when it is important that rural people are physically strong and there are few competing requirements for labour-time. Farmers plan ahead and manage their resources so as to try to conserve grain and other foods for this critical time. In famine, many do not succeed, and have to borrow money or food at high rates of interest, work for money during at least some of the time, travel to distant markets to buy grain, or scour the hills looking for wild foods. All of these activities prevent them from cultivating and cut into their future harvest.

Most small villages are inaccessible by vehicle during the rains. A wet-season food distribution would have to be based on central distribution points, with villagers coming to collect their rations. The villagers would travel at the expense of tending their fields, or else ignore the relief food. If the distributions are unpredictable, rural people will have difficulty planning their wet-season strategies. A farmer who wrongly expects a relief distribution may fail to build up reserves of food, and become unexpectedly desperate in the middle of the season, leading him or her to sell animals or take out debts unnecessarily. Likewise, a farmer who wrongly does not expect a distribution may decide to plant only a small area and take paid work to buy food to build up a reserve, only to find later that the reserve was unnecessary. An uncertain distribution may therefore make a farmer use the household's labour-time inefficiently, and possibly jeopardize their future subsistence. It is important that when rural people are given a resource, such as food, they are given it in such a way that they can make best use of it, by integrating it into their strategies for resource management. Therefore it is best to inform people of how much food relief they are to receive, and give it to them in a single donation. The most effective form of free food relief would be to give farmers about two months' supply of grain, in a single donation, just before the start of the rains.

The giving of food to rural people should be seen as an income transfer, and not as a means of nutritional support. Many rural people will sell part of the food they receive. Most relief agencies currently disapprove of such sales. However, famine relief can only be truly effective if the recipients are able to use the resources they are given as they see fit, and this may well include selling them.

One category of people who require free food consists of those who are incapacitated or 'labour-poor'. This includes people who are old, disabled, or chronically ill, or households with one working member and a large number of dependents. Such people cannot maintain themselves, even in normal times. They are the major recipients of traditional forms of charity from *zaka* distributions, and are the main constituency of local charitable organizations such as Red Crescent committees. The ideology, tradition, and institutions for helping such people thus exist, and the problems are ones of shortage of relief supplies and lack of infrastructural and management support.

Whether or not free food distributions are made, food policy during famine is important. The high price of grain may not be the only critical factor in vulnerability to famine, but it is one factor. Many townspeople rely on buying food from the market, have little or no access to wild foods, have a fixed income, and have few assets to sell. They are particularly vulnerable to rises in the price of grain. Artisans and rural labourers are in a comparable position. Food policy for an area vulnerable to famine should aim at making grain available at a reasonable price to such people.

Legal controls on the price of grain cannot work during a food shortage unless grain is also released on to the market. A food security policy to combat famine must be based upon reserve stocks of grain, built up and maintained during non-famine years, which can be sold at a subsidized price when need arises. The grain should be sold in the principal markets, that is in the towns. It could also be sold in rural markets where the price of grain is very high, under the aegis of market committees. Restrictions will have to be placed on bulk-buying and speculative storage of grain by merchants. It is important to emphasize what such a food security policy can and cannot do. It can provide grain at a reasonable price to townspeople and those who migrate to the towns for seasonal work. It can keep down the price of grain in towns, where most of the consumers of marketed grain live. This will in turn keep down the price of grain in the rural markets which normally sell grain to the towns. It will also prevent urban interests from crushing the power of rural market committees which try to restrict the price and movements of grain. But the policy cannot provide grain to the poorest; neither to the incapacitated and very poor, nor to drought-stricken farmers and herders. It cannot save the lives of poor rural children. Also, it cannot keep down the price of grain in rural markets which are very remote or are not linked to urban markets. A food security policy based on market intervention is no substitute for programmes specifically aimed at saving lives, preserving livelihoods, or sustaining the very poor.

Early Warning

Since the famines of 1984/5 in Africa, huge amounts of money have been spent on building 'famine early-warning systems' for various African countries, including Sudan. Early-warning systems are based on the indisputable principle that timely intervention in an impending famine is better than late intervention. The logic of these systems is that a famine can be seen in advance by collecting and analysing data on rainfall, animal and crop production, and socio-economic indicators such as grain prices and volumes of livestock sales. By studying these 'early-warning indicators', governments and relief agencies should have sufficient advance warning of an impending famine to be able to intervene in a timely manner. Their establishment has led to the collection and analysis of large amounts of such data (Eldredge, Salter, and Rydjeski 1986). This in itelf has proved a valuable exercise, as it has made data for famine-prone areas widely available in a way that did not exist previously.

Early-warning systems have their ancestry in the Indian famine codes of the late nineteenth and early twentieth centuries (Drèze 1988). In India they enjoyed some success, but attempts to introduce the system to Africa, such as in the Sudan Famine Regulations of

1920, were less successful. The reasons for the success in India but failure in Sudan are instructive. India had high population density, well-integrated markets, and a developed infrastructure. Famine-prone Indian populations typically owned few assets, had little grain in storage, and relied heavily on wage-labour. Consequently famines could be rapid in onset. Following a harvest failure on account of flood or drought, or a collapse in access to grain through the market, rural people might become stricken by famine in a period of a few weeks. Because of this and the well-integrated market, the signs of an impending crisis, such as grain-price inflation and high demand for employment, were relatively clear and uniform, and could be assessed far more quickly than objective indicators such as size of the harvest. Above all, India had a professional civil service operating in rural areas which could perform all the necessary monitoring and reporting tasks. In such a situation, it was both easy and essential to monitor these indicators, so that interventions could be implemented swiftly.

In Sudan, by contrast, the population density is low, the markets are fragmented, the infrastructure poor, and the administration thin on the ground. Famines have a long period of gestation, because many rural people have many disposable assets, particularly animals, and stored grain and wild foods are available. Because of this and the fragmented and imperfect markets, the signs of an impending crisis are variable, both in space and through time, and ambiguous. The signs are difficult to monitor and difficult to intepret. Monitoring these indicators is also redundant, because someone who is in a position to understand what they mean will certainly know whether or not a famine is coming anyway. The difficulties of collecting and analysing the data mean that they are neither quicker not more accurate indicators of approaching famine than the assessment of objective indicators such as crop production. The slow onset of famine removes the need for intervening in a matter of weeks, and in any case, interventions can only be implemented very slowly. Local government in Sudan employed few professional civil servants, and instead relied heavily on the work of untrained 'native administrators', especially village sheikhs. Such people could not be expected to perform the monitoring and reporting tasks required. The Condominium administration in Sudan consequently found that the Famine Regulations were an inefficient and ineffective instrument. They had been designed for conditions that did not obtain in most of Sudan. Instead, the government adopted a warning system based upon a heterogeneous set of channels of communication. These varied from area to area. They included harvest assessments by agricultural officers, signs of distress observed by district officers, and most importantly, the representations of sheikhs and other rural leaders, who came forward with requests for assistance (Civsec 19/1/ 1–2).

Modern famine early-warning systems appear to be following a similar path. In early days there was optimism that such systems would provide a 'technical fix' to the problem of predicting famines and facilitating their relief. Some people even appeared to believe that a simple and uniform predictor of an impending famine, such as a rise in the price of grain, would be found. This was of course not so. More recent work on early-warning systems has argued that local mechanisms of representation and communication are the best way of giving warning for almost all cases in which relief is needed (Eldredge and Rydjeski, 1988).

The case of the Darfur famine of 1984/5 demonstrates this well. During the early 1980s there were few data available for prices, production, and other indicators of approaching crisis. Most of the rainfall stations in north Darfur had even ceased sending in reports. Yet, despite the absence of such data, everybody knew that famine was approaching. Rural people of course knew. The merchants knew, and the broadsheets published by the various Chambers of Commerce in Kordofan and Darfur contained detailed information and accurate predictions. The politicians knew: the governor, Ahmad Diraige, made a public stand on the issue as early as 1983. Even USAID was aware, and its commitment of emergency relief sorghum for Darfur was made in September 1984, less than a month after the failure of the 1984 rains became apparent. The problem was not lack of knowledge, nor a failure of communication, but a failure in democratic accountability at the highest level. President Nimeiri refused to recognize the existence of the crisis, and throughout 1983/ 4 even obstructed the delivery of relief grain that had already been committed for Darfur.

It follows that the core of an effective early-warning system for Darfur should consist in strengthened democracy. Channels of communication and representation between villagers and their district councils and MPs should be improved. Local charitable institutions and local newspapers should be developed. Regional issues should be higher on the national agenda. Aid agencies currently prefer to support specific projects that have clear and tangible results. Yet the most pressing need is for the rehabilitation of the core institutions of local government in rural areas.

I have discussed the shortcomings of technically based early-warning systems in more detail elsewhere (de Waal 1988). The argument is that the role of technical information should not be to predict *when* a famine will occur, which is a task that it cannot do effectively, and need not do anyway. Instead, it should identify which groups of people are vulnerable to dying or being rendered destitute, where and how, should a famine occur. A warning system for preventing excess deaths would concentrate on collecting the information on public health that is essential for planning the health programmes mentioned above. A warning system for preventing destitution would similarly collect information on livestock market-ing, fodder and water needs of animals, labour markets, etc. Improved agricultural statistics would also provide an essential cross-check to local claims of harvest failure. This would also help to overcome the principal problem of a warning system based on local democracy, which is that groups who are more vocal or more influential are likely to receive more assistance than others. Such information would also be of use for planning development projects in non-famine years.

What is emphatically not required is a high-technology, central-ized data-collection system, using standardized techniques and over-simplified models of famine. Nutritional surveillance is probably the worst such early-warning method, being technically almost useless, conceptually misleading, obscuring the value of other methods of assessment, and implying a need for the wrong kinds of intervention (food relief). Unfortunately, such techniques have a spurious air of objectivity and credibility. However, they stand in the way of local democracy, and hence they are a disservice to rural people, and ought to be stopped.

Conclusion

Effective famine relief is not going to be easy. It is going to be complicated. It is going to require long-term planning and long-term commitment. It is going to need a wide variety of professional and political skills. Some interventions, such as security stocks of food and improved public health, should be started at once, even with no famine on the horizon. At all stages it will require detailed research and detailed planning, and considerable management skills. There will be no easy solutions, no quick technical fixes, and problems will not be solved by liberal helpings of enthusiasm, goodwill, and free sorghum. Some humility is in order. It is becoming fashionable for foreigners to admire rural people's skills, but there is no indication of it becoming fashionable to recognize, let alone admire, the skills and ethics of local politicians and government officials in countries such as Sudan. There is a danger that admiration for rural people's knowledge and skills will become another stick with which to beat the government, which will result in little good. Note that the policy of food relief which I am advocating looks more like that designed by the Regional Government of Darfur in 1983/4, than that imposed by USAID and the relief agencies in 1985–6.

The proposals in this section are essentially proposals for ways in which rural people can come to have greater access to the state and its resources. It follows that they will work only if designed in consultation with rural people and the institutions of local government. For that reason, these programmes are merely suggestions. They should be items on the agenda for discussion, rather than a new orthodoxy to be imposed on rural people by the central state and foreign agencies. Programmes of this sort are likely to be adopted and implemented most rapidly and enthusiastically in the towns and in rural areas such as Dar Berti where people have become adept at handling governments. Elsewhere, they may be successful, after a slower start. Rural people say that 'The unlucky one sees the consequences in himself and the lucky one sees them in others' (quoted by Mustafa 1988, p. 133). Rural people will wait and see how the programmes work, and it is possible that they will consider the risks of a closer association with the state to be greater than the benefits they will obtain, and mostly abstain from participation in such programmes. It is possible that they will be right to do so.

9

Other Famines

General Conclusions

There are two levels of conclusion for this book. One is at an abstract level. This is that English-speakers have consistently misunderstood famines because we have been misled by an inappropriate concept of what famine is. Instead we must recognize that 'famine' is not a single, cohesive concept, and famines are not a natural kind. Analysis of individual famines must precede attempts to understand the general phenomenon of famine. This analysis emphatically must take into account the understandings of the famine articulated by the people who are suffering it.

The second conclusion is at the level of the general model of understanding and responding to famine that has been developed here for Darfur. At the core of this are the constituent concepts of *'maja'a'*, as understood in Darfur: hunger, destitution, and death. Relief is a possible extra element. These can be summarized:

(1) Hunger, which you just put up with.
(2) Destitution, which you do your utmost to prevent.
(3) Death, which is beyond your power to influence.

In addition there is (4) relief, which you do not rely upon.

This approach has proved productive in explaining how rural people responded to the famine as they did. The most important general conclusion is that people's principal aim during the famine was to preserve the basis of an acceptable future way of life, which involves not only material wellbeing but also social cohesion. More specific elements include attempting to explain differences in responses between people of different locations, groups, and classes, and between men and women. These follow differences in economic opportunities, ecology, structures of power and authority, and differences in ideology and understanding. Indigenous understandings of phenomena such as drought, desertification, the national economy, and the prevalence of disease are also important. Though the causes that people ascribe—God's wrath causing drought, God's arbitrary choices determining mortality—may fit ill with scientific thinking, these causal models are often based on accurate empirical observations. Indigenous models can often contribute to our understanding of these issues. Even when they cannot, for instance on the occasions when the empirical observations are misleading or inaccurate, this does not detract from their value in helping to explain responses to famine.

The remainder of this chapter will form a postscript, attempting to see how much of the model can be applied to other famines. To investigate this issue, we can start modestly. In Darfur during 1984/5, not one but three famines occurred, separate but overlapping. The analysis up to now has concentrated almost exclusively on the 'main' famine. By looking at what was happening simultaneously on the western and southern borders of Darfur, we can see which aspects of the analysis are entirely specific to one particular set of circumstances, and which can be generalized. To anticipate the findings, the answer is that a similar society afflicted by a famine with slightly different causes requires a different model of analysis, as does a different kind of society stricken by a famine with similar causes. Any generalization from the experience of Darfur must proceed with extreme caution.

The Famine in Dar Masalit

The first example of the 'other famines' in Darfur in 1984/5 is the famine that struck Dar Masalit, otherwise known as El Geneina District. During 1984 and early 1985 the famine in Dar Masalit was sufficiently similar to that in other parts of Darfur to consist in merely another variation on the themes already discussed. But, during the rains of 1985 the famine developed in such a different manner that Dar Masalit deserves to be regarded as a separate 'epicentre' of famine.

The Last Place in Sudan

Arara is a village lying in the southern part of Dar Masalit, two miles from the border with Chad (see Fig. 9.1). It is as close to the coast of west Africa in Cameroon as it is to Port Sudan. The captain of the army post grumbled that it was 'the last place in Sudan'. It could also

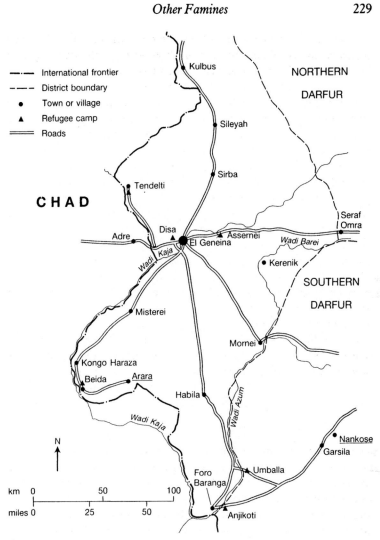

Fig. 9.1. *Dar Masalit*

be called 'the first place in Chad': more than half of the 20,000 people served by the market in Arara live in Chad.

Dar Masalit has a wetter climate and a less degraded ecology than other areas of Darfur on the same latitude. The southern part has rich alluvial soils, with basement hills in between, and big *wadi* villages of several thousand people. Arara is one of these villages, poorer than the average. The north and central areas are thickly settled fertile *goz*, with larger numbers of smaller villages. The population density is among the highest in Darfur, and land-holdings are correspondingly small. One response to this problem, followed in Arara, has been to acquire land in Chad.

The frontier between Sudan and Chad is a central fact of life in Arara.

In cultural terms the border has a limited existence. Many ethnic groups straddle it, the Masalit being one of them. The Masalit on the Sudanese side subscribe to much the same set of values concerning subsistence and belonging as the other communities in Darfur which have been discussed. On the Chadian side the people, whether Masalit or others, are similar.

In political terms, the border is ambiguous. Dar Masalit, in the sense of the homeland of the Masalit, consists of areas on both sides of it. Between the Mahdiya and the French military expeditions of 1909–10 the whole of Dar Masalit was ruled as an independent state, headed by a sultan. The French and Anglo-Egyptian forces only completed their occupation and partition of the sultanate in 1922. Most of Dar Masalit, including the sultan's allegiance, fell on the Anglo-Egyptian side. Thereafter the Condominium Government practised indirect rule, on the northern Nigerian model, through the sultan (Davies 1924; Kapteijns 1982). The present sultan, Bahr el Din, was the only member of the native administration to retain his position after the reform of local government in 1971. He claims allegiance from people on both sides of the border, although he has no legal status in Chad. Bahr el Din has followed what is in effect an independent foreign policy, giving support and sanctuary to various factions in Chad, notably Hissene Habre in 1979–80. He has maps of Dar Masalit and Africa on the wall of his court, but no map of Sudan. Dar Masalit does not recognize itself as part of Dar*Fur*, in the sense of 'country of the Fur'.

In economic terms, the border provides an opportunity, perhaps the principal opportunity. Sudan has neglected Dar Masalit, and economic links with the rest of Sudan have been intermittent and tenuous. Farmers grow few cash crops other than grain, apart from what can be sold locally, because of the prohibitive cost of transport. Commerce in Dar Masalit was hampered by the fact that it was a 'closed district' until 1956, and traders found it difficult to obtain licences. The first riverain Sudanese 'Jellaba' traders arrived in rural areas only during the decade of Independence. They are still few in number. Arara market, though serving a large population, is very rarely visited by commercial trucks. Instead the merchants concentrate on importing consumer goods from Chad, and exporting cattle and the leather goods produced by the artisans of El Geneina town.

The principal link with Sudan is long-term male out-migration to *Dar Sabah*. This migration has been going on since the 1920s. The average household size in Arara is 4.4 people (in Darfur it is 5.5), almost half of the households are headed by women, and there is a lack of adult men. One quarter of the Darfurians in central and eastern Sudan come from Dar Masalit. The pattern of this migration differs slightly from that found among the Fur emigrants from Jebel Si. The Fur tend to go to Gezira, wheras the Masalit tend to go further east, to Gedaref Province, where they settle as smallholders and work for money on the mechanized farming schemes. Remitting money across the entire breadth of Sudan is not easy, and in most cases the cash income earned in eastern Sudan only affects Dar Masalit if and when the migrant returns home.

Economic ties across the border with Chad have been much stronger, though also intermittent (Doornbos 1983; 1984). Dar Masalit is the granary for much of eastern Chad. On the Sudanese side of the border there is a string of markets, through which grain and consumer goods move west and livestock moves east. This process of cross-border integration was helped by the beginnings of the Chadian civil war in 1966, because it became difficult to supply eastern Chad from N'Djamena. In the early 1970s there were armed camel caravans leaving Beida for Chad daily. But in the longer term the war stifled the prosperity of the border area. The 1970s saw increased insecurity, and between 1979 and 1982 the Chadian rebel coalition, in exile in El Geneina, embargoed trade through Beida and Arara. The insecurity and embargoes affected large traders more than smaller donkey-traders, who were less visible, and who continued to thrive. In 1982–3 there was a general upswing in trade in the border area, and the beginnings of a recovery among richer smallholders. Animal numbers grew fast during these years (in contrast to other parts of Darfur): numbers of cattle rose by 20 per cent, sheep and goat numbers doubled.

Famine in Dar Masalit 1984/5

Dar Masalit suffered drought from 1982 to 1984. With the exception of 1973, these were the three driest years on record. The southern areas were hit less badly than the central and northern *goz* areas, and on some alluvial soils the harvest of 1984 was close to normal. In Arara the 1983 harvest was above average for only 4.5 per cent of farmers. The 1984 crop met only one third of needs. Forty-five per cent of the animals died in 1984/5. Thus the harvest failure and animal deaths were not as severe as in northern Darfur, but worse than most parts of southern Darfur. The large class of artisans in El Geneina town were particularly badly hit by the famine, being dependent on a highly elastic demand for their products, and having to buy grain from the market.

During 1984 and the first three months of 1985 the price of grain was lower than the average for Darfur. It was comparable to the price in areas such as Nankose. In normal times the price of grain is lower in western than in eastern Darfur. This is related to the poor marketing and very low cash incomes in the area, which persisted over the famine. All the income to Arara in the *seif* of 1985 would have bought 4.3 per cent of the village's grain needs, by far the least of any of the villages studied.

At this time Dar Masalit was hosting 120,000 refugees from Chad. It might be expected that their presence, which swelled the population by a quarter, would have inflated the grain prices. It did not. One reason was that many people in eastern Chad normally bought grain from Dar Masalit, the only difference in 1984/5 being that they did not return to Chad after leaving the market-place. Another reason was the (intermittent) supply of relief grain to the refugee camp at Assernei. A third reason was that many of the refugees were moving eastwards to Zalingei, Nyala, and central Sudan. In mid-1985 Tendelti camp held 10,000 people, but only 200 adult males: the remainder of the men had left for *Dar Sabah*.

Up until the rains of 1985, the people of Dar Masalit had the same concerns as those elsewhere in Darfur: to preserve their animals and plant their land. In this they were as successful as people elsewhere. The area planted in Arara rose by 1 per cent between the 1984 and 1985 seasons. This figure conceals the fact that the richer half of the population increased their area by 15 per cent and the poorer half decreased their area by 24 per cent. There was scarcely any unplanted land. Only one sampled household fell below subsistence through failing to plant. Five fell below subsistence through having land confiscated (by the Sudanese army post) or having crops stolen or destroyed (in Chad). There was the familiar two-peak pattern of animal sales, and no one fell below normative subsistence through these sales.

The Dar Masalit Famine during the Rains of 1985

The Dar Masalit famine was similar to that in the rest of Darfur until the end of the dry season. It was a second crisis, superimposed on the first, that created appalling conditions up until September and even October 1985. This crisis came at the point when recovery was beginning in most parts of Darfur; during June and July 1985 grain prices began to fall, animal prices began to recover, and people began to move away from the low-status activities. In Dar Masalit the opposite happened.

The grain price rose. In April–May it passed £s200, and continued to rise, fluctuating wildly and reaching prices of £s300 per sack and even more. For the first, and so far the last time, grain was more expensive in Dar Masalit than anywhere else in Darfur. Meanwhile the market in low-status trades, already overfilled by unemployed artisans, famine migrants, and refugees, collapsed entirely. There were estimated to be 250,000 people in El Geneina town, four times the normal population (Simon Mollison, personal communication). Bands of beggars roamed the town, forcing the police to post guards at grain stores, and forcing the closure of restaurants. The town council had to employ a carter to circle the market every morning to take away the corpses. In rural areas this market collapsed too. In Arara only eight sampled households (5 per cent) were able to earn an income from low-status trades, and then only an average of one trade per household, a drop of over 90 per cent on the dry season. Much of this trade was selling *mukheit*. Numbers of animals sold fell in most of Darfur; in Dar Masalit the 'second peak' of sales was prolonged until the end of the rains. In Arara it accounted for 55 per cent of the sales during the whole year. Only one household, however, became destitute through this.

Why did this happen? The underlying reason was war in Chad. Southern Darfur was host to large numbers of 'refugees' from northern Darfur in early 1985, but these people returned north for the rainy season. The Chadian refugees in Dar Masalit did not leave when the rains came. On the contrary, more of them continued to arrive, especially in Beida. Others had been sent back from Nyala westwards by UNHCR. If the Chadians had been 'drought refugees', they would have left to plant their farms. I interviewed fifty of them individually in 1985: they said that they were not returning to Chad for fear of their lives. We have every reason to believe them (also see Ruiz 1987). The war in Chad was bringing a famine to Dar Masalit. At the same time, relief food was failing to reach the refugees, due to flooded *wadis*. For once, the transport constraint was real.

The presence of the refugees confounded expectations of the course of the famine. They sold animals, bringing down livestock prices. They bought grain, inflating grain prices. They ate wild foods, in some areas effectively ending free access to them. They overwhelmed the low-status trades. In Darfur itself the worst was over by July; in Dar Masalit the worst was still occurring in September and October.

This makes a different analysis of responses to famine in Dar Masalit necessary. In other parts of Darfur people planned their responses to the famine on the assumptions that the rains would start in June, and that from then on things would improve. In Dar Masalit the second of these expectations was confounded. People followed a normal pattern of strategies during the dry season, but experienced appalling hardship during the wet season. By then the success or failure of the main objective of the famine strategies was already decided: normative subsistence was either lost or assured. The crops were growing, and grazing was available for animals. Farmers needed no further expenditure to be certain of a harvest; they merely had to guard their crops and stay alive. They could sell animals and take out loans knowing that their survival for a year ahead was assured.

Therefore, in Arara during the rains of 1985 we might expect to find that people followed pure 'survival strategies', in the sense of strategies with the sole or overwhelming aim of obtaining food. This is a test of the conditions under which physical survival alone becomes people's main objective.

'Last year I should have died,' said one man in Arara in 1986. The last assault of the famine, during the rains of 1985, certainly produced unequalled horrors. A survey by the Red Cross in Beida in September found that 93 per cent of refugee children and 53 per cent of local children were moderately or severely 'malnourished', according to anthropometric classification. These rates are some of the worst ever recorded. Arara is close to Beida, but it was inaccessible and no surveys were done there until the harvest was coming in.

We can calculate the extent of the grain market in Arara during the rains using the 'residual' and 'income' methods for the sample of 168 households which were interviewed. The 'residual' method leaves us with ten households, which is a drop from thirty-five during the dry season. In addition, eleven households were buying wild foods from the market. The 'income' method gives a figure of 6.9 per cent of needs that could have been supplied, at a price of £s300 per sack. This figure represents twice the cash income during the dry season. The increase is remarkable in view of the decline in income from low-status trades over the same period. Twenty-three per cent of households went into debt in the famine year, most of them at the start of the rains. Most of the borrowing was not of money but of sacks of grain. Animal sales were high throughout the rains, up 10 per cent on the dry season. Eight sampled households even sold donkeys, an exceptionally high number, and a signal of desperation. Elsewhere in northern Darfur fewer households were taking out loans and sales of animals were declining.

Arara suffered from an absolute shortage of *'esh* during the rains, because it simply could not be transported there, except by helicopter. (USAID chartered helicopters to fly in relief food, but very little was sent to Arara.) Also, the severity of the shortage was unanticipated. Hence the argument that it was possible to obtain access to grain through the market does not hold in this case. There was also a shortage of wild foods, which resulted in a thriving market in *mukheit*. The income to Arara would have bought 30 per cent of the village's food energy needs if it had been spent on *mukheit*, as much of it was.

The increases in sales of animals and in debts show an increase in concern with immediate survival. This concern is echoed in remarks such as the one quoted above. Yet at the same time, remarkably few households in Arara crossed the critical threshold into normative destitution during the rains. Only one household sold animals critical to subsistence. Five sampled households worked in the wet season, as farm labourers, and thereby failed to cultivate enough of their own land. These represent six of the twenty-six households that became destitute during the famine: the other twenty had succumbed already in the dry season. This shows that the increase in cash income was not obtained at the expense of normative subsistence. Even when households had assured their survival for a year ahead, they were not prepared to jeopardize the basis for their livelihood even further into the future.

Conclusion

The first point of the conclusion follows directly. The evidence for hunger and destitution during the rains appears to show that even when the famine was prolonged and worsened, households clung on to the base of their future livelihood. The aim of avoiding destitution persisted in the face of hunger that equalled even the worst of Mawashei. The increase in expenditure on food also suggests that the aim of subsistence and the toleration of hunger should be seen as relative. There comes a point when the balance between them begins to swing in the direction of meeting immediate food needs. This may occur when severe undernutrition, with its corollary of increased susceptibility to disease, is likely. It is notable that mortality did not increase significantly above dry-season levels during the rains in Arara, and that, as elsewhere, there were no effects of wealth or production explaining differences in mortality.

The second point is to challenge the supposition that the wet-season severity was unexpected. Were expectations really confounded if people were able to continue through the rains without significantly endangering their future livelihood? The answer is, perhaps not. The worsening of the famine in the rains in Dar Masalit was markedly different from what happened in other parts of Darfur, but that does not mean it was unexpected. The rains of 1985 were very good, but if they had been poor, many people would not have left southern areas to return north, the grain price would not have dropped, and distress sales would have continued. Chapter 4 showed that people are pessimistic about the likelihood of a failure of

NEXT WEEK — READING

Ch. 7 & Preface

        ↳ p. xi – 2nd full ¶
           (rd. before ch. 7)

Concepts: disaster tourism
         structural violence
         data + policy

Measuring suffering
- participant observation / ethical issue w/studying this suffering

De Waal's Famine That Kills: Darfur, Sudan
In-class Exercise, Chapters 1-6

Form groups of no more than 3 people. Try to avoid being in the same group as your civic engagement team members. Choose one person to be the rapporteur for your group. Hey! Why not someone different from last time! You have 15ish minutes.

Part I: Prepare a 3 minute summary of the author's main point of your assigned chapter and a description of the evidence he uses to support his position.

Part II: Decide which of the following questions are most pertinent to your assigned chapter, discuss, and be prepared to state your position to the rest of the class.

  d) What has changed between the 1984-85 famine and the current conflict in Darfur?
  e) Has the international humanitarian regime learned to respond effectively to famines, crises of massacre, and mass displacement? What has improved? What is still lacking?
  f) What augers of the current violence can be detected in the ethnography of 1984-85?

the rains. Elsewhere in Darfur the wet season also saw increased distributions of relief food, which rural people had not expected. Things did start to improve in June and July, but until then there was an expectation that they might well continue to get worse. Only in Dar Masalit, for the quite contingent reasons of the refugee population, did this actually happen, but it could have been typical.

The case of Arara therefore shows that rural people could be even more resilient in the face of famine than most of them, in the event, needed to be. When the nadir of the famine was reached in most of Darfur, in about May–June, the famine could have continued to intensify without a fundamental change in peoples' strategies and priorities.

The final point that is demonstrated by the case of Dar Masalit is that the causes of a famine can be highly particular to the area and time in question. Geographically, socially, and economically Dar Masalit has many similarities with the rest of Darfur. The notions of 'famine', of 'hunger', '(normative) destitution', and 'death' held in Dar Masalit are similar to those held in other parts of Darfur, and the same mode of socio-economic analysis works for peoples' responses to the famine. Yet an understanding of why the famine developed the way it did requires us to look at very local and very singular factors.

Famine in Western Bahr el Ghazal

An Unnoticed Famine

The 'third famine' in Darfur during 1984/5 occurred in the far south of the region. So far the village of Legediba has been the most southerly site discussed. It is notable that the harvest failure of 1984 was more severe there than in the other sites in southern Darfur, which lie well to the north. Impoverishment and destitution were greater there too. In fact, the whole of the southern part of Buram District suffered more than almost any other part of southern Darfur, and Buram town had one of the worst famine camps in the whole region, at Hujerat.

The reason for this was a third 'epicentre' of famine, lying to the south of Darfur, caused by drought and harvest failure. In 1984 a band of drought stretched across the southernmost parts of Darfur and into Bahr el Ghazal. Legediba lay at the northern edge of this band. What of places that lay well within it?

All of Darfur suffers from a data problem, but this dwindles into relative insigificance when compared with the data problem involved in studying western Bahr el Ghazal. During Anglo-Egyptian rule, different estimates for the population of Bahr el Ghazal varied by factors of five or more. In 1910 the population was estimated at 315,000, in 1922 at 2,500,000, and in 1936 at 475,000. Even the Censuses of 1953 and 1956 differed by 30 per cent, six times their largest disagreement elsewhere in Sudan. These remote and mobile populations proved impossible to enumerate. This problem has become worse since Independence, with more or less continual insecurity in the province. In Bahr el Ghazal during 1984/5 the government and aid agencies were confined to the towns and were unable to provide useful information on rural areas.

The situation was rendered worse by the conflict between Rizeigat and Dinka, which flared during the famine, and reached full-scale war by 1987. Part of the reason for the conflict were disputes over grazing. In Chapter 6, I mentioned the course of a dispute between the Fellata and the Habbaniya concerning grazing and cattle movements, which was finally arbitrated and resolved by the local authorities. A similar dispute between Rizeigat and Dinka could have been peacefully resolved by negotiation and arbitration, as had happened in the past. The national politics of Sudan during the 1980s prevented this. The dispute escalated into armed conflict, systematic raiding, and the massacre of over 1,000 Dinka people in Ed Da'ien in March 1987 (Ushari and Baldo 1987). In this case extreme violence was not a cause but, in part, a consequence of the famine.

There are huge problems involved in attempting to study this famine. The absence of data has been mentioned. Another difficulty is that an attempt to understand it using the explanatory model that I have been propounding is doomed to failure. This model was developed for the savannas of Darfur. It fitted a famine with different causes in Dar Masalit, but fails to fit a famine with similar causes on the borderlands of Darfur and Bahr el Ghazal.

Sabola, Dar Binga

Sabola is a small village of fifty-two households that is administratively part of Darfur but culturally, demographically, and economically akin to Bahr el Ghazal. It lies in a forest clearing a few yards to the south of the Umbelasha river. According to a neglected clause in the agreement of 1972 which ended the first civil war, the river forms the frontier between Darfur and Bahr el Ghazal. The area is known as Dar Binga, after the people who live there. It therefore can give some clues as to the pattern of famine in areas of the same latitude that unequivocally lie within Bahr el Ghazal.

Dar Binga is not affected by the war in Bahr el Ghazal. But it has its own data problem. This is due to its complex and little documented history, and because informants are unwilling to talk about the most important aspects of the economy because they are mostly illegal.

Dar Binga and the adjacent part of Bahr el Ghazal are areas that were dominated by Dar Fur during the sultanate, up to the conquest of Bahr el Ghazal by the slave-trader Zubeir Pasha in the mid-nineteenth century. Dar Fur had a large slaving post and trading town nearby at Kafia Kinji, until it was destroyed by the British in the 1930s, and copper mines at Hofrat en Nahas, where there was another important town. Both towns had large trading populations, including west Africans, Egyptians, and Riverain Sudanese. The Fur state maintained tribute-paying states headed by sultans in this area, the largest being Dar Feroge and the Kresh kingdom. The whole area was known as Dar Fertit. Fertit was the name the Fur state gave to its enslavable southern neighbours.

The origins of the Binga are unclear. O'Fahey (1982) classed them as a people indigenous to Darfur who were partially assimilated to the Fur and partly pushed further south by Fur expansion. The Binga of Sabola gave an account of their origins which claims that they lived beside the Fur, but were forced to leave for the south after being unable to pay reparations to the Fur following a dispute. Santandrea (1964, p. 234) wrote that the name *Binga* 'is probably a foreign denomination, comprising a number of sections and clans closely linked together . . . that only in later years have attained tribal unity'. Dar Binga as a polity appears to date from the appointment or confirmation of Adam Sabun as sultan of the Binga by Ali Dinar.

The states of Dar Fertit lived uneasily as client states of Dar Fur. They were polities created by Dar Fur to mediate in the slaving business. Informants in Dar Binga were forthcoming, not to say strident, in the exposition of their history and the injustices which had been meted out to them. It is likely that these origins are evident in the current organization of society, but to research this topic would have required more time than was available. An intriguing clue was provided by a discussion by Binga informants on the subject of the Mandala people. Mandala was the name given by Baggara Arabs to their actual or potential slaves; they were thus in a similar position to the Binga, and Binga people were prepared to discuss issues with reference to them that they would not discuss with reference to themselves. Binga informants insisted that a Mandala woman, divorcing her Mandala husband, keeps the children with her. This was variously attributed to Mandala ethnicity being matrilineal and to the fact that in the past a slave-owner who owned a female slave also owned any children she might have. In Dar Rizeigat this was disclaimed (any mention of the Mandala caused much embarrassment there) but was reported by Governor Lampen during the 1920s (Civsec 66/2/13). (Lampen gave the 'slave origins' account.) Binga informants insisted that they themselves were patrilineal and would not comment on their own divorce arrangements. The Binga of this area continue, however, to have a client relationship with the Arabs. They host large numbers of Habbaniya who bring their cattle down to the Umbelasha during the dry season, and exchange wild honey, meat, and contraband for animals.

The British were not happy about these little sultanates with their elusive identities and client status. British policy towards southern Sudan was to isolate it so far as possible from Arab and Moslem influence. There were even suggestions of federating the region with Uganda. One way in which this policy was pursued was by the creation of a cordon sanitaire between Moslem northern and western Sudan and non-Moslem south Sudan. This policy was put into effect in the early 1930s (Civsec 66/4/35). The Binga, along with other Fertit, lay in the middle of the proposed no man's land. The British response to this problem was to propose that the Moslems be removed northwards and the non-Moslems southwards, and to burn the town of Kafia Kinji. Four non-Moslem sections of the Binga moved south and three Moslem sections moved north, leaving (briefly) a gap between them.

The Binga, however, are not principally farmers and are hard to pin down in one place. They keep livestock, but numbers and herding strategies are limited because the area has little ground-water, and most of it is infested by tsetse fly. Millet and sorghum can be grown, but clearing and weeding are difficult because the area is so thickly forested and so wet. The area is well known for marijuana, though statistics are not easy to obtain. Waged employment was once intermittently available at the copper mines of Hofrat en Nahas, though there has been none now for over a decade. Hunting and gathering are important. While there were still elephants the trade in ivory was very profitable, and leopard and lion skins continue to provide an illegal income; hunting also provides meat. Gathering includes not only wild fruits and grains to eat but honey, which commands a high price in Darfur's urban markets. This part of Darfur may be a long way away and unreachable by vehicle for six months of the year, but this has not prevented the economy from being integrated into all the adjacent economies: Darfur, southern Sudan, and Central Africa. Kafia Kinji, to the south, and Songo, just over the river from Sabola, were both important centres for the pilgrimage to Mecca from west Africa (Birks 1978, pp. 20–3, 101). Traders come down this way to buy the products of the forest, legal and illegal. Baggara herders bring their cattle herds down this way and the Binga profit from them. Zaghawa herders come this way too in poor seasons. Several from Angabo went to Hofrat en Nahas, and at least one household came all the way from Furawiya, a 1,000 mile round trip. The Binga themselves migrate for seasonal work northwards to the new commercial farms of southern Darfur and to the towns. They trade northwards with Darfur, eastwards with Bahr el Ghazal, and westwards with Central Africa.

The Binga have a different attitude to famine to that which is found in the rest of Darfur. Famines are not named, and informants seemed puzzled even by the idea of them. Only Juma Abdel Rahman, a Tunjur who had deserted from Ali Dinar's army in 1916 and was still living as an escapee in Songo, could tell us of past famines, and then only of *Julu*, which occurred when he was living in El Fasher. Binga informants knew of *Julu* as *Ja'ali*, believing that this was a place where the famine had occurred—presumably the land of the Ja'aliyiin Arabs. One said that Dar Binga had received 'refugees fleeing from Ja'ali', which could be dated to about 1914. By contrast raidings and enforced movements were well remembered. Zubeir Pasha was recalled, but the most vividly recalled events were the forced removals of the Condominium Government in the 1930s, which continue to provoke violent emotions.

According to the concept of 'famine' held by people in the savanna societies of Darfur, the Binga are in a state of perpetual famine. They are in client relationships with their northern neighbours. They depend on gathering and hunting, and petty trading. Some share-crop. Many do not even claim to be Moslems. The Binga have mostly not adopted the 'Darfur ideology'. Their lack of recognition of famines may also be related to the chronic insecurity of the area, always raided or disrupted by the Fur, or the Arabs, or one of the governments of Sudan. The notion of famine as 'dearth' or 'doing unpleasant things to survive' does not apply in an area where this is the norm. They have few crops to wither and few animals to die. The concepts of normative destitution and subsistence as used in Darfur do not apply where hunting, gathering, and share-cropping are preferred activities. Understanding responses to famine in Dar Binga would require an entirely separate project: this was not undertaken.

Dar Binga suffered drought in 1984, and it is possible to trace some of the effects of this. There was production of millet adequate for less than half of needs. Livestock numbers dropped by about 40 per cent. But household strategies bore no clear relationship to level of subsistence or destitution. Eighty per cent took paid labour, including share-cropping. All but one ate wild foods; but here these foods are a normal part of the preferred diet. Excluding commercial credit to hunters, 70 per cent of the households in Sabola went into debt in 1984/5. This is a higher level of access to credit than was found elsewhere in Darfur, and illustrates the mercantile nature of this apparently isolated community. In one sense these are the 'same' responses as are found in other parts of Darfur, but they were undertaken with different considerations and had different meanings.

One very striking fact about Sabola was the high number of deaths. The annual death rate during 1984–6 was 48 per thousand. This was the highest rate found. As mentioned in Chapter 7, Sabola belongs demograhically in Bahr el Ghazal, where normal death rates are as much as twice those prevailing in Darfur. The sample was also small, being fifty-two households. Taking these facts into consideration, it is not possible to infer that famine mortality in this area was exceptionally high.

Nevertheless, the example of Sabola illustrates the dangers of analysing famines primarily as episodes of excess deaths. If a larger study of Dar Binga were to replicate what was found in Sabola, the implications would be considerable. A study with a 'focus on death' would conclude that the famine here was more severe than elsewhere in Darfur, because the rate of excess deaths was higher. A study which used the notions of 'famine' current in Dar Binga might conclude the opposite: that the famine was less severe here than elsewhere. This would follow from the findings that the episode posed little threat to the Binga way of life, and that the Binga people did not recognize it as a famine. A study of a famine must combine both approaches.

Conclusion

This section has not served as another fragment of the pattern of responses to famine in Darfur in 1984/5: a whole new account of the theory of famine and subsistence would be needed to explain what occurred in this area. Instead, the discussion of Dar Binga and Sabola serves as a reminder of how specific these patterns of response are to the ecology and the social economy of a particular area, and to societies with a particular set of values. The 'Darfur model' of understanding and responding to famine, derived from the 'core' societies of the mountains and savannas of Darfur, will not work here. It may be that in Dar Binga and western Bahr el Ghazal people went hungry so as to preserve an acceptable way of life: this study has not developed the tools for analysing that.

Coda

This book could be concluded with any number of platitudes. I could mention the resilience and humanity of the people of Darfur in the face of great suffering (in contrast to the portrayal of the Ik by Colin Turnbull). There is also the need to examine the concepts we use to analyse other peoples' societies, and the role of these same concepts in our own ideologies. There is the almost tangible feeling of relief that pervaded the countryside as the post-famine harvest was brought in at the end of 1985, and how, with astonishing rapidity, the famine was over. There is the rallying cry of 'never again!'. Following that, the book could be concluded with definite proposals for a programme of action, with specified roles for various institutions. Better endings might stress the need for further research ('Now we may begin', or alternatively, to paraphrase Lewis Carroll: 'We don't know much, and that's a fact.') This is exemplified by the case of the agricultural experts who sadly shook their heads over the degraded *goz* surrounding El Fasher in late 1985 and advised the farmers that millet would never grow there again; the farmers predictably ignored their advice and by late 1986 ripe millet stood, head high, from horizon to horizon.

The subject of famine lends itself to profound, moral, and sombre concluding sentences. But any such ending would have a note of completeness, even satisfaction, which would be inappropriate. Famines consist in unease, failure, lost opportunity, and dissatisfaction. It was a miserable famine.

REFERENCES

Abel, W. (1980). *Agricultural Fluctuations in Europe from the 13th to the 20th Centuries* (London, Methuen).

Achebe, C. (1966). *A Man of the People* (London, Heinemann).

Adams, M. E. (1975). 'A Development Plan for Semi-Arid Areas in Western Sudan', *Experimental Agriculture*, 11, 277–87.

Alamgir, M. (1980). *Famine in South Asia: the Political Economy of Mass Starvation* (Cambridge, Mass., Oelgeshlager, Gunn and Hain).

Appleby, A. B. (1978). *Famine in Tudor and Stuart England* (Liverpool, Liverpool University Press).

Anderson, D. M., and Johnson, D. H. (1988). 'Introduction, Ecology and Society in Northeast African History', in D. H. Johnson, and D. M. Anderson, (eds.), *The Ecology of Survival, Case Studies from Northeast African History* (London, Lester Crook).

Arkell, A. J. (1940). 'The Coinage of Ali Dinar, Sultan of Darfur 1898–1916', *Sudan Notes and Records*, 23, 151–160.

—— (1951a). 'The History of Darfur 1200–1700 AD (I)', *Sudan Notes and Records*, 32, 37–70.

—— (1951b). 'Medieval History of Darfur (II)', *Sudan Notes and Records*, 32, 207–38.

—— (1952a). 'The History of Darfur 1200–1700 (III)', *Sudan Notes and Records*, 33, 129–55.

—— (1952b). 'The History of Darfur 1200–1700 (IV)', *Sudan Notes and Records*, 33, 244–75.

Autier, P. (1988). 'Nutrition Assessment Through the Use of a Nutritional Scoring System', *Disasters*, 12, 70–80.

Balamoan, G. A. (1976). *Migration Policies in the Anglo-Egyptian Sudan 1884–1956* (Cambridge, Mass., Harvard University Centre for Population Studies).

Barbour, K. M. (1950). 'The Wadi Azum from Zalingei to Murnei', *Sudan Notes and Records*, 31, 105–28.

Baring, A. (1969). 'Political Institutions in Darfur', B.Litt. thesis (University of Oxford).

Barth, F. (1967a). 'Human Resources: Social and Cultural Features of the Jebel Marra Project Area' (Rome, FAO).

—— (1967b). 'Economic Spheres in Darfur', in R. Firth (ed.), *Themes in Economic Anthropology* (London, Tavistock).

al Bashir, A-R. A. (1978). 'Problems of the Settlement of Immigrants and Refugees in Sudanese Society', D.Phil. thesis (University of Oxford).

Bayoumi, A. (1979). *The History of the Sudan Health Services* (Nairobi, Kenya Literature Bureau).

Beaton, A. C. (1939). 'Fur Rain Cults and Ceremonies', *Sudan Notes and Records*, 22, 186–203.

—— (1948). 'The Fur', *Sudan Notes and Records* 29, 1–39.

Bede, the Venerable (1969). *Ecclesiastical History of the English People*, ed. B. Colgrave and R. Mynors (Oxford, Clarendon Press).

Behnke, R. H. (1985). 'Rangeland Development and the Improvement of Livestock Production' (Nyala, WSDC).

Berry, A. (1985). 'Famine Food and the Process of Adaptation to Extreme Food Shortages' (London: London School of Hygiene and Tropical Medicine).

Birks, J. (1978). *Across the Savannas to Mecca: The Overland Pilgrimage Route from West Africa* (London, Hurst).

Bonar, J. (1895). *Malthus and his Work* (London, Macmillan).

Browne, W. G. (1806). *Travels in Africa, Egypt and Syria from the Year 1792 to 1798*, 2nd edn., (London, Cadell and Davies).

Buckley, R. (1987). 'Results from the Household Survey undertaken by the SCF Information Department in Darfur Region, Sudan from March–July 1986' (London, SCF).

—— (1988). 'Food Targeting in Darfur: Save the Children Fund's Programme in 1986', *Disasters*, 12, 97–103.

Burckhardt, J. L. (1819). *Travels in Nubia* (London, J. Murray).

Buxton, J. C. (1963). *Chiefs and Strangers, A Study of Political Assimilation among the Mandari* (Oxford, Clarendon Press).

Caldwell, J. C. (1975). 'The Sahelian Drought and its Demographic Implications' (Washington, DC, Overseas Liaison Committee Paper No. 8).

—— (1977). 'Demographic Aspects of Drought: An Examination of the African Drought of 1970–74', in D. Dalby, R. J. Harrison-Church, and F. Bezzaz (eds.), *Drought in Africa 2* (London, International African Institute, African Environment Special Report No. 6).

Chambers, R. (1983). *Rural Development, Putting the Last First* (London, Longman).

Chen, L. C., Chowdhury, A. K. M. A., and Huffman, S. L. (1980). 'Anthropometric Assessment of Protein-Energy Malnutrition and Subsequent Risk of Mortality among Pre-school Aged Children', *American Journal of Clinical Nutrition*, 33, 1836–45.

Clift-Hill, A. (1986). 'Darfur Historical Rainfall Records' (Zalingei, JMRDP).

Cordell, D. D. (1985). *Dar al-Kuti and the Last Years of the Trans-Saharan Slave Trade* (Madison, University of Wisconsin Press).

Cossins, N. J. (1972). 'No Way to Live: A Study of the Afar Clans of the North-East Rangelands' (Addis Ababa, Livestock and Meat Board).

Crosse-Upcott, A. R. W. (1958). 'Ngindo Famine Subsistence', *Tanganyika Notes and Records*, 50, 1–20.

Currey, B. (1978). 'The Famine Syndrome: Its Definition for Relief and Rehabilitation in Bangladesh', *Ecology of Food and Nutrition*, 7, 87–98.

Davies, R. (1924). 'The Masalit Sultanate', *Sudan Notes and Records*, 7, 49–62.

de Waal, A. (1987*a*). 'Famine that Kills, Darfur 1984–85', (London, SCF).

—— (1987*b*). 'The Perception of Poverty and Famines', *International Journal of Moral and Social Studies*, 2, 251–62.

—— (1988). 'Famine Early Warning Systems and the Use of Socio-Economic Data', *Disasters*, 12, 81–91.

—— (1989). 'Famine Mortality: A Case Study of Darfur, Sudan 1984–5', *Population Studies*, 43, 5–24.

Decalo, S. (1977). *Historical Dictionary of Chad* (Meiuchen, NJ, Scarecrow Press).

Demeny, P. (1968). 'The Demography of Sudan: An Analysis of the 1955/6 Census', in W. Brass, (ed.), *The Demography of Tropical Africa*, (Princeton, Princeton University Press).

Dessalegn Rahmato, (1987). 'Famine and Survival Strategies: A Case Study from Northeast Ethiopia' (Addis Ababa, Institute of Development Research, Food and Famine Monographs No. 1).

Doornbos, P. (1983). 'Some Aspects of Smuggling between Chad and Sudan', (Khartoum, Development Studies and Research Centre, Discussion Paper No. 33).

—— (1984). 'Trade in Two Border Towns: Beida and Foro Baranga (Darfur Province).', in L. O. Manger (ed.), *Trade and Traders in the Sudan*, (Bergen, Bergen Occasional Papers in Social Anthropology No. 32).

—— (1986). 'Regionalisation and the Quest for Revenue: Darfur Region', in P. van der Wel and M. Ahmed Abdel Ghaffer (eds.), *Perspectives on Development in the Sudan, Selected Papers from a Research Workshop in The Hague, July 1984* (The Hague).

Douglas, M. (1966). *Purity and Danger* (London, Routledge and Kegan Paul).

Drèze, J. (1988). 'Famine Prevention in India' (London, London School of Economics, Development Economics Research Programme, Discussion Paper No. 3).

Eldredge, E. and Rydjeski, D. (1988). 'Food Crises, Crisis Response and Emergency Preparedness: The Sudan Case', *Disasters*, 12, 1–4.

—— Salter, S., and Rydjeski, D. (1986). 'Towards an Early Warning System in Sudan', *Disasters*, 10, 189–96.

Eldridge, C. (1988). 'Food for Thought: Suggestions for a Systematised Approach to Emergency Food Distributions' (London, SCF).

Farah, A-A., and Preston, S. H. (1982). 'Child Mortality Differentials in Sudan', *Population and Development Review*, 8, 365–83.

Faulkingham, R. H. (1977). 'Ecological Constraints and Subsistence

Strategies: The Impact of Drought in a Hausa Village, a Case Study from Niger', in D. Dalby, R. J. Harrison-Church, and F. Bezzaz, (eds.), *Drought in Africa 2*, (London, International African Institute, African Environment Special Report No. 6).

Firth, R. (1959). *Social Change in Tikopia* (New York, Macmillan).

Flinn, M. (ed.). (1977). *Scottish Population History from the 17th Century to the 1930s* (Cambridge, Cambridge University Press).

Flood, G. (1976). 'Nomadism and Its Future: the Afar', in A-M. Hussein, (ed.), *Rehab: Drought and Famine in Ethiopia* (London, International African Institute, African Environment Special Report No. 2).

Foster, S. O. (1984). 'Immunizable and Respiratory Diseases in Child Mortality', *Population and Development Review*, Supplement to 10, 119–40.

—— and Pifer, J. M. (1971). 'Mass Measles Control in West and Central Africa', *African Journal of Medical Sciences*, 2, 151–8.

Franke, R. W. and Chasin, B. H. (1980). *Seeds of Famine: Ecological Destruction and the Development Dilemma in the Sahel*, (New York, Universe Books).

Fraser, L. (1911). *India under Curzon and After* (London, Heinemann).

Greene, M. H. (1974). 'Impact of the Sahelian Drought in Mauritania, West Africa', *Lancet*, i, 1093–7.

Grove, A. T. (1973). 'A Note on the Remarkably Low Rainfall of the Sudan Zone in 1913', *Savanna*, 2, 133–8.

Haaland, G. (1972). 'Nomadism as an Economic Career among Sedentaries of the Sudan Savanna Belt', in I. Cunnison and W. James (eds.), *Essays in Sudan Ethnography* (London, G. Hurst).

Harrell-Bond, B. E. (1986). *Imposing Aid: Emergency Assistance to Refugees* (Oxford, Oxford University Press).

Hartwig, G. W. (1978). 'Louse-Borne Relapsing Fever in Sudan 1908–51', in G. W. Hartwig and K. D. Patterson (eds.), *Disease in African History*, (Durham, NC, Duke University Press).

Hewitt, K. (1983). 'The Idea of Calamity in a Technocratic Age', in K. Hewitt (ed.), *Interpretations of Calamity, from the Viewpoint of Human Ecology* (Boston, Allen and Unwin).

Hill, A. G. (1985). 'The Recent Demographic Surveys in Mali and their Main Findings', in A. G. Hill (ed.), *Population, Health and Nutrition in the Sahel* (London, KPI).

Hill, P. (1972). *Rural Hausa: A Village and a Setting* (Cambridge, Cambridge University Press).

Hollingsworth, T. H. (1969). *Historical Demography* (London, Hodder and Stoughton).

Holt, P. M. (1958). *The Mahdist State in the Sudan* (Oxford, Clarendon Press).

Holy, L. (1974). *Neighbours and Kinsmen: A Study of the Berti People of Darfur* (London, Hurst).

—— (1980). 'Drought and Change in a Tribal Economy: The Berti of Northern Darfur', *Disasters*, 4, 65–72.

—— (1987). 'Decline of Reciprocal Farm Labour among the Berti', in L. O. Manger (ed.), *Communal Labour in the Sudan* (Bergen, Bergen Occasional Papers in Social Anthropology No. 41).

Hoskins, W. G. (1964). 'Harvest Fluctuations and English Economic History 1480–1619', *Agricultural History Review*, 12, 28–46.

—— (1968). 'Harvest Fluctuations and English Economic History 1620–1759', *Agricultural History Review*, 16, 15–31.

HTS (1977). Hunting Technical Services, 'Agricultural Development in the Jebel Marra Area, Sudan', (Borehamwood, HTS Working Paper No. 3).

Hurst, H. E. (1923). 'The Rains of the Nile Basin and the Nile Flood of 1913', (Cairo, Government Press, Physical Department Paper No. 12).

Hussein, A-M., (ed.). (1976). *Rehab: Drought and Famine in Ethiopia* (London, International African Institute, African Environment Special Report No. 2).

Ibrahim, F. N. (1984). *Ecological Imbalance in the Republic of the Sudan— with Reference to Desertification in Darfur*, (Bayreuth, Bayreuther Geowissenschaftliche Arbeiten).

Iliffe, J. (1987). *The African Poor, A History* (Cambridge, Cambridge University Press).

JMRDP (1984). Jebel Marra Rural Development Project, 'Migration into the Project Area', (Zalingei, JMRDP).

—— (1986). 'Annual Report 1985/6, Annex II, Monitoring and Evaluation Department' (Zalingei, JMRDP).

Jernudd, B. (1968). 'Linguistic Integration and National Development, A Case Study of the Jebel Marra Area, Sudan', in J. A. Fishman, C. A. Ferguson, and J. Das Gupta (eds.), *Language Problems of Developing Nations* (New York, J. Wiley).

Kameir, el W., and Karsany, I. (1985). *Corruption as the 'Fifth' Factor of Production in the Sudan* (Uppsala, Scandanavian Institute for African Studies, Report No. 72).

Kapteijns, L. (1982). *Mahdist Faith and Sudanic Tradition, A History of Dar Masalit 1870–1930* (Amsterdam, University of Amsterdam).

Kasongo Project Team, (1983). 'Anthropometric Assessment of Young Children's Nutritional Status and Subsequent Risk of Dying', *Journal of Tropical Paediatrics*, 29, 69–75.

Keen, D, (1986). 'The Incidence and Origins of Food Crises in Darfur, Sudan, Since the Second World War', M.Sc. Thesis (London School of Economics).

Kershaw, I. (1973). 'The Great Famine and Agrarian Crisis in England 1315–22', *Past and Present*, 59, 3–50.

Khan, M. (1986). *Always Hungry, Never Greedy: Food and the Expression of Gender in Melanesian Society* (Cambridge, Cambridge University Press).

Kloth, T. I., Burr, W. A., Davis, J. P., Epler, G., Kolff, C. A., Rosenberg, R. L., Staehling, N. W., Lane, J. M., and Nichaman, M. Z. (1976). 'Sahel Nutrition Survey 1974', *American Journal of Epidemiology*, 103, 383–90.

Koopman, J. S., Fajardo, L., and Bertrand, W. (1981). 'Food, Sanitation, and the Socio-Economic Determinants of Child Growth in Colombia', *American Journal of Public Health*, 71, 383–90.

Ladurie, E. LeR. (1979). 'Amenorrhoea in Time of Famine', in *The Territory of the Historian*, trans. B. and S. Reynolds (Brighton, Harvester).

Lampen, G. D. (1950). 'History of Darfur', *Sudan Notes and Records*, 31, 177–209.

Laya, D. (1975). 'Interviews with Farmers and Livestock Owners in the Sahel', *African Environment*, 1, 49–93.

Leonard, E. M. (1900). *The Early History of English Poor Relief* (Cambridge, Cambridge University Press).

Lofchie, M. F. (1975). 'Political and Economic Origins of African Hunger', *Journal of Modern African Studies*, 13, 551–67.

Lovejoy, P. E. (ed.). (1981). *The Ideology of Slavery in Africa* (Beverley Hills, Sage).

Lundstrom, K. J. (1976). *North-Eastern Ethiopia: Society in Famine*, (Uppsala, Scandanavian Institute of African Studies, Research Report No. 34).

MacMichael, H. A. (1915). 'Notes on the Tribes of Darfur' (Khartoum, National Records Office, file no. Civsec 112/3/9).

—— (1920). 'The Tungur-Fur of Dar Furnung', *Sudan Notes and Records*, 3, 24–32.

Malthus, T. R. (1890). *An Essay on the Principle of Population*, 6th edn., originally published 1826, (London, Ward, Lock, and Co.).

—— (1926). *First Essay on Population*, originally published 1798, (London, Macmillan).

Martorell, M., and Ho, T. J. (1984). 'Malnutrition, Morbidity and Mortality', *Population and Development Review*, supplement to 10, 49–68.

Maurice, G. K. (1932). 'The Entry of Relapsing Fever into Sudan', *Sudan Notes and Records*, 15, 97–118.

Meillassoux, C. (1974). 'Development or Exploitation: Is the Sahel Famine Good for Business?', *Review of African Politican Economy*, 1, 27–33.

Mesfin Wolde Mariam (1986). *Rural Vulnerability to Famine in Ethiopia 1958–1977* (London, Intermediate Technology Publications).

Miers, S., and Kopytoff, I. (eds.). (1977). *Slavery in Africa* (Wisconsin, University of Wisconsin Press).

Mohammed el Hassan (1980). 'Pre-Settlement Sociology Surveys' (Nyala, WSDC).

—– (1983*a*). 'A Report on El Amud el Akhdar 1980–1983' (Nyala, WSDC).

—— (1983*b*). 'Goz Afin' (Nyala, WSDC).

Murray, M. J., and Murray, A. B. (1977). 'Suppression of Infection and its Activation by Refeeding: A Paradox?', *Perspectives in Biology and Medicine*, 20, 471–83.

—— —— Murray, N. J., and Murray, M. B. (1975). 'Refeeding Malaria and Hyperferraemia', *Lancet*, i, 653–4.

Mustafa Babiker Ahmed (1988). 'Primary Export Crop Production and the Origins of the Ecological Crisis in Kordofan, The Case of Dar Hamar', in D. H. Johnson, and D. M. Anderson (eds.), *The Ecology of Survival, Case Studies from Northeast African History* (London, Lester Crook).

Nabarro, D., and Chinnock, P. (1988). 'Growth Monitoring: Inappropriate Promotion of an Appropriate Technology', *Social Science and Medicine*, 26, 941–8.

Nachtigal, G. (1971). *Sahara and Sudan, vol. iv, Wadai and Darfur*, originally completed 1874, (London, G. Hurst).

Nicholson, S. E. (1979). 'The Methodology of Historical Climate Reconstruction and its Application to Africa', *Journal of African History*, 20, 31–50.

O'Brien, J. (1985). 'Sowing the Seeds of Famine', *Review of African Political Economy*, 33, 23–32.

O'Fahey, R. S. (1980). *State and Society in Dar Fur*, (London, G. Hurst).

—— (1982). 'Fur and Fartit: The History of a Frontier', in J. Mack and P. Robertshaw (eds.), *Culture History in the Southern Sudan: Archeology, Linguistics, Ethnohistory* (Nairobi, British Institute in Eastern Africa).

—— and Abu Salim, M. I. (1983). *Land in Dar Fur: Charters and Related Documents from the Dar Fur Sultanate* (Cambridge: Cambridge University Press).

Pankhurst, R. K. and Johnson, D. H. (1988). 'The Great Drought and Famine of 1888–92 in Northeast Africa', in D. H. Johnson and D. M. Anderson (eds.), *The Ecology of Survival, Case Studies from Northeast African History* (London, Lester Crook).

Post, J. (1977). *The Last Great Subsistence Crisis of the Western World* (Baltimore, Johns Hopkins University Press).

Postan, M. M. (1950). 'Some Economic Evidence for the Declining Population in the Later Middle Ages', *Economic History Review*, 2nd ser., 2, 221–46.

Rangasami, A. (1985). 'Failure of Exchange Entitlements Theory: a Response', Paper given at International Workshop 'Women's Role in Self-Sufficiency and Food Strategies' (Paris).

Ravallion, M. (1987). *Markets and Famines*, (Oxford, Clarendon Press).

Raynaut, C. (1977). 'Lessons of a Crisis', in D. Dalby, R. J. Harrison-Church, and F. Bezzaz (eds.). *Drought in Africa 2* (London, International African Institute, African Environment Special Report No. 6).

Relief and Rehabilitation Commission (1974). 'Hararghe under Drought: A Survey of the Effects of Drought upon Human Nutrition in Hararghe Province, Ethiopia' (Addis Ababa, Relief and Rehabilitation Commission).

Republic of the Sudan (1959). *First Population Census of Sudan, 1955/6: Final Report, vol. i* (Khartoum, Department of Statistics, Population Census Office).

—— (1980). *Second Population Census, 1973, vol. ii* (Khartoum, Population Census Office).

Richards, P. (1983). 'Ecological Change and the Politics of Land Use', *African Studies Review*, 26, 1–72.

Rivers, J., Holt, J., Seaman, J., and Bowden, M. (1976). 'Lessons for Epidemiology from the Ethiopian Famines', *Annales Société Belge de Médecine Tropicale*, 56, 345–57.

Ruiz, H. (1987). 'When Refugees Won't Go Home: The Dilemma of Chadians in Sudan' (Washington, DC, US Committee for Refugees).

Santandrea, S. (1964). *A Tribal History of the Western Bahr el Ghazal* (Bologna, Nigrizia).

Schove, D. J. (1977). 'African Droughts and the Spectrum of Time', in D. Dalby, R. J. Harrison-Church, and F. Bezzaz (eds.), *Drought in Africa 2* (London, International African Institute, African Environment Special Report No. 6).

Scott-Villiers, H. (1984). 'Land Use change in Qoz Ma'aliya, southern Darfur, Sudan' (Nyala, WSDC).

Seaman, J. and Holt, J. (1975). 'The Ethiopian Famine of 1973–4. 1: Wollo Province', *Proceedings of the Nutrition Society*, 34, 114A.

—— —— Rivers, J., and Murlis, J. (1973). 'An Enquiry into the Drought Situation in Upper Volta', *Lancet*, ii, 774–8.

Sen, A. K. (1981). *Poverty and Famines: An Essay on Entitlement and Deprivation* (Oxford, Clarendon Press).

Shawcross, W. (1984). *The Quality of Mercy, Cambodia, Holocaust and Modern Conscience* (London, Deutsch).

Sheets, H., and Morris, R. (1974). *Disaster in the Desert: Failures of International Relief in the West African Drought,* (Washington, DC, Carnegie Endowment for International Peace).

Shepherd, A. W. (1984). 'Nomads, Farmers and Merchants: Old Strategies in a Changing Sudan', in E. P. Scott (ed.), *Life Before the Drought* (Boston, Allen and Unwin).

Shoham J. (1987). 'Does Nutritional Surveillance have a Role to Play in Early Warning of Food Crises and in the Management of Relief Operations?', *Disasters*, 11, 282–5.

Simmel, G. (1971). 'The Poor' originally published as *Der Arme*, 1908, in *On Individuality and Social Forms*, trans. D. Levine, (Chicago, University of Chicago Press).

Simms, J. Y. (1976). 'The Impact of the Russian Famine of 1891–2: A New Perspective', Ph.D. thesis (University of Michigan).

Smith, K. (1951). *The Malthusian Controversy* (London, Routledge and Kegan Paul).

Sorokin, P. (1975). *Hunger as a Factor in Human Affairs*, originally completed 1922 (Gainesville, University of Florida Press).

SCC (1974). Sudan Council of Churches, 'Report on Mission to Darfur and Kordofan' (Khartoum, SCC).

Theobald, A. B. (1965). *'Ali Dinar, The Last Sultan of Darfur 1898–1916* (London, Longmans).

Tobert, N. (1985). 'The Effect of Drought among the Zaghawa in Northern Darfur', *Disasters*, 9, 213–23.

Tomkins, A. M. (1986*a*). 'Protein-Energy Malnutrition and Risk of Infection', *Proceedings of Nutrition Society*, 45, 289–304.

—— (1986*b*). 'Nutrient Intake during Diarrhoea in Young Children', in N. G. Taylor and N. K. Jenkins (eds.), *Proceedings of the XIIIth International Congress of Nutrition, 1985* (London, J. Libbey).

Topps, J. H. (1977). 'Adaptation of Cattle to Drought Conditions and their Requirements for Food and Water', in D. Dalby, R. J. Harrison-Church, and F. Bezzaz, (eds.), *Drought in Africa 2* (London, International African Institute, African Environment Special Report No. 6).

Tubiana, M-J., and Tubiana, J. (1977). *The Zaghawa from an Ecological Perspective* (Rotterdam, Balkena).

el Tunisi, M. (1854). *Travels of an Arab Merchant in Soudan.* Abridged and trans. B. St John, (London, Chapman and Hall).

Turnbull, C. (1972). *The Mountain People* (New York, Simon and Schuster).

Turton, D., and Turton, P. (1984). 'Spontaneous Resettlement After Drought: An Ethiopian Example', *Disasters*, 8, 178–189.

Ushari Mahmoud and Baldo, S. A. (1987). *Al Diein Massacre and Slavery in the Sudan* (Khartoum).

van Apeldoorn, G. J. (1981). *Perspectives on Drought and Famine in Nigeria* (London, Allen and Unwin).

Vaughan, M. (1987). *The Story of an African Famine: Gender and Famine in 20th Century Malawi* (Cambridge, Cambridge University Press).

Watkins, S. C., and Menken, J. (1985). 'Famines in Historical Perspective', *Population and Development Review*, 11, 647–76.

Watts, M. J. (1983). *Silent Violence: Food, Famine and Peasantry in Northern Nigeria* (Berkeley and Los Angeles, University of California Press).

Wilson, R. T. (1976*a*). 'Studies on the Livestock of Southern Darfur, Sudan, III: Production traits in Sheep', *Tropical Animal Health and Production*, 8, 103–14.

Wilson, R. T. (1976*b*). 'Studies on the Livestock of Southern Darfur, Sudan, IV: Production Traits in Goats', *Tropical Animal Health and Production*, 8, 221–232.

—— (1979). 'The Incidence and Control of Livestock Diseases in Darfur, Anglo-Egyptian Sudan, during the Period of the Condominium, 1916–1956', *International Journal of African Historical Studies*, 12, 62–82.

—— and Clarke, S. E. (1975). 'Studies on the Livestock of Southern Darfur, Sudan, I: The Ecology and Livestock Resources of the Area', *Tropical Animal Health and Production*, 7, 165–87.

—— (1976). 'Studies on the Livestock of Southern Darfur, Sudan, II: Production Traits in Cattle', *Tropical Animal Health and Production*, 8, 47–57.

Woodham-Smith, C. (1962). *The Great Hunger, Ireland 1845–49* (New York, Harper and Row).

Wrigley, E. A., and Schofield, R. S. (1981). *The Population History of England 1541–1871, A Reconstruction* (London, E. Arnold).

York, S. (1985). 'Report on a Pilot Project to Set Up a Drought Information Network in Conjuction With the Red Crescent Society in Darfur', *Disasters*, 9, 173–8.

Young, M. W. (1986). 'The Worst Disease: The Cultural Definition of Hunger in Kalauna', in L. Manderson (ed.), *Shared Wealth and Symbol* (Cambridge, Cambridge University Press).

Archives in National Records Office, Khartoum

Civsec 122/1/3, 'Darfur (Campaign): Narrative of Events' (1916).

Civsec 19/1/2, 'Famine', with extracts from 1920 Famine Regulations (1937–49).

Civsec 56/3/26, 'Zaka and Fitr' (1906, 1922).

Civsec 64/2/11, 'Economic Development Darfur Province' (1945).

Civsec 64/6/42, 'Control of Markets Darfur Province' (1928–9).

Civsec 66/2/13, 'Mandala of Darfur Province' (1929).

Civsec 66/4/32, 'Beni Hussein' (1928).

Civsec 66/4/35, 'Grazing: Dinka-Humr-Rizeigat', with Kafia Kinji policy (1930–41).

Civsec 112/2/5, 'Darfur Intelligence' (1910).

Civsec 112/2/6, 'Military Intelligence, Darfur' (1914–15).

Civsec 112/2/7, 'Intelligence: Ali Dinar' (1911–14).

Civsec 122/1/1, 'Patrol 99: Southern and Western Darfur (1)' (1921).

Civsec 122/1/3, 'Darfur (Campaign): Narrative of Events' (1916).

Darfur 1/33/169, 'Events in Darfur, 1898–1916'.

Darfur 6/5/12, 'Darfur Province Reports, 1948–50'.

Darfur 6/6/17, 'Handbook on Western Darfur by Mr Beaton' (1938), with additional material added (1939–47).

Intel 2/1/6, 'Rizeigat, 1913–14'.

Intel 6/8/24, 'Sudan Intelligence Report, 1914–15'.

INDEX